"AQUITANIA"

THE QUADRUPLE-SCREW TURBINE-DRIVEN CUNARD LINER "AQUITANIA" ON THE CLYDE.

THE

QUADRUPLE-SCREW   TURBINE-DRIVEN

CUNARD   LINER

"AQUITANIA"

CONSTRUCTED   AND   ENGINED   BY

MESSRS. JOHN BROWN AND CO., LTD.,

SHEFFIELD   AND   CLYDEBANK.

Reprinted   from   "ENGINEERING."

Patrick Stephens

For my grandparents
Josephine and Zygmont Rawdan
who were married in 1914.

Originally published in 1914
PSL edition first published in 1988

British Library Cataloguing in Publication Data

The Quadruple-screw turbine-driven Cunard
liner 'Aquitania'.—2nd ed.
1. Passenger transport. Shipping. Steam
liners. Aquitania (Ship), 1913-1914
I. Warren, Mark D.   II. Engineering
magazine
387.2'432

ISBN 1-85260-022-5

Patrick Stephens is part of the
Thorsons Publishing Group,
Wellingborough, Northamptonshire, NN8 2RQ, England

Reproduced from the original. Additional material
photoset in 8 on 8½ pt Century Old Style by
Harper Phototypesetters Limited, Northampton.

Printed in Great Britain by
Butler & Tanner Limited, Frome, Somerset

1 3 5 7 9 10 8 6 4 2

INTRODUCTION

This book is primarily a facsimile reprint of a special volume published in 1914, comprising a series of articles that had appeared in *Engineering** magazine, describing in great detail the construction and launch of the RMS *Aquitania*. This scarce volume, along with the better-known *Shipbuilder* special issue on the *Aquitania*, contains the most comprehensive published contemporary account of the design and construction of the ship, even though, unlike previous special volumes on individual ships published by *Engineering*, the *Aquitania* publication originally did not include interior photographs of the vessel.

This volume is now republished in celebration of the forthcoming seventy-fifth anniversary of the *Aquitania*'s maiden voyage on 30 May 1914. It now features three blueprint plans and 72 additional photographs, including 66 interior views. Most of these have been added in the form of an appendix beginning with Plate XIV. Additional new illustrations, which are not included in the appendix, are: the photograph of the 'First-Class Smoking Room Fireplace' on page viii, the '*Aquitania*' on page ix, the 'First-Class Georgian Lounge' on page x, the '*Aquitania*' on page xiii, the 'First-Class Salon Entrance' on page xv, the two photos of the '*Aquitania*' on pages 80 and 84, and 'Plate A' on page 85. Plates VII and VIII have been deleted but are preserved as entries in the General Index.

Perhaps the most admired and successful liner of all time, the *Aquitania* was also one of the most beautiful, from her elegant, well-proportioned, classic profile, to her artistically discriminating interiors which, from the outset, earned her a reputation as 'Ship Beautiful', 'Aristocrat of the Atlantic' and 'World's Wonder Ship'.

The last of the four-funnelled liners to serve the North Atlantic, the *Aquitania*'s legendary career involved 442 transatlantic voyages, spanning 35½ years, with the distinction of serving admirably in both World Wars, and carrying approximately 1,200,000 passengers 3,000,000 miles. Historically, the *Aquitania* never quite surpassed the *Lusitania*'s fame or the *Mauretania*'s achievement as the longest holder of the Blue Riband, yet she was an enduring institution, loved and respected by all who had the honour of escorting her through her many years.

When Cunard's Board of Directors met on 16 December 1909 and 'decided to prepare plans of [a] new steamer [of] 88′ beam, [and] 23 knot speed'†, competition for passenger revenue on the North Atlantic had already reached historic proportions. The Directors wanted Cunard to be the first steamship company with a three-ship weekly express service, which would not only give the company a decided edge over White Star and the Hamburg-Amerika Line, who were also in the process of planning or building their respective trios of super-liners,** but also would finally fulfil Samuel Cunard's original 1838 intention of a three-vessel, transatlantic service.†† This much larger, albeit slightly slower, consort for the enormously successful twin express steamers, *Lusitania* and *Mauretania*, would also replace the *Caronia*, *Carmania* and ageing *Campania* on the Liverpool to New York run. According to the 'General Conditions' of the 'Proposed New Steamer' outlined in a confidential letter to John Brown & Company, dated 9 September 1910, Cunard required that 'The hull, outfit, equipment, engines, boilers, auxiliary machinery, etc, are to be constructed of the very best materials, finished complete in a first-class style of workmanship to the entire satisfaction of the Owners, without any charge over the contract price, unless previously agreed in writing'.*** Since Cunard already had the two fastest ships in the world, speed was no longer as important as the increased revenue the company could now expect with the more than 1,000 additional passengers that the *Aquitania* would carry beyond that of her 'sisters'.

* *Engineering: An Illustrated Weekly Journal*, 18, 25 April 1913; 17 April, 8, 15, 22, 29 May and 19 June 1914.

† From handwritten notes on the official agreement between John Brown & Company and The Cunard Steamship Company, 31 January 1911. UCS1 Collection, Glasgow University Archives. Crown Copyright.

** White Star Line: *Olympic*, *Titanic* and *Britannic*; Hamburg-Amerika Line: *Imperator*, *Vaterland* and *Bismarck*.

†† Samuel Cunard had originally hoped to establish a fortnightly service with three vessels. However, with the advent of the *Aquitania*, this service would now be possible weekly.

*** UCS 1 Collection, Glasgow University Archives. Crown Copyright.

Cunard had already become so prosperous as a result of the popularity of the *Lusitania* and the *Mauretania* that the cost of constructing this new liner was to be absorbed totally by the company. In comparison, the building of the *Lusitania* and the *Mauretania* had largely been financed through a government subsidy, with the hope that their performances might win back for Britain the prestige that had passed to the Germans, with the loss of the Blue Riband, ten years earlier. Without much effort, that hope was promptly realized with the *Lusitania*'s second westbound voyage, and again with the *Mauretania*'s eastbound maiden voyage. It was these and other record-breaking voyages by the *Lusitania* and the *Mauretania* that brought Cunard the success it had aimed for, and the recognition it had not known since the sensation made by her last Blue Riband winners, the *Campania* and the *Lucania*, in 1893.

In addition, between the completion of the *Lusitania* in 1907 and the *Aquitania* in 1914, Cunard's fleet expanded a remarkable 70 per cent with eight new vessels totalling 141,021 gross tons.* In comparison, during the same period the tonnages of both the White Star Line† and the Hamburg-Amerika Line increased only 20 per cent, while that of Norddeutscher Lloyd increased 24 per cent.**

Among Cunard's new vessels were the 18,150 ton *Franconia*, which began operating between Liverpool and New York in February 1911, and the 18,099 ton *Laconia*, which followed in January 1912. These two popular intermediates incorporated many innovations, including Cunard's first shipboard gymnasiums, and running water in the First-Class stateroom wash basins instead of previously standard 'folding lavatories'. The *Laconia* was also the first British passenger liner to be fitted with Frahm's anti-rolling tanks, while the *Franconia* was the first British ship to feature movable chairs in the First-Class Dining Room, instead of traditional bolted-down swivel chairs. The significance of this innovation was fully publicized only four months later when the world's newest and largest ship, White Star Line's *Olympic*, also boasted this amenity. The designers of the *Aquitania*, however, took this evolutionary step one further by also furnishing the Second-Class Dining Saloon with comfortable movable chairs.

Cunard was able, in addition, to buy the Thomson Line in 1911, the Anchor Line in 1912†† and the Royal Line in 1916, thus expanding their service to Canada for the first time since 1867, and increasing to four the number of distinct services now offered.*** Two new 13,405 ton steamers, the *Alaunia* and *Andania* were completed in 1913 to join the *Ausonia* and *Ascania* which had been built for the Canadian route in 1911. And now, with the maiden voyage of the *Aquitania* on 30 May 1914, Cunard finally reached its greatest aspiration as the first steamship company to have a three-ship weekly service on the North Atlantic, even though, with the outbreak of the First World War in August, the triumph was to be short-lived.

The terms of the 1903 contract between Cunard and the Government had required that the forthcoming *Lusitania* and *Mauretania*, as well as all other Cunard vessels capable of 17 knots, be planned and built with the same strict Admiralty supervision as that of military vessels. In the event of war, these vessels could be taken over by the Admiralty at prescribed rates and converted into auxiliary cruisers or transports, which would be better equipped to withstand extraordinary damage while minimizing losses. Cunard's naval architect, Leonard Peskett, was required, therefore, to incorporate the most advanced fire prevention system with a sophisticated watertight subdivision of the hull.

* This figure does not take into account the loss of the *Slavonia* in 1909.

† This figure does not include the *Titanic*, or the *Britannic*, which was not completed until 1915. If the *Titanic* had survived and been included in this figure, the increase in White Star's tonnage during this period would have been 32 per cent.

** The *Columbus* (later *Homeric*) is not included in this figure, as she was only 80 per cent completed when work stopped in August 1914.

†† The Anchor and Donaldson Lines amalgamated in 1916, of which Cunard owned the Anchor portion.

*** Liverpool-New York; Liverpool-Queenstown-Boston; London and Plymouth to Montreal and Quebec or Portland; Adriatic-Mediterranean-New York.

The design of the *Aquitania*'s hull began with a double cellular bottom that extended the full length of the ship and well up the bilge, which was 5 ft 4 in deep under the boiler rooms and holds, and 6 ft 3 in deep under the engine rooms. In total, the double bottom contained 41 separate watertight compartments, which allowed for trimming of the vessel in any direction. Above this, the hull was divided by 16 watertight transverse bulkheads, many of which extended 19 ft above the load waterline.* Six of these transverse bulkheads were subdivided by port and starboard watertight longitudinal bulkheads, which not only separated each of the four turbine engines, but also created an inner hull 18 ft from the outer shell plating which, when further divided into compartments 27 to 33 ft in length, would serve as coal bunkers. The transverse bulkheads between boiler rooms 1, 2 and 3 formed deep watertight compartments which also would be used as coal bunkers, with the corresponding space between boiler rooms 3 and 4 occupied by the Turbogenerator Room. These transverse coal bunkers were possible because of the ship's length, greater than that of both the *Lusitania* and the *Mauretania*. What resulted was the separation and insulation of each of the four boiler rooms, thereby minimizing the possibility of flooding or explosion due to damage. They were also designed to carry fuel oil if conversion should take place at a later date.

For extra safety, all trunks and hatchways as well as 'G' Deck the full length of the ship, were also made watertight, creating a total of 84 watertight compartments. This subdivision, theoretically, would allow the first five consecutive compartments forward, or the last five compartments aft, to be flooded without sinking the ship, provided all portholes were closed. If there were damage amidships, the nine watertight longitudinal coal bunkers lining the port or starboard sides of the four boiler rooms, and the wing engine and condenser compartments could also be flooded without seriously endangering the ship.†

As the *Aquitania* was built in an atmosphere of impending war, her hull was also completely subdivided by transverse diaphragms fitted with fireproof doors, as well as special watertight firescreen bulkheads. As with the *Lusitania* and the *Mauretania*, gun rings were installed by the Admiralty on the *Aquitania*'s decks, which were reinforced to support twelve 6 in quick-firing guns, should conversion to an armed merchant cruiser be necessary.

The same foresight that the Admiralty had displayed in the planning of these potential military assets, Cunard demonstrated in the business of maximizing passenger profits. While other steamship companies had ignored the steerage passenger's comfort, Cunard had realized the importance of the lucrative immigrant trade by having introduced for the first time, vastly upgraded Third-Class accommodations in the *Lusitania* and the *Mauretania*. This was a sensible decision, as immigration statistics for the years between 1907 and 1913 show that 27.37 per cent of all passengers arriving in the USA were in the First and Second Classes, while the remaining 72.63 per cent were in Third Class or steerage.** During those years, statistics for people leaving the United States, however, represented a different ratio, as 34.45 per cent of the outbound passengers were in the First and Second Classes, while the remaining 65.55 per cent travelled in Third Class or steerage. The difference in these two sets of figures

* Peskett's first meeting with Lloyd's regarding the height of the transverse bulkheads was held on 23 March 1910, more than two years before the *Titanic* tragedy.

† The watertight subdivision of the *Aquitania*'s hull was so thoroughly planned by the Admiralty, that following the *Titanic* disaster, the cost of making modifications to the watertight subdivision of the hull amounted to only £6,180 ($30,076), as compared to an estimated £250,000 ($1,216,675) required to correct the design of the *Titanic*'s sister ship, the *Olympic*, which originally had only a 'single-skin' hull.

** Third Class had cabin accommodations, even if austere, while steerage passengers were housed without privacy in open berths.

prompted Cunard to create 'interchangeable' staterooms in the *Aquitania*, which allowed for the first time more flexibility in conforming to the alternating immigration statistics in each class.* Specifically, 60 staterooms with a capacity of 216 persons were designed to be used by either First-Class or Second-Class passengers. On the Lower Deck 'F', 48 rooms accommodating 112 people could alternately be used for Second-Class or Third-Class passengers. Another 40 rooms, on 'F' Deck, could accommodate either 100 Second-Class or 172 Third-Class passengers.† By upgrading the Second-Class and Third Class accommodation to a more uniform standard, for the first time class divisions were substantially reduced. This change, coincidentally, strongly reflected the outraged public sentiment which followed the *Titanic* disaster.

The normal division of classes on the *Aquitania* was 38.14 per cent in the First and Second Classes, and 61.86 per cent in Third. These figures correspond closely with immigration statistics for people leaving the USA in 1913, as 39.35 per cent were in First and Second Class, and 60.65 per cent were in Third. The number of people entering the USA in 1913, however, show First-Class and Second-Class arrivals amounting to only 28.61 per cent, with 71.39 per cent in Third. By fully utilizing the interchangeable staterooms, Cunard could now roughly match these figures if desired, with 30.9 per cent in the First and Second Class, and 69.1 per cent in Third.

In addition to providing interchangeable staterooms, the planners of the *Aquitania* managed to allocate an unusually high proportion (98.22 per cent) of the 394 spacious, permanent First-Class staterooms exclusively to single and double berths, as 179 (45.43 per cent) had a single berth, and 208 (52.79 per cent) had two berths. Only five rooms (1.27 per cent) were fitted with three berths and the remaining two cabins had four berths. With the exception of those five three-berth cabins, no First-Class stateroom was fitted with upper berths, which uniformly gave the rooms the appearance of 'luxurious hotel suites'. In keeping with Cunard's original intention of maximizing profits, the lucrative immigrant trade was not forgotten, as there was also accommodation for 1,998 in Third Class. In all, the *Aquitania* had a capacity of 4,202 persons with 3,230 passengers in 1,719 rooms, and a crew of 972.

In comparison, the *Aquitania*'s closest competitor in both size and purpose, the *Olympic*,** had a total capacity of 3,300 with 2,435 passengers in 762 rooms, and a crew of 865. In addition, only 60.66 per cent of the *Olympic*'s 333 First-Class staterooms were furnished with single or double berths, while 38.14 per cent (127 rooms) were fitted with three berths. The Third Class was also smaller, as only 1,026 passengers, or 48.64 per cent less than the *Aquitania*, could be accommodated.†† One explanation for this diminished capacity can be the *Olympic/Titanic*'s enormous reciprocating engines, which rose through three decks of passenger accommodation. The *Aquitania*, on the other hand, was required by contract to locate all engines, machinery and steering mechanisms below the waterline, with the result that more room was created for passengers.

James Millar, the man responsible for designing the *Lusitania*'s public rooms, was again awarded that privilege in conjunction with the *Aquitania*. Through an agreement worked out between Cunard and the Hamburg-Amerika Line, Arthur Davies, of the prestigious London firm of Mewès and Davies was chosen as architect for the *Aquitania*'s large public rooms.*** The agreement stipulated that with regard to work on the *Aquitania*, their partnership would have to be split because Charles Mewès, the famous grand hotel architect, was still under contract to the Hamburg-Amerika Line. Consequently, the architects were not allowed to work together.

Mewès and Davies's career together began in 1903 when Albert Ballin, the Director of the Hamburg-Amerika Line, commissioned Mewès (who in turn enlisted Davies) to design the interior of the *Amerika*, the world's largest, and Hamburg-Amerika's newest, ship. Together they created the most fashionable and innovative vessel yet to cross the Atlantic. Given their experience designing exclusive hotels, Mewès and Davies knew what the wealthy wanted and demanded in service and accommodation. Consequently, they incorporated smart innovations in the *Amerika*, such as an exclusive *à la carte* restaurant, a trellised winter garden lounge, and the first shipboard elevators, all of which would become standard features on many liners, including the *Titanic* and the *Aquitania*.

Besides adapting the most popular features from the *Amerika*, Davies's design of the *Aquitania* basically began with an expanded version of the *Lusitania* and *Mauretania*'s classic floor plan. From there he freely borrowed the best elements from other liners, especially the *Olympic* and *Titanic*, and incorporated them into the *Aquitania* along with many of his own unique ideas, so that her design represented not only the culmination of a tried and true arrangement, but also included all the newest improvements and trends in passenger accommodation.

Among the most notable features Davies borrowed from the *Titanic* was the enclosing of both sides of the forward end of the First-Class Promenade on 'A' and 'B' Decks with sliding glass windows to protect passengers from the elements. This was done in much the same way as the builders of the *Titanic* had done on her Promenade Deck only a month before her maiden voyage.

Within the enclosed section on the *Aquitania*'s 'A' Deck, Davies then installed on both sides, with vestibules at each end, a 123 ft long, 20 ft wide, trellised 'Garden Lounge', complete with potted plants and wicker furniture, almost certainly modelled after *Titanic*'s Café Parisian. It must have given Davies great satisfaction to see his original idea of a small, indoor winter garden lounge on the *Amerika*, evolve in less than ten years into a space encompassing 4,878 sq ft on the largest British liner in the world.

Another appropriation from both the *Olympic* and the *Titanic* was the floor plan of the First-Class Dining Saloon which, along with the general arrangement of tables, was very similar to that of the *Aquitania*. Even the width of all three dining rooms, as well as their location, sandwiched between the second and third funnel casing, was the same. However, in structure and decor, the *Aquitania*'s two-storey dining room found its origins not with the *Olympic/Titanic*, but with the *Amerika*, as both had open, balustraded wells which rose to staterooms on the deck above.

As previously mentioned, both White Star liners and the *Aquitania* had exclusive *à la carte* restaurants, with their own kitchens and staff, where for an extra price, the élite could sumptuously dine far removed from the bustle of the First-Class Dining Saloon. This concept was not unknown to Davies, who along with Mewès, had designed in 1904 an *à la carte* restaurant on the *Amerika* that had its own separate kitchens and staff, managed solely by the famous hotel firm of Ritz-Carlton.

Not by coincidence, at this time Mewès himself was busy in Germany designing the most notable of all Ritz-Carlton restaurants — those on the *Imperator* and *Vaterland*. Davies's creation, however, would be decidedly English as he chose to decorate the *Aquitania*'s 'Grill Room' in the same early Jacobean style as that of the *Titanic*'s First-Class Dining Room.

Even though Mewès and Davies were forbidden by contract to work together on their respective projects, collaboration between the two, or, at the very least, their long-standing relationship, was revealed by the striking similarities between the *Aquitania* and *Imperator*'s First-Class Grand Staircases.

One unique feature found on the *Aquitania*, which distinguished her from other popular liners of the day, was an imaginative system for allowing natural light and fresh air into two inner rows of First-Class staterooms on 'C' Deck. By elevating 'B' Deck almost 2 ft over the middle row of 'C' Deck cabins, transom windows placed high inside the staterooms permitted fresh air and light to enter the cabins from the open promenade above. This raised terrace, which was 189 ft long and 7 ft wide, also allowed First-Class passengers an unobstructed view of the ocean from their deckchairs.

For a smoother and steadier voyage, a Frahm's anti-rolling tank was installed in the *Aquitania* below 'G' Deck, between boiler rooms 2 and 3. This recently perfected innovation had proven so effective on the *Laconia* that bilge keels were no longer necessary, as the amplitude of the roll was reduced an average 60 per cent.

As assurance to the *Aquitania*'s passengers, there were 22 wooden and 58 collapsible lifeboats with a capacity for 4,584 persons — 382 more than the ship was designed to carry. In addition were two 30-ft motor launches, made to tow the open boats and equipped with wireless sets capable of transmitting between 120 and 150 miles and receiving transmissions from up to 300 miles.

The wireless installation on the *Aquitania* was the most powerful shipboard wireless when originally installed in the ship's 'Marconi Office', high on the Boat Deck. It had a range of about 650 miles during the day, and over twice that at night, which enabled the ship's two wireless operators to maintain contact in mid-ocean with both sides of the Atlantic simultaneously. In the 1920s, the ship's wireless capability was considerably upgraded and the complement of operators increased to eleven.

Located directly below the Marconi Office on 'A' Deck was the 'Long Gallery', at that time another unique concept for the *Aquitania*. This 148 ft long, 14 ft 6 in wide, 'late eighteenth-century-style' corridor connected the First-Class Smoking Room with the First-Class Lounge, and was noted for its engraved portraits and prints of English seaports, as well as the four large vitrines containing various *objets d'art*. Adjoining the First-Class Secondary Stairway and passenger lift, the Long Gallery also originally accommodated the Barber's Shop, complete with a striped pole, the Typist's Office, and the upper pantry for the Maid's Dining Room on the deck below. However, in the 1920s, this area was transformed into small shops selling men's clothes, women's perfumes, chocolates and tobacco, as well as jewellery.

The main entrance to the largest room on 'A' Deck, the First-Class 'Carolean' Smoking Room was located at the aft end of the Long Gallery. Monumental in size, this 'room' actually consisted of six rooms, all tastefully decorated with a nautical flavour in the period of Charles II, and measuring in total 77 by 53 ft. The most spacious central room, adapted from one of the finest in the Greenwich Hospital, was luxuriously panelled in oak. It was 50 ft long by 33 ft wide at the centre, with a magnificent 18-ft-high plaster ceiling. At the forward end, surmounting a marble fireplace, hung Sir Godfrey Kneller's full length portrait of James II. This was bordered by high relief ornamental trophies carved in limewood. Elegant to the last detail, even the andirons — cast in silver, and massive — were faithful copies of originals found at Knole.

Dominating both sides of the room, were two enormous paintings — 'Embarkation of St Ursula' and a 'Seaport with Figures', copies of Claude Lorrain's originals in the National Gallery. These were set in ornately carved frames over richly sculpted, 7 ft 6 in long marble-topped console tables. Softly illuminating both paintings were two pairs of pedestal electric lamps which were patterned after a seventeenth century ship's stern lantern. Also decorating the walls were sculpted cartouches and motifs from old ships and naval trophies largely copied from Grinling Gibbon's finest. These blended well with limewood carved copies of the Royal Arms and the Arms of London. The coats-of-arms and armorials of New York, Boston, Quebec, Belfast, Dublin, Glasgow, as well as those of Liverpool, Queenstown and other British commercial centres completed the wall decoration. Period reproduction furniture rested on a vast carpet of Persian design. During the day, sunlight suffused the room through clerestory windows above wide Doric columned doorways.

Bounding the central room on three sides were five very masculine, oak-clad rooms that were decorated with bas-relief panels carved of solid oak. These depicted nautical trophies and coats-of-arms, many of which had been copied from the 1637 ship, *Sovraigne of the Seas* — the largest and most opulently decorated vessel of her time. Spherical lights copied from a seventeenth-century Dutch ship hung from the high oak-beamed ceiling, even though the rooms were already well lit by large, two-tiered, glass panelled windows.

One of the most splendid rooms was the universally acclaimed First-Class 'Georgian' Lounge, which could be reached through the forward end of the Long Gallery. Often referred to as the 'Palladian Lounge', the room was actually decorated in an eclectic Queen Anne/Georgian Revival style. It measured 72 ft 6 in by 52 ft 6 in, and was remarkable for its elegantly proportioned Ionic colonnade and entablature, on which rested a lofty 18-ft-high vaulted ceiling with circular and tripartite lunette clerestory windows. Equally noteworthy were the period ceiling paintings, bordered by high relief plaster molding, the centre panel an original Van Cuygen dated 1716.

At the forward end, under a recessed coffered arch, nautical swags expertly carved from single blocks of limewood counterbalanced the prominent wall clock above the fireplace of rare 'Breccia Africanae' marble. Positioned on either side under limewood swags, pairs of deep shell niches sheltering life-sized busts were set between carved, fluted columns. A semi-elliptical apse displaying a Mortlake tapestry depicting the Battle of Solebay dominated the aft end of the room. Although this area was originally intended as a small stage, complete with raised platform and two

* The concept of interchangeable staterooms exclusively for passengers was first introduced on the *Titanic*, which had 40 staterooms on 'G' Deck that could be used by either Second-Class or Third-Class passengers. This certainly was an improvement over those on the *Olympic*, which had 22 'Portable' staterooms on 'G' Deck which could be used for either Third Class or cargo.

† While the *Aquitania* had been designed with flexibility to reflect immigration statistics, the *Lusitania* and *Mauretania* had been built with more concern for the élite eastbound American passenger. This was principally due to the very nature of the twin express steamers. They were built for speed, and speed was a luxury few Third-Class passengers could afford in 1907. The *Lusitania* was designed to carry 46.04 per cent First-Class and Second-Class passengers, and 53.96 per cent in Third-Class. The *Mauretania* had 47.44 per cent reserved for the First and Second Classes, while Third Class occupied 52.56 per cent. These figures correspond roughly with immigration statistics for the years 1903 to 1906 inclusive, which show 40.14 per cent of all passengers departing the US were in either First or Second Class, while 59.86 per cent were in Third. However, in comparison, those same years showed only 17.33 per cent of all passengers arriving in the US were in First or Second Class, while 82.67 per cent were in Third Class or steerage.

** The *Aquitania* and the *Olympic*, as well as the *Titanic*, were all built for comfort, not speed, and although the *Aquitania* was 19 ft longer and some 323 gross registered tons greater than the *Olympic*, she was only 682 GRT less than the *Titanic*.

†† Although nearly identical to the *Olympic* in overall dimensions, the *Titanic* was certified to carry 3,547 persons, with at least 2,603 passengers in 788 staterooms, including 905 First Class in 373 staterooms, and a crew of 900.

*** Mewès and Davies were paid £5,000 for their services, as well as an additional £271 11s 4d for travelling expenses.

hidden dressing rooms, it resembled a Roman basilica. At both ends, spandrels decorated with allegorical representations of the four elements, 'Earth', 'Air', 'Fire' and 'Water', were carefully copied from originals by Jean Baptists Van Lee.

Both sides of the central room were flanked with Ionic colonnades suggesting a Roman loggia. Under an 11-ft-6-in-high ceiling, each side had tables and chairs along with four alcoves containing comfortable settees providing a view of the Garden Lounge through large Georgian windows. A captivating warmth of colour was achieved by the celadon grey mahogany walls, the predominently wine red upholstered furniture, and the deep red Savonnerie carpet.

Forward, port and starboard First-Class Lounge entrances led directly into the two First-Class Writing Salons through glass-panelled doors. These elegant rooms in the style of Louis XVI had curved corners and measured 15 by 30 ft. They were mirror images of each other. Grey panelled walls heightened with gilt mouldings and sconces provided a worthy setting for the two large landscape paintings after Hubert Roberts, displayed on either side of an arched, recessed mirror. Illuminated by fancy cut-glass light fixtures, and resting on a camel-coloured carpet, reproductions of Bergére chairs, as well as small tables and a settee, faced three writing desks, each beneath a large window draped with purple and gold.

The twin forward entrances of the Writing Salons, consisting of massive, seven ft thick and seven ft wide arches with *trompe l'oeil* coffered ceilings, led directly into the First-Class Grand Entrance. This Louis XVI room, painted in French grey, measured 54 by 33 ft and was distinguished by its slender, carved Corinthian columns and pilasters that fringed the perimeter of an enormous, oval wrought iron and glass skylight, measuring 17 by 20 ft. The ornate wrought iron and glass twin elevator gates and matching balustrade faced an original oil painting by Giovanni Antonio Pannini, showing the Arch of Constantine and the Colosseum, with statues in the foreground.

The last room accessible forward the First-Class Grand Entrance was the pastel blue, First-Class Adam Drawing Room and Library, which measured 45 ft by 36 ft 6 in. This authentically reproduced Adam room was divided by fluted Corinthian columns with the reading section on the left, and writing tables on the right.

The reading section was particularly memorable for its 23 ft 6 in by 16 ft domed oval skylight, containing 16 circular, leaded-glass lunettes, as well as for the reproduction Cipriani painting that hung over the statuary marble fireplace. A large three-frame mirror, a reproduction of one made by the Brothers Adam for the Earl of Bute, rested on a table copied from one found in the Duke of Northumberland's Sion House. The blue carpet was supplemented with Persian rugs, and the walls were decorated with framed eighteenth-century mezzotints accented by twin light sconces. A gracefully executed scrollwork frieze connected the tall Corinthian pilasters.

The main entrance hall of the ship, the First-Class Foyer or 'Reception' Room, as well as the Purser's Bureau, were located three decks directly below, on 'D' Deck. Decorated in the style of Louis XVI and measuring 87 by 46 ft, the Foyer was not only the first room passengers encountered when entering the ship, but also its main stairway. Twin passenger lifts provided access to all other First-Class decks. Besides the collection of framed late eighteenth-century engravings were two paintings of the Colosseum and the Arch of Constantine. These were set in light grey painted walls with sculpted garland reliefs. French windows curtained in pale rose silk, and cane-backed settees cushioned in velvet, completed the appropriate setting for entrance into the *Aquitania*'s largest room, the First-Class 'Louis XVI' Restaurant.

This grand space, which measured 92 ft by 140 ft 6 in and encompassed 10,602 sq ft, was panelled in light grey mahogany. It was famous for 'The Triumph of Flora', an oval, Baroque-styled ceiling mural after Jacques Lagrenée, placed almost 19 ft above the floor and crowning the centre of the 23 by 41 ft, rectangular open well. Concealing the fore and aft funnel casings were two large, rectangular canvases depicting early perspective views of Versailles's 'Parc du Grand Trianon' and 'Jardins du Petit Trianon'. Beneath these paintings were large marble-topped console tables flanked by paired marble pilasters. Matching these canvases, and also framed by pairs of marble pilasters, were four smaller paintings showing the 'Orangery', the 'Pavilion of Play and Conversation', the 'Temple of Love', and 'Migne's Belvedere or Music Room'. In addition, 20 neoclassical arabesque panels after Francois Prieur, which matched the design surrounding the oval ceiling painting, decorated the room's vents and bulkhead walls.

The room was accentuated by the heavy, smoothly polished *jaunne de Sienna* marble columns with Ionic capitals that supported the 10-ft lower ceiling. The lighter, second-floor arched pillars and elaborate wrought iron balustrade containing Cunard's monogram hid the recessed orchestra platform at the aft end. To complete the desired

TABLE A	*Mauretania*			*Aquitania*		
	Decoration	Furnishings	Total	Decoration	Furnishings	Total
First-Class Library	£6,910 ($33,629)	£1,400 ($6,813)	£8,310 ($40,442)	£2,547 ($12,395)	£1,502 ($7,310)	£4,049 ($19,705)
First-Class Lounge	£8,910 ($43,362)	£2,800 ($13,627)	£11,710 ($56,989)	£5,546 ($26,991)	£4,129 ($20,095)	£9,675 ($47,086)
Main Stairway	£21,350 ($103,904)		£21,350 ($103,904)	£10,300 ($50,127)		£10,300 ($50,127)
First-Class Smoke Room	£8,835 ($42,997)	£2,484 ($12,089)	£11,319 ($55,086)	£6,185 ($30,100)	£2,621 ($12,756)	£8,806 ($42,856)
First-Class Dining Room	£13,408 ($65,253)	£3,301 ($16,065)	£16,709 ($81,318)	£10,950 ($53,290)	£6,463 ($31,454)	£17,413 ($84,744)
Total:	£59,413 ($289,145)	£9,985 ($48,594)	£69,398 ($337,739)	£35,528 ($172,903)	£14,715 ($76,615)	£50,243 ($244,518)

TABLE B	*Lusitania*	*Mauretania*	*Aquitania*
Total Cost of Hull	£690,000 ($3,358,023)	£992,736 ($4,831,348)	£1,014,046 ($4,935,058)
Total Cost of Machinery	£589,000 ($2,866,486)	£834,930 ($4,063,354)	£521,051 ($2,535,800)
Total:	£1,279,000 ($6,224,509)	£1,827,666 ($8,894,702)	£1,535,097 ($7,470,858)

Abstracted and adapted from UCS1 Collection, Glasgow University Archives. Crown Copyright.
Note: The cost of Heating, Ventilation, Electric Lighting, Grounding etc is not included in Table A.

effect, a huge, tiered, oblong table for fancy desserts and pastries dominated the centre of the room, along with two circular tables supporting sizeable ornate lamps. Dotting the blue carpeted main floor, 458 comfortable satinwood chairs upholstered in yellow and blue silk *petit point* tapestry, accommodated passengers around the 156 smaller, more intimate lighted tables.

The exclusive First-Class 'Jacobean' Grill Room was located on the port side of 'D' Deck, aft of the Louis XVI Restaurant. It could easily be reached through an early seventeenth-century panelled hallway leading from the Louis XVI Restaurant, as well as from the First-Class Secondary Stairway or adjoining lift. Measuring 71 ft 6 in by 33 ft, and divided into two rooms by a wall with three open window bays and a doorway, the Grill Room was decorated in the style contemporary with James I. It was copied from an early Jacobean room at the Victoria and Albert Museum, having been removed from the Palace at Bromley-by-Bow. Its oak-panelled walls painted in ivory, featured paired pilasters and a frieze covered with intricately carved fretwork. Rectangular columns of the same design with corbelled capitals, supported a fine moulded plaster ceiling. Beneath it, heavy walnut chairs upholstered in English needlepoint accommodated 118 passengers around small, widely spaced tables lit with antique spiral candlestick lamps. Ivory-coloured curtains of an Elizabethan needlepoint design hung from the 14 recessed, arched windows and, completing the decoration were blue Delft ceramics, seventeenth-century framed prints of English monarchs, and a wall clock of the Cromwellian era.

It is interesting to note that while the *Aquitania* was some 30 per cent larger than the *Mauretania*,* the cost of her construction, as well as the decoration of her public rooms, was considerably less. However, more money was spent on the furnishings of the *Aquitania*'s public rooms. This was chiefly due to the change in tastes that followed the end of the Edwardian era, with the shift towards simpler, less-ornamented walls, and more emphasis on furnishings. Table 'A' above, compares the costs of decorating and furnishing the principal public rooms of the *Mauretania* and *Aquitania*, and Table 'B' provides a breakdown of the vessels' total construction costs.†

It is not surprising that the most expensive suites of the *Aquitania* were named after Van Dyck, Holbein, Velasquez, Rembrandt, Romney, Raeburn, Gainsborough and Reynolds. Located on 'B' Deck, the latter four suites featured private verandas, and all eight groups of apartments included separate sitting rooms whose walls were decorated with framed prints of the respective artists' best-known works.

Built at John Brown & Company in the same berth as the *Lusitania*, the *Aquitania* never drew much attention to herself. Her long career, though not uneventful, always seemed to be overshadowed by the current events of the day. Yet she was a vital participant, known best for her reliability, durability and devotion to service that firmly established her as a cornerstone of twentieth century transatlantic travel. The excitement of her maiden voyage was sadly stifled by news of the loss of the *Empress of Ireland* the day before — a disaster which claimed 1,024 lives.

The Great War erupted on 4 August 1914, and within four days the *Aquitania*, having completed only three voyages to New York, was stripped of her beautiful fittings in Liverpool and converted into an armed merchant cruiser carrying six-inch guns. But it was not until 25 August that the Admiralty realized the risks of using large liners in this capacity. On that day, the *Aquitania* sustained heavy bow damage following a collision with the Leyland liner *Canadian*. On 26 August, the recently converted auxiliary cruiser *Kaiser Wilhem Der Grosse* was scuttled by her crew after a duel with the British cruiser HMS *Highflyer*. Germany's *Cap Trafalgar* inflicted heavy damage on another auxiliary cruiser, Cunard's *Carmania*, before she sank following a fierce battle on 14 September. In light of these incidents, it was decided that the *Aquitania* be converted into a much-needed troop transport, and painted a blue and khaki dazzle scheme that was unique to merchant vessels of the First World War.

After shuttling some 30,000 troops to the Dardanelles Campaign between May and August 1915, both the *Aquitania* and the *Mauretania*, were refitted as hospital ships, painted white with buff funnels and green ribands. The *Aquitania* alone transported 25,000 wounded between August, 1915 and the end of 1916.

Too expensive and too risky to operate, the *Aquitania* lay idle in Liverpool for most of 1917, but with the entry of the United States into the war in April, she eventually began transporting American and Canadian troops to France. On 9 October 1918, while transporting 8,000 American soldiers, the *Aquitania* inadvertently collided with the destroyer USS *Shaw*, shearing it in two, with the loss of 12 Americans. By the time the armistice was signed on 11 November 1918, the *Aquitania* had transported approximately 120,000 troops, yet until early 1919 she remained in Government service to repatriate soldiers.

Six months after her first commercial 'austerity' sailing between her new home port of Southampton and New York on 14 June 1919, the *Aquitania* was sent to Newcastle for a complete renovation, and restoration of her original fittings. At a cost of £400,000, her boilers were converted to oil-firing, subsequently reducing her boiler room crew from 350 to 50, and a Gyro compass was installed — the first ever in a merchant vessel. Resumption of regular service commenced in August 1920 and in May 1922 the *Aquitania* was joined by the *Berengaria* (ex-*Imperator*). With these ships and the *Mauretania*, Cunard once again proudly provided a reliable three-ship weekly service.

The next major change occurred in 1926 with the introduction of a new 'Cabin' and 'Tourist' Class, which necessitated a complete change in passenger accommodation to 610 in Cabin Class, 950 in Second Class, and 640 in Tourist (Third) Class.

* Based on GRT.
† It is worth noting here that contrary to popular belief, at the time of her maiden voyage, the *Titanic* was not the most costly vessel ever constructed. Built at a cost of £1,564,606 ($7,614,472) between 1909-12, the *Titanic* cost £263,059 ($1,280,230) less than the *Mauretania* built between 1904-07, and only £29,510 ($143,614) more than the *Aquitania*.

Pound conversions here and in Tables A and B are based on a standard conversion rate that includes all phases of construction. By averaging the official annual exchange rates of the pound to the dollar between the years 1903 and 1913 inclusive, we arrive at £1 = $4.8666995.

THE QUADRUPLE-SCREW TURBINE-DRIVEN CUNARD LINER "AQUITANIA."

FIRST-CLASS SMOKING ROOM FIREPLACE.

Most new Cabin-Class staterooms were enlarged and redecorated so that two or three former First-Class staterooms now became one Cabin-Class stateroom. On 'B' Deck, 24 staterooms were extended outward incorporating the 2,646 sq ft of the raised deckchair terrace on the Promenade. In total, 131 original First-Class staterooms on that deck, excluding 2 suite dining rooms and 4 private verandas, were transformed into 97 Cabin-Class staterooms. On 'C' Deck, 263 former First and Second-Class staterooms were converted into 139 new Cabin-Class staterooms.

In 1933, it was decided that the height of the Second-Class Dining Saloon's open well on 'D' Deck allowed the installation of a movie theatre with seating for 188 passengers. An enclosed snack bar was also installed on the First-Class Promenade adjoining the aft end of the port side Garden Lounge.

In August 1936 the *Queen Mary* captured the Blue Riband, and in order to help keep pace, the *Aquitania* was fitted with new propellers, which raised her speed often to over 24 knots. At about that time, the First-Class Grill Room was gutted for 13 new Tourist-Class staterooms.

In total, between the two World Wars, the *Aquitania* ferried 530,749 passengers on 582 crossings with an occasional cruise to South America or the Mediterranean, and it seemed her life was completed as it was rumoured she would be scrapped with the appearance of the new *Queen Elizabeth*. However, the outbreak of the Second World War on 3 September 1939 changed all that, as her period of greatest service was about to begin.

After making one more commercial voyage, for a second time the great Cunarder trooped Canadian soldiers from Halifax to Southampton, between November 1939 and early 1940. Then she was entirely overhauled in New York and fitted with four rocket launchers, two six-in guns, and 27 smaller guns. Her next assignment, in March 1940, was to transport troops from Australia and New Zealand to Bombay and Alexandria.

Once based in Sydney in 1941, 'Old Granny', as she was fondly called by troops, made frequent trips to Wellington, Port Moresby, Singapore, Colombo, Bombay and Madagascar. In April, out of Sydney, she joined one of the great convoys, which included the *Queen Mary*, the *Queen Elizabeth*, the *Mauretania* (2) and the *Nieuw Amsterdam*. After the Japanese attacked Pearl Harbor in December, the *Aquitania* made an emergency voyage evacuating American women and children from Hawaii to San Francisco, a frightening voyage that lasted a full month.

In May 1943, escorted by the two *Queens*, the *Aquitania* made one trip from Sydney to New York via Cape Town and Rio de Janeiro, and later, 17 transatlantic voyages to England, heavily laden with troops. In all, the *Aquitania* transported over 384,000 people 526,000 miles during the Second World War — the only major liner to serve in and survive both World Wars.

Remaining in Government service returning troops until March 1948, the *Aquitania* began the final phase of her life. She transported settlers from Southampton to Halifax, with tourists on the return leg, until Cunard announced on 14 December 1949 that the *Aquitania* would be withdrawn from active service.

Broken up in Scotland between February 1950 and November 1951, her withdrawal marked not only the end of a ship with a remarkable career, but also the end of an era. The last of the great four-funnelled liners and all they represented was gone forever.

MARK D. WARREN
NEW YORK, OCTOBER 1988

ACKNOWLEDGEMENTS

I would like to acknowledge the assistance of those people who helped me in compiling the photographs and plans in the new section, as well as in the production of the book. They include: in London, England, Mr Peter Twist, Messrs Martin Taylor and Terry Charman of the Imperial War Museum; in Princeton, New Jersey, Mr Jeffrey Clarke; in Liverpool, England, Mr Michael Cook, MA, University Archivist, University of Liverpool; and in Belfast, Northern Ireland, Mr Rodney McCullough of Harland and Wolff, PLC.

Special thanks for most generous assistance go to: Mr Frank Trumbour of Ridgewood, New Jersey; Laura Brown of the Steamship Historical Society of America, Inc, at the University of Baltimore Library, Baltimore, Maryland; Mr Everett E. Viez of Boynton Beach, Florida; Messrs Frank R. Gerety, PE, and Thomas W. Coffey of New York City; Mrs Andrea D. Owens of the Cunard Archives, the University of Liverpool, Liverpool, England; Mrs Alma Topen of the Archives, University of Glasgow, Glasgow, Scotland; Mrs Catherine Stecchini of Princeton, New Jersey; and Mr Darryl Reach, Editorial Director of Patrick Stephens Ltd, Wellingborough, England.

PHOTOGRAPHIC SOURCES

The Cunard Archives at the University of Liverpool supplied the following photographs: pages viii, x, xv, and Plates XVI-XXXII, with the following exceptions which were taken from : 'The Cunard Quadruple-Screw Liner *Aquitania* — Souvenir Number Of The Shipbuilder'. Newcastle, 1914: Plate XIX, Fig. 209; Plate XXII, Fig. 220; and Plate XXVIII, Fig. 243. The following photographs and plans are from the UCS 1 Collection, Glasgow University Archives: Pages 80, 84, Plates A, XIV and XV. Photographs on Pages ix, xiii, Plate XXXIII and Page 144 are from the Private Collection of Everett E. Viez in Boynton Beach, Florida. Original advertisement on Page 144 is from the booklet: 'RMS *Aquitania* — Interior Views', n.p., n.d. (*circa* 1913). Front cover: 'The Cunard Quadruple-Screw Liner *Aquitania* — Souvenir Number Of The Shipbuilder'. Back cover: 'Souvenir of the Launching of RMS *Aquitania* — April 1913', UCS1 Collection, Glasgow University Archives.

BIBLIOGRAPHY

The Great Cunarder RMS Aquitania — The World's Wonder Ship booklet, The Cunard Steam Ship Company Ltd, n.p., n.d. (*circa* 1914). *Presbrey's Information Guide For Transatlantic Travellers* Ninth Edition: Frank Presbrey Co, New York, 1914. *The Cunard Quadruple-Screw Liner 'Aquitania' — Souvenir Number Of The Shipbuilder*, first published in Newcastle, June 1914 and reprinted in 1971 by Patrick Stephens Ltd. Bowen, Frank C., *A Century Of Atlantic Travel 1830-1930*: Little, Brown and Co, Boston, 1930. Babcock, F. Lawrence, *Spanning The Atlantic*: Alfred A. Knopf, New York, 1931. Diggle, Captain E.G., RD, RNR; *The Romance Of A Modern Liner*: Oxford University Press, New York, n.d., Grattidge, Captain Harry, *Captain Of The Queens*: E. P. Dutton & Co, Inc, New York, 1956. Shaum, John H. Jr, and Flayhart, William H. III, *Majesty At Sea*: Patrick Stephens Ltd, Cambridge, 1981. Maxtone-Graham, John, *The Only Way To Cross*: Patrick Stephens Ltd, Cambridge, 1983. Eaton, John P., and Haas, Charles A., *Titanic — Triumph and Tragedy*: Patrick Stephens Ltd, Wellingborough, 1986.

OUTBOUND "AQUITANIA" LEAVING NEW YORK CIRCA 1930.

THE QUADRUPLE-SCREW TURBINE-DRIVEN CUNARD LINER "AQUITANIA."

First-Class Lounge.

GENERAL INDEX.

LIST OF ILLUSTRATIONS.

RARE VIEW OF THE "AQUITANIA" IN NEWCASTLE, CIRCA 1920, AFTER CONVERSION TO OIL, WITH FOREPEAK PAINTED WHITE. RAISED WHEELHOUSE IS SHOWN BEFORE ORIGINAL WHEELHOUSE WINDOWS WERE ENCLOSED WITH PORTS.

LIST OF ADDITIONAL ILLUSTRATIONS

* Stateroom Photograph Pre-First World War

* Stateroom Photographs Pre-First World War

THE QUADRUPLE-SCREW TURBINE-DRIVEN CUNARD LINER "AQUITANIA."

First-Class Salon Entrance, Port Side

THE LOG OF THE "AQUITANIA'S" FIRST ROUND VOYAGE.

BY way of foreword we give the logs of the first outward and homeward voyages of the Aquitania. That a vessel, in the machinery of which so many important improvements in detail were introduced, attained such remarkably good results on a maiden trip, notwithstanding that she had only been under steam previously for about forty-eight hours, proves the highly satisfactory character of the design and the skill and experience of the workmen as well as the prescience and knowledge of the builders and owners. The guarantee was that the vessel should, within a year, attain an average speed of 23 knots on the Atlantic trip; this she did on the first voyage, and would have done still more had it not been necessary to steam "dead slow" for three hours on the fourth day out from Liverpool, owing to fog suggesting the proximity of ice. The mean speed on the outward voyage was 23.17 knots, and on the homeward run 23.45 knots. It will be seen that on three days the rate was over 24 knots. The coal consumption on the round voyage was most satisfactory. The logs are as follow :—

CUNARD R.M.S. "AQUITANIA."

ABSTRACT OF LOG FOR FIRST ROUND VOYAGE.

WESTWARD FROM LIVERPOOL TO NEW YORK :—
Passed North-West Lightship 4.26 p.m. May 30, 1914 (G.M.T.)

Up to Noon	... May 31, 1914	475 knots = 23.19 knots	Moderate winds, smooth sea
Do.	... June 1, ,,	576 ,, = 23.1 ,,	Do. do. foggy
Do.	... June 2, ,,	602 ,, = 24.3 ,,	Variable winds, smooth sea
Do.	... June 3, ,,	527 ,, = 21.57 ,,	Very foggy, ice region, reduced speed
Do.	... June 4, ,,	602 ,, = 24.19 ,,	Moderate wind and sea, fine and clear
Up to 5.09 a.m. ... June 5, ,,		399 ,, = 22.43 ,,	Do. do.

Passed Ambrose Channel Lightship 5.09 a.m. (N.Y.T.)
Total distance, 3181 nautical miles. Average speed, 23.17 knots.
Time for Westward passage, 5 days, 17 hours, 43 minutes.

EASTWARD FROM NEW YORK TO LIVERPOOL :—
Passed Ambrose Channel Lightship 12.17 p.m. June 10, 1914 (N.Y.T.)

Up to Noon	... June 11, 1914	541 knots = 23.69 knots	Moderate wind and sea
Do.	... June 12, ,,	550 ,, = 23.7 ,,	Moderate S.W. breeze and sea
Do.	... June 13, ,,	544 ,, = 23.34 ,,	Do. do.
Do.	... June 14, ,,	535 ,, = 23.01 ,,	Do. do.
Do.	... June 15, ,,	541 ,, = 23.31 ,,	Light variable winds and sea
Up to 5.15 a.m. ... June 16, ,,		384 ,, = 24.34 ,,	Do. do.

Passed Strumble Head, Fishguard, 5.15 a.m. (G.M.T.)
Total distance, 3095 nautical miles. Average speed, 23.45 knots.
Total time for Eastward passage, 5 days, 11 hours, 58 minutes.

THE CUNARD TURBINE-DRIVEN QUADRUPLE-SCREW ATLANTIC LINER "AQUITANIA."

THE new Cunard liner Aquitania, built by Messrs. John Brown and Co., Limited, at their Clydebank Works, left Liverpool on the 30th May on her first voyage to New York. Her appearance on the ocean marks the completion of another link in the chain of Empire forged by the steamship line which takes the leading place, not so much by reason of the magnitude of its fleet as of its stimulating influence on marine construction, and its continuous promotion of our maritime supremacy. The Aquitania is a further gratifying evidence of the fact that the prestige of our premier steamship line, and through it of British shipping generally, is being admirably maintained, if not extended, under the stimulus and experience of Mr. A. A. Booth, who is so well fitted to succeed a long line of illustrious men as Chairman of the Cunard Company. The Aquitania is remarkable, not only for her great size, but principally for the embodiment in her of all the qualities which experience has proved to conduce to the three great essentials of the ocean steamship—reliability and safety in service, economy in propulsion, and speed. In all of these respects we understand Mr. Booth has personally exerted influence on the design, having had almost unique opportunities of acquiring sound knowledge of the features in design necessary to achieve these *desiderata*; in fact, from his youth upwards he has devoted all his time to the study of steamship construction and management. Details which affect ease in management of the ship, economy of control, and the health and comfort of passengers have also had special consideration, and to these full reference will be made when we come to deal with structural details, passenger accommodation, and the equipment of the ship.

No stronger combination than that of the Cunard Company with Messrs. John Brown and Co., of Clydebank, could be made for the realisation of the essentials enumerated. Since their formation in 1840 the Cunard Company have accumulated an experience in steamship design, equipment, and management, which is unexcelled, and their technical staff have, under the encouraging stimulus of the Chairman and Directors, utilised their great opportunities for testing new ideas and collating results, so that by the process of elimination and deduction, associated with a true spirit of enterprise and conservative courage, they have led the way in the development of the Atlantic steamship along safe and approved lines. The accompanying table, giving particulars of notable Cunarders since the formation of the company to the present day, is proof of what we have written, especially when taken in conjunction with the fact that, notwithstanding the millions of passengers carried across the ocean, not a single life has been lost owing to the loss of a Cunard ship.

As regards the builders, there is equally striking evidence in support of their right to a first place among ship-constructors. Without attempting to enumerate the many successful ships built for other lines, significance is attached to the vessels included in the list of notable Cunarders which were built at Clydebank. Amongst these are the China, Russia, Servia, Saxonia, Carmania, Caronia, Lusitania, and Aquitania, all marking distinct steps on the way of evolution of the Atlantic liner, along which other builders have followed. Again, they have done much pioneer work in connection with turbine design and construction, and during the past ten years have completed, or have now in progress at Clydebank or allied works abroad, turbine machinery totalling 1,160,000 shaft horse-power. In warship construction they have shown corresponding enterprise; of almost every type of fighting craft notable examples have emanated from the Clydebank yard, and alongside the Aquitania there were constructed the largest battleship and battle-cruiser and several of the fastest torpedo-boat destroyers yet built for the British Navy. Again, the pioneer work done at their Atlas Works at Sheffield, in the development of steel manufacture for forgings, castings, and armour, has given them a prominent place in the history of metallurgy. The Sheffield Works supply much of the material required for the completion of ships and machinery at Clydebank, notably the rotors and other massive parts of large turbines. The consequence is the accumulation at Sheffield, as well as at Clydebank, of experience and data which are specially useful for evolving new designs and ideas in the experimental department of the works, and the rearing of a staff of officials, managers, foremen, and men capable of realising the best results.

THE DESIGN OF THE "AQUITANIA."

The aim in building the Aquitania was to provide a third ship which would be equally acceptable to the travelling public as the Lusitania and Mauretania have proved to be. There is no need to adduce any evidence of the popularity of these two ships, nor of the regularity with which they maintain the service. Both vessels have on the ocean maintained a speed of 26 knots for the whole voyage, and by their good sea qualities and the regularity with which, under normal service steaming, they arrive at port have established themselves as first favourites on the Atlantic. Three vessels, however, are required to maintain a weekly service, and it was therefore decided to build the Aquitania. It will be remembered that the two earlier vessels were built under agreement with the Government, who provided a sum of 2,600,000*l.*, secured on debentures at $2\frac{3}{4}$ per cent. interest, for the construction of the hulls, and a sum of 150,000*l.* per annum for the maintenance of the ships in service. The Cunard Company, on their part, agreed to ensure that the two ships would be capable of maintaining a minimum average ocean speed of $24\frac{1}{2}$ knots in moderate weather; this agreement they have fulfilled to the letter. It was felt, however, that a third ship, equally fast, could not be made financially successful without corresponding subvention, and the management of the Cunard Company had to decide what was the highest sea speed attainable consistent with reasonable monetary return on the capital involved. On the other hand, consideration had also to be given to the speed necessary to ensure that there would be sufficient time at the terminal ports to enable the vessel to "turn about," so that, leaving Liverpool on Saturday, the ship could be ready to depart on the return trip from New York on the Tuesday week following. Great things have been done—notably by the Cunard Company—in facilitating re-coaling, re-victualling, and otherwise preparing their ships between arrival and departure; but

TABLE I.—PARTICULARS OF HISTORICAL VESSELS OF THE CUNARD COMPANY'S FLEET, 1840–1914.

Name of Ship.	Material of Construction.	Means of Propulsion.	Moulded Dimensions. L. (ft.)	Moulded Dimensions. B. (ft. in.)	Moulded Dimensions. D. (ft. in.)	Indicated Horse-Power.	Sea Speed.	Corresponding Draught (ft. in.)	Corresponding Displacement.	Tonnage. Gross.	Tonnage. Net.	Weight. Hull.	Weight. Machinery.	Total Dead weight.	Coal in Permanent Bunkers.	Persons Carried. 1st.	2nd.	3rd.	Crew.	Total.	Date Entering.
Britannia	Wood	Paddles and sails	207	34 2	22 4	740	8.4 to 10.4	—	2,370	1,139	—	—	—	—	640	115	—	—	—	—	1840
Hibernia	,,	Paddles and sails	219	35 9	24 2	1,040	8.9	—	2,950	1,422	—	—	—	—	740	115	—	—	—	—	1843
America	,,	Paddles and sails	251	38 0	25 3	1,040	10.1	—	3,520	1,825	—	—	—	—	840	140	—	—	—	—	1848
Arabia	,,	Paddles and sails	285	40 8	27 7	3,000	12.5	—	4,650	2,402	—	—	—	—	1400	140	—	—	—	—	1852
Persia	Iron	Paddles and sails	376	45 3	31 6	3,600	12.9	—	8,166	3,300	—	—	—	—	1640	250	—	—	—	—	1855
Scotia	,,	Paddles and sails	379	47 8	—	4,900	14.4	—	6,871	3,871	—	3,205	944	2,722	1800	300	—	—	—	—	1862
China	,,	Screw and sail	326	40 5½	—	2,250	13	—	5,180	2,529	—	—	—	—	1100	160	—	—	—	—	1862
Russia	,,	Screw and sail	358	42 6	—	2,800	13	—	5,300	2,959	—	2840		2,460	1180	430	—	—	—	—	1867
Abyssinia	,,	Screw and sail	331	42 0	—	2,480	12.5	—	5,500	3,253	—	—	—	—	1180	202	—	1060	—	—	1870
Bothnia	,,	Screw and sail	420	42 0	—	2,780	13	—	6,530	4,556	—	3898		2,632	940	310	50	1100	155	1615	1874
Gallia	,,	Screw and sail compound	430	44 0	36 0	4,750	15	24 0	8,188	4,808	2,897	—	—	—	1044	380	50	1100	174	1704	1879
Servia	Steel	Screw and sail compound	515	52 0	40 9	9,500	16.5	28 5	13,645	7,391	3,971	6,874	1031	5,740	1780	462	160	200	252	1074	1881
Umbria	,,	Screw and sail compound	500	57 0	40 0	15,000	19.5	28 0	13,071	8,127	3,699	6,274	2500	4,297	2185	250	—	720	—	—	1885
Campania	,,	Twin-screw triple-expansion	600	65 0	41 6	27,650	21.75	29 8	21,628	12,884	5,526	10,500	4935	6,193	3163	523	295	548	450	1816	1893
Ultonia	,,	Twin-screw triple-expansion	500	57 0	37 0	4,440	13.1	29 3¼	18,036	10,402	6,593	5,740	1010	11,286	891	nil	98	1940	210	2248	1898
Ivernia	,,	Twin-screw quadruple-expansion	580	64 3	41 6	10,945	16	32 0	24,789	14,066	9,058	9,820	2110	12,859	1485	340	220	1228	300	2088	1900
Saxonia	,,	Twin-screw quadruple-expansion	580	65 0	41 6	9,950	15.5	31 10	25,100	14,270	9,054	10,250	2050	12,800	1460	360	220	1190	310	2080	1900
Carpathia	,,	Twin-screw quadruple-expansion	540	64 0	40 6	7,385	13.9	31 4½	23,245	13,603	8,660	8,850	1860	12,435	1046	200	130	2150	315	2795	1903
Pannonia	,,	Twin-screw triple-expansion	485	59 0	36 0	5,000	13.06	28 6½	17,490	9,851	6,210	5,926	1014	10,550	899	86	83	1723	235	2127	1904
Carmania	,,	Triple-screw turbine	650	72 0	52 0	21,000	18.5	33 3½	30,918	19,524	9,982	14,682	3918	12,318	2665	297	330	1830	480	2937	1905
Caronia	,,	Twin-screw quadruple-expansion	650	72 0	52 0	20,644	18.56	33 3½	31,155	19,687	10,306	14,455	4145	12,555	2665	368	290	1780	480	2918	1905
Lusitania	,,	Quadruple-screw compound turbine	760	87 6	60 0	72,500	26	36 0	41,440	30,396	12,611	20,145	9936	11,359	6029	580	450	1120	850	3000	1907
Mauretania	,,	Quadruple-screw compound turbine	760	87 6	60 6	72,500	26	36 2½	41,550	30,704	12,799	19,758	9402	12,390	6354	570	460	1120	850	3000	1907
Franconia	,,	Twin-screw quadruple-expansion	600	71 0	52 3	12,349	16.53	29 6	24,290	18,150	11,247	11,540	2850	9,900	2910	240	630	1940	450	3260	1911
Laconia	,,	Twin-screw quadruple-expansion	600	71 0	52 3	11,776	15.6	29 6	24,290	18,098	11,225	11,800	2850	9,640	2509	250	600	1940	450	3240	1912
Andania	,,	Twin-screw quadruple-expansion	520	63 9	46 0	7,244	14.4	28 2	19,400	13,404	8,275	8,444	1750	9,206	1665	nil	522	1560	340	2422	1913
Transylvania	,,	Twin-screw geared turbine	548	66 3	45 0	10,000*	15.5†	27 6	19,480	14,500*	9,000*	9,500*	1700*	9,080*	2600*	340	158	1960	350	2808	—
Aquitania	,,	Quadruple-screw triple expansion turbine	865	97 0	64 6	56,000*	23	34 0	49,430	46,150*	17,500*	29,150*	9000*	11,280*	6000*	618	614	1998	972	4202	—

* Approximate figures. † Designed speed.

prudence suggested that more liberal time than "record performances" should be allowed. It was therefore decided that the new vessel should have a speed on the ocean of 23 knots, to enable her to do the crossing in 5½ days, which leaves four days between arrival and departure. The contract for the new ship was made with Messrs. John Brown and Co., Limited, for a trial-trip speed of 24 knots. What this meant in space and weight of machinery is suggested by the fact that while the 26 knots of the Lusitania required 158,350 sq. ft. of heating surface in the boilers, the 24 knots of the larger Aquitania only requires 138,595 sq. ft. The weight of the machinery is 10 per cent. less, being 9000 tons in the case of the Aquitania, as against 9936 tons in the case of the Lusitania.

It was decided, in order to increase the revenue, to make greater provision for cargo and for a larger number of passengers, particularly in the third-class. Although the reduction in area for, and in the weight of, machinery assisted towards the finding of greater space to ensure this increased earning capacity, it was still necessary to increase the superficial area available for passenger accommodation, and increased length of still greater proportion. The displacement considerably exceeds 53,000 tons for a draught of 36 ft., whereas in the case of the Lusitania it was 41,440 tons for the same draught. Increased displacement, of course, involves higher power for the same speed. For 24 knots the power required by the Lusitania is 50,000 shaft horse-power, equal to 1.266 shaft horse-power per ton, whereas in the Aquitania the designed power for 24 knots is 60,000, equal to 1.2 horse-power per ton displacement. The Lusitania, on the other hand, requires 72,500 horse-power for 26 knots, so that the proportion of power to displacement tonnage becomes, for the higher speed, 1.77.

The dimensions of the Aquitania, along with what might be called contemporaneous leviathan high-speed ships, are given in Table II. There are always difficulties in making comparisons, because the length over all may be influenced by features which are scarcely essential to the structure of the ship, while the length between perpendiculars is more or less arbitrarily fixed, as the perpendicular point may vary with the idiosyncrasy of the designer. Again, as regards the gross tonnage, this may be affected by the coefficient of fineness exhausting into a turbine on the centre shaft, the other ships are fitted with turbines on all shafts. The Aquitania has three turbines working in series, the high-pressure turbine exhausting into the intermediate high-pressure turbine, which latter passes steam to the two low-pressure turbines mounted on the inboard shafts ; while on the wing shafts there are high-pressure astern turbines, and on the inboard shafts low-pressure astern turbines, each of very great power.

The dimensions and other particulars were evolved as a result of many conferences between the Cunard Company and the builders. The question of stability under abnormal conditions—which includes the ingress of the sea through accident to any part of the ship—had special consideration in the design of this as of all other Cunard ships. Before even the dimensions were fixed upon, this matter was closely investigated. In the double bottom, which extends from bow to stern, there are 41 water-tight compartments, while in the moulded structure of the ship above this there are 84 water-tight compartments formed by transverse and longitudinal bulkheads and water-tight decks. The transverse bulkheads have been

TABLE II.—SHOWING DIMENSIONS OF "AQUITANIA" AND OTHER LARGE SHIPS OF VARIOUS NATIONALITIES.

Name of Ship	"Aquitania."	"Britannic."	"Vaterland."	"Imperator."	"Olympic."	"La France."	"Lusitania."*	"Kronprincessin Cecilie."
Name of builders	John Brown and Co., Clydebank	Harland and Wolff, Belfast	Blohm and Voss, Hamburg	Vulcan Company, Hamburg	Harland and Wolff, Belfast	S. des Chantiers et Ateliers de St. Nazaire	John Brown and Co., Clydebank	Vulcan Company, of Stettin
Name of owning company	Cunard	White Star	Hamburg-Amerika	Hamburg-Amerika	White Star	French	Cunard	North German Lloyd
Year when built	1914	1914	1914	1912	1910	1910	1907	1907
Length over all	901 ft. 6 in.	882 ft. 9 in.	950 ft.	905 ft.	883 ft.	714 ft.	785 ft.	706 ft. 4 in.
Length between perpendiculars or moulded	865 ft.	850 ft.	—	880 ,,	—	685 ft.	760 ft.	682 ft. 9 in.
Breadth	97 ,,	93 ft. 6 in.	100 ft.	98 ,,	92 ft.	75 ft. 9 in.	88 ft.	72 ft.
Depth, moulded	64 ,,	64 ft. 3 in.	63 ft.	62 ,,	64 ft. 3 in.	52 ft. 10 in.	60 ft. 4½ in.	44 ft. 2 in.
Gross tonnage	46,500	48,000	54,190	52,117	45,000	24,448	32,000	19,400
Draught	36 ft.	34 ft. 7 in.	38 ft. 6 in.	35 ft. 6 in.	—	30 ft.	33 ft. 6 in.	30 ft.
Displacement	53,000 tons	53,000 tons	63,100 tons	57,000 tons	—	27,000 tons	38,000 tons	27,000 tons
Number of passengers—first	618	790	672†	700	730	535	552	729
,, ,, second	614	836	535	600	560	442	460	318
,, ,, third	1998	953	2392‡	2690	1200	908	1186	740
Machinery makers	John Brown and Co.	Harland and Wolff	Blohm and Voss	Vulcan Company	Harland and Wolff	S. des Chantiers, St. Nazaire, &c.	John Brown and Co., Clydebank	Vulcan Company, of Stettin
Type of engine	Four-screw steam-turbines	Reciprocating, with turbine on centre shaft	Turbines	Four-screw steam-turbines	Reciprocating, with turbine on centre shaft	Four-screw steam-turbine	Parsons turbine	Four sets, four-cylinder quadruple-expansion
Number of cranks	—	8	—	—	8	—	—	6
Diameters of cylinders	—	Two of 54 in. ; two of 84 in. ; and four of 97 in.	—	—	Two of 54 in. ; two of 34 in.; four of 97 in.	—	—	Four of 37.40 in.; four of 49.21 in.; four of 74.80 in.; four of 112.20 in.
Stroke of pistons	—	75 in.	—	—	75 in.	—	—	70.87 in.
Number and type of boilers	21 cylindrical : double-ended	29 cylindrical : 24 double-ended ; 5 single-ended	46 water-tube	46 water-tube	29 cylindrical : 24 double-ended ; 5 single-ended	11 double-ended ; 8 single-ended	25 cylindrical : 23 double-ended ; 2 single-ended	12 double-ended ; 7 single-ended
Number of furnaces	168	159	138	46	159	120	192	124
Steam pressure	195 lb.	215 lb.	235 lb. per sq. in.	235 lb. per sq. in.	215	199 lb. per sq. in.	195 lb. per sq. in.	220.5 lb. per sq. in.
Total heating surface	138,595 sq. ft.	150,958 sq. ft.	210,440 sq. ft.	203,009 sq. ft.	144,142 sq. ft.	99,303 sq. ft.	158,350 sq. ft.	101,900 sq. ft.
,, grate area	3,541 ,,	3,461 ,,	3,843 ,, ,,	3,763 ,,	3,466 ,,	2,555 ,,	4,048 ,,	2,970 ,,
System of draught	Howden's	Natural	Howden's	Howden's	Natural	Howden's	Howden's	Open stokehold
Total indicated horse-power	60,000	50,000	—	76,250	46,000	46,370	68,000	45,000
Speed on service	23.5 knots	—	22.5 knots	22½ knots	22¾ knots	23.6 knots	25 knots	23.5 knots
Revolutions per minute	165	77 and 170	180 to 190	185	77.5	241.5	180	82

* The Cunard liner Mauretania is practically of the same dimensions as the Lusitania ; she was built by Messrs. Swan, Hunter and Wigham Richardson, Limited, Wallsend-on-Tyne, and engined by the Wallsend Slipway and Engineering Company, Limited.

† In addition there are 80 berths for servants and 110 Pullman berths.

‡ This figure includes 1542 fourth-class passengers.

hull became necessary. As a consequence, the Aquitania is designed for a population of 4202, as compared with 3000 in the Lusitania, the Aquitania being arranged to take 3230 passengers, as compared with 2150 in the Lusitania. The number of first-class passengers has been increased from 580 to 618, the second-class passengers from 450 to 614, and the third-class passengers from 1120 to 1998, while the crew—principally because of the increase in staff required for the passengers—has been augmented by the addition of 122—from 850 to 972. Increased beam had to be given as well as increased length.

The moulded dimensions, therefore, of the Aquitania are 865 ft., as compared with the 760 ft. of the Lusitania, while at the same time the beam was increased from 87 ft. 6 in. to 97 ft., and the depth, moulded, from 60 ft. to 64 ft. 6 in. These are most favourable conditions, not only for speed, but for stability, the metacentric height of the vessel when loaded being about 4 ft., as compared with 3 ft. 6 in. in the Lusitania. This, while satisfactory as to safety, is accompanied by easy motion in a seaway. The result of the enlarged dimensions has been to increase the weight of the hull from 20,145 tons to 29,150 tons, while the dead-weight capacity for cargo, &c., is considerably increased, by reason principally of the less quantity of coal to be taken for the voyage, as the power is reduced 22 per cent., and, by reason of higher economy in the engines, the coal consumption will be lessened in of the ship. As regards displacement tonnage, the question to be determined is as to whether the draught to be taken into account is in the loaded or unloaded condition, or the mean draught on the voyage, or the draught at the beginning or end of the voyage. The coal carried in the bunkers, if included, may make a difference of 5000 or 6000 tons to the displacement tonnage. These limitations should be carefully borne in mind in any comparison that may be made of the dimensions as set out in tabular form. It will be seen that the Aquitania has a length over all—and in this no excrescences are included—of 901 ft. 6 in.; the Britannic—to which the same remark applies—is 882 ft. 9 in. ; the Imperator is 905 ft. ; and the Vaterland, just completed for the Hamburg-Amerika line, is 950 ft. As regards beam, the Aquitania is 97 ft.; the Britannic, 93 ft. 6 in. ; the Imperator, 98 ft. 3 in. ; and the Vaterland, 100 ft. The gross tonnage of the Aquitania is 47,000 tons ; of the Britannic, 48,000 tons ; of the Imperator, 52,117 tons ; and of the Vaterland, 54,190 tons. The German ships are obviously intended to be faster, as the machinery is of much greater power. Thus, while the Aquitania has a designed power of 60,000 shaft horse-power, and the Britannic of 50,000 horse-power, the Imperator has to develop 76,250 horse-power, and the Vaterland a still greater amount. While the Britannic is fitted with a combination system of machinery, having two reciprocating engines on the wing-shafts, carried up to an unusual height, and this, in conjunction with the longitudinal and horizontal divisions, make the conditions such that should the fore part of the ship for the first five compartments, or the after part of the ship for the six after compartments, or the five centre compartments, be open to the sea, the ship would still remain in a perfectly stable condition. Indeed, everything possible that scientific knowledge could devise has been carried out to make this ship safe.

The question of stability, &c., did not stand alone in determining the dimensions. There are many purely extraneous circumstances which affect the issue, not the least important being the limitations in the depths of channels, notwithstanding the enterprise of harbour authorities. Deep draught is the constant dream of the naval architect, but it is a costly idea for the harbour engineer. Length and beam have therefore to be relied upon by the ship-designer, and even here there are limitations. In the general dimensions of the Aquitania, therefore, the increases are in length and beam, and in connection with the final proportions, and particularly the coefficient of fineness and generally the lines, the Cunard Company availed themselves of the experimental tank at the Clydebank Works, Messrs. John Brown and Co. being the only firm capable of building a vessel of the size of the Aquitania who possess such an experimental tank. Calculations previously made for determining the power required to drive the vessel, as well as the design of propellers best suited to utilise that power efficiently, were thus confirmed, and the form and dimensions of the Aquitania finally fixed.

THE BUILDING OF THE SHIP.

The order for the Aquitania was placed with Messrs. John Brown and Co., Limited, in December, 1910, and arrangements were at once proceeded with for the preparation of the berth for the construction of the ship. Enough has already been said to establish the claim of the builders to the right for such preference as was shown by the Cunard Company; but although the Lusitania had been most successfully built, launched and navigated to the sea, the great increase in size in the Aquitania involved the making of a new berth. The Clydebank yard has a frontage to the river of nearly 3200 ft., in the centre of which is the fitting-

yet ordered; and H.M.S. Barham, which belongs to the Queen Elizabeth class, and is therefore the embodiment of the highest achievement in battleship design.

Owing to the line of keel-blocks for the Aquitania being at a more acute angle to the river than were those of the Lusitania, additional piling had to be carried out, especially at the lower end of the berth, in order particularly to take up the thrust from the fore poppets of the cradle when the stern of the ship was first water-borne. Careful calculation was made from past experience in the launching of long ships to determine the moment when the stern would float, and the position at which the downward thrust forward would be exerted on the standing ways and berth. Close piling was driven over an extensive area, and heavy walings secured the piling together, as shown in the photograph reproduced on page 5, Fig. 5. This again

suitable foundation plate and a top plate, to which the guys are attached. The jib is of rolled-steel sections and plates; the bottom boom consisting of two rolled-steel channels arranged to form a track for the trolley. The latter is constructed of steel plates, and mounted on four single-flange wheels. It is racked up the jib by means of a four-part rope, and returns by gravity to the minimum radius. The racking-rope is wound or unwound on a cast-iron drum, driven by a motor through the medium of suitable reductions of gearing.

Suitable stairs and platforms are provided to give access to all parts requiring attention. The driver's cabin is situated immediately under the slewing gear, where the man has complete control of the operations and a clear view.

The motors are of the totally-enclosed reversing type, especially designed for crane service. They

Photo by Burton, Leicester.

LORD ABERCONWAY, CHAIRMAN OF MESSRS. JOHN BROWN AND CO., LIMITED

Photo by Lafayette, Manchester.

MR. A. A. BOOTH, CHAIRMAN OF THE CUNARD COMPANY.

out basin; to the east were the six old berths on which all the large ships built had been constructed, while to the west are several new berths for the building of light cruisers, Channel steamers, and the like. In order to accommodate the Aquitania with the minimum of disorganisation of the other large berths, it was decided to embrace in the one berth the width formerly occupied by two berths, so that the six berths have become five. At the same time several buildings, formerly at the head of two of the berths, and accommodating various departments connected with the completion of ships—plumbing, painting, &c.—had to be demolished, but the range of platers' and fitters' machine-tool shops still continues along the head of the rearranged berths. It is significant of the importance of the work undertaken at Clydebank that there were simultaneously on the rearranged berths the Aquitania, the largest merchant ship built; H.M.S. Tiger, the greatest battle-cruiser

was completely surrounded by concrete. The piling was carried under the area later occupied by the keel-blocks and standing ways.

The crane arrangements made are illustrated in the same view and in several of the views of the ship in progress (see also pages 4 and 5). It will be seen that along each side of the berth are seven derrick cranes, which were supplied and erected by Sir William Arrol and Co., Limited, Glasgow. Owing to their great height and radius these are of special interest, and drawings of them are produced in Figs 1 to 4, on page 4. The maximum load is 5 tons at an extreme radius of 55 ft. The load can be racked in to a minimum radius of 11 ft. 6 in. The height of lift above the berth level is 111 ft., and the total height of the mast is 135 ft. over all. Slewing gear is provided to turn the jib through an angle of 205 deg.

The mast is built up of rolled-steel sections, well braced and riveted together, and provided with

are rated so that after a half hour's run under full load the temperature rise above that of the surrounding atmosphere does not exceed 90 deg. Fahr. Each motor is provided with a tramway-type reversing controller, having the vertical contact barrel mounted on ball-bearings to ensure ease of operation. The jib-slewing motor drives a spur-wheel attached to the jib foot-bearing through reductions of gearing. The load is lifted on a single-part best plough-steel wire rope, winding on to a cast-iron drum, driven by a motor, through the medium of three reductions of spur-gearing. A double set of gear is provided for the last reduction in order that the two specified speeds of hoisting may be obtained. Change of gear is effected by means of a claw-clutch. The hoisting-drum is of large diameter, turned and grooved to take the full amount of rope in a single lap. Two brakes are provided; one is an automatic electric brake, operated by means of a solenoid magnet connected in such a manner that the brake is released directly the motor is started, and is applied directly the current is cut off, or fails for any reason. This brake is also arranged so that it may be released by hand, and the loads allowed to descend by gravity. A foot-brake is fitted on the hoisting-motor spindle, so that in the event of failure of the solenoid brake, this brake may be applied by the operator. The speeds of working are:—Hoisting, 5 tons at 60 ft. per minute and 3 tons at 100 ft. per minute ; racking, 5 tons at 35 ft. per minute ; and slewing, 5 tons at 200 deg. per minute.

On this berth, and with the assistance of these cranes, the great leviathan steadily grew, but the actual work of construction we will deal with presently when describing the hull. Suffice it here to say that she was launched on the 21st of April, 1913.

THE LAUNCH OF THE SHIP.

In view of the great experience of the management of the works in the launching of immense ships, it was anticipated that there would be brought to bear upon the solution of one of the most fascinating problems presented to the naval architect, every precautionary measure which past operations of a kindred nature suggested, and, as a result, although the vessel is the largest yet built in this country, there was not for one moment any feeling of anxiety by those responsible, who had a full knowledge of the precautionary measures taken. For two or three minutes before the vessel actually started, she was "creeping," but this was a direct consequence of the leaving in position of more of the keel-blocks than is usual so as to retard the speed during the initial period of the launch, and to obviate too great a momentum being developed. The speed of the ship on the ways did not at any time exceed 15 knots, and the mean velocity was just over 10 ft. per second.

We reproduce on page 6 drawings of the most important part of the launching cradle—the forward part ; a perspective view of this is reproduced in Fig. 14, page 7. The drawings reproduced in Figs. 8 to 13 are of special interest because they show the provision made for taking the great stress not only on the structure of the ship forward, but on the forward cradle, when the stern first became water-borne. Heavy piling, with horizontal and diagonal timbers buried in ferro-concrete, had been put in, during the preparation of the berth, in order to take the pressure through the launching-ways. Thus it was ensured that there would be no yielding of the foundation at any part, and particularly at the point where the downward thrust was exerted by the bow when the stern became water-borne. The ways had a width of 6 ft. 6 in., and at the forward end the thickness of the sliding-ways was 20 in., and for the remaining part of the length 10 in. On the two-page Plate I. we reproduce an admirable view of the ship immediately before the launch ; and one of the many interesting features which may be seen is the considerable overhang forward of the bow cradle, due to the very fine entry of the ship. Abaft, as shown in the view on Plate I, it was possible to house the poppets of the cradle immediately under the inner propeller brackets. The normal load on the ways was reduced to 2.2 tons per square foot, which, it will be recognised, is far below the limit.

The heads of the poppets in the forward cradle were housed partly against the shell-plating, and partly, in the case of the outer poppets, in recesses in heavy built-up steel brackets riveted to the shell-plating and frames of the ship, as shown in Figs. 8 and 9. The poppets were made up for the most part of 15-in. by 15-in. timbers, the innermost timbers being 15 in. by 18 in. The brackets were braced by longitudinal channels or flanged plates, as shown in Figs. 10 to 13. The poppets were braced horizontally and diagonally by 9-in. by 6-in. ribbons and by steel plates 12-in. wide. There was a series of tie-rods extending, under the keel of the ship, from port to starboard side, as shown in Fig. 8. These were bolted up through a horizontal ribbon with 3-in. bolts passing through the spaces between the poppets, as shown in Fig. 9. This construction extended for about 32 ft. of the length of the cradle. Abaft this the poppets were at greater intervals apart, and there was substituted for the tie-rods chain lashings between the port and starboard poppets.

CRANES FOR THE BUILDING BERTH OF THE "AQUITANIA."

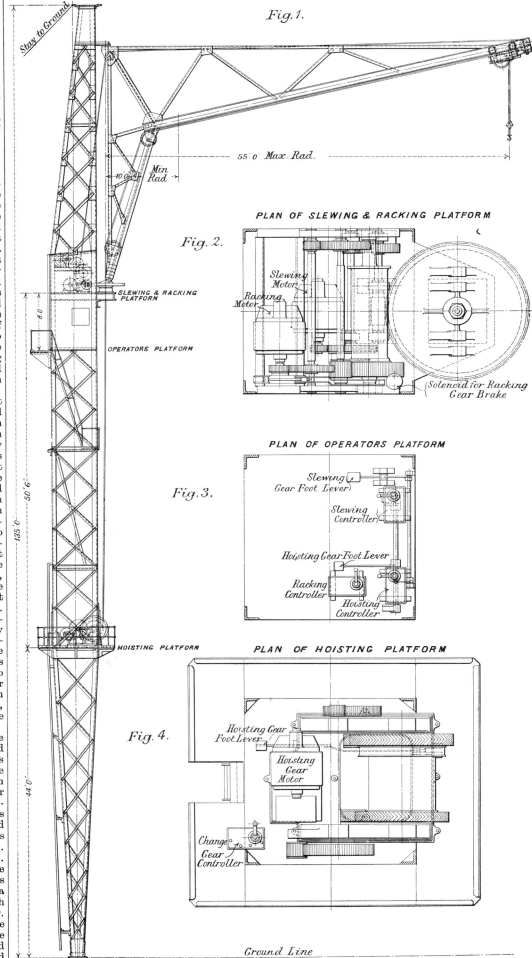

Fig. 1.

Stay to Ground

55'.0" Max. Rad.

40'.0" Min. Rad.

Fig. 2.

PLAN OF SLEWING & RACKING PLATFORM

Slewing Motor

Racking Motor

Solenoid for Racking Gear Brake

SLEWING & RACKING PLATFORM

OPERATORS PLATFORM

Fig. 3.

PLAN OF OPERATORS PLATFORM

Slewing Gear Foot Lever

Slewing Controller

Hoisting Gear Foot Lever

Racking Controller

Hoisting Controller

HOISTING PLATFORM

Fig. 4.

PLAN OF HOISTING PLATFORM

Hoisting Gear Foot Lever

Hoisting Gear Motor

Change Gear Controller

135'.0"   50'.6"   8'.0"   44'.0"

Ground Line

The provision made for holding the ship and the sliding ways stationary after the bilge-blocks had been removed, and after as many of the keel- applied; it consists of an hydraulic cylinder, the ram of which retains in a vertical position a centrally pivoted forged trigger, the upper part of this trigger the vertical to the horizontal position, freeing the sliding-ways. The valves of all three pairs of cylinders are actuated simultaneously by electrical gear.

The honours of the occasion were in the hands of the Countess of Derby, who herself takes a deep interest in all that concerns the prosperity of Liverpool. Moreover, the Earl of Derby had a direct interest, because he was the Lord Mayor of the City. The electric gear actuating the exhaust-valves of the cylinders was operated simultaneously with the mechanism for throwing the christening-bottle against the side of the ship. When the triggers was released there was no perceptible movement for quite three minutes, but there was evidence in the creaking noise that the laws of gravity were steadily asserting themselves. Thus, after fully 3 minutes' creeping, for reasons which we have already explained, the ship began to move, and from the first indication of perceptible motion until she was afloat 1 minute 31 seconds elapsed, which gives an average speed, as we have said, of about 10 ft. per second. To check the vessel there were eight piles of chains on each side of the berth, and these were connected by wire ropes secured to very heavy eye-bolts riveted temporarily to the sides of the ship. These may be discerned in the view of the vessel reproduced on Plate I. The collective weight of these chain-drags was just under 1400 tons, and the aftermost drag came into effect just before the bow of the ship had left the ways. Thus the brake was very gentle and gradual in its application. That it was effective is proved by the fact that the vessel was pulled up when only about 150 ft. from the end of the ways, and that two of the piles of drags on each side were never moved. The total time taken from the electric release of the exhaust-valves until the vessel dipped from the end of the ways was 5 minutes 10 seconds. The draught forward was found to be 13 ft., and aft 21 ft., the launching weight, without the ways or cradle, being about 22,000 tons. The vessel was at once taken in charge by seven tug-boats, and moved into the fitting-out dock at the works, being moored within an hour of the launch.

At the luncheon which followed there was general congratulation at the success of the launch, a success which only conformed with the traditions at the Clydebank Works. It was gratifying to note, on the part alike of Mr. A. A. Booth, the chairman of the Cunard Company, and of Lord Aberconway, the chairman, and Mr. Charles Ellis, the managing director, of the builders' company, a generous but well-won recognition of the efforts of the technical

Fig 5. View of Berth, showing also Piling for Keel-Blocks and Standing-Ways.

Fig. 6. The "Aquitania" Taking the Water.

blocks had been knocked out as it was determined to remove, consisted of hydraulic triggers. There were three separate pairs, placed at considerable distances apart, in the length of the ways. The mechanism is now well known, and very widely holding the standing ways in position by locking into a recess of heavy forged steel built into the bottom of the sliding-way. Release of the pressure water in the cylinder causes the ram to recede and enables the centrally-pivoted trigger to tilt from officers of both companies towards the work which had culminated in the launch of the ship. Another point regarding which there was justifiable recognition was the enterprise of the Clyde Navigation Trustees and the Clyde Lighthouse Board, and the

FORWARD LAUNCHING CRADLE FOR THE "AQUITANIA."

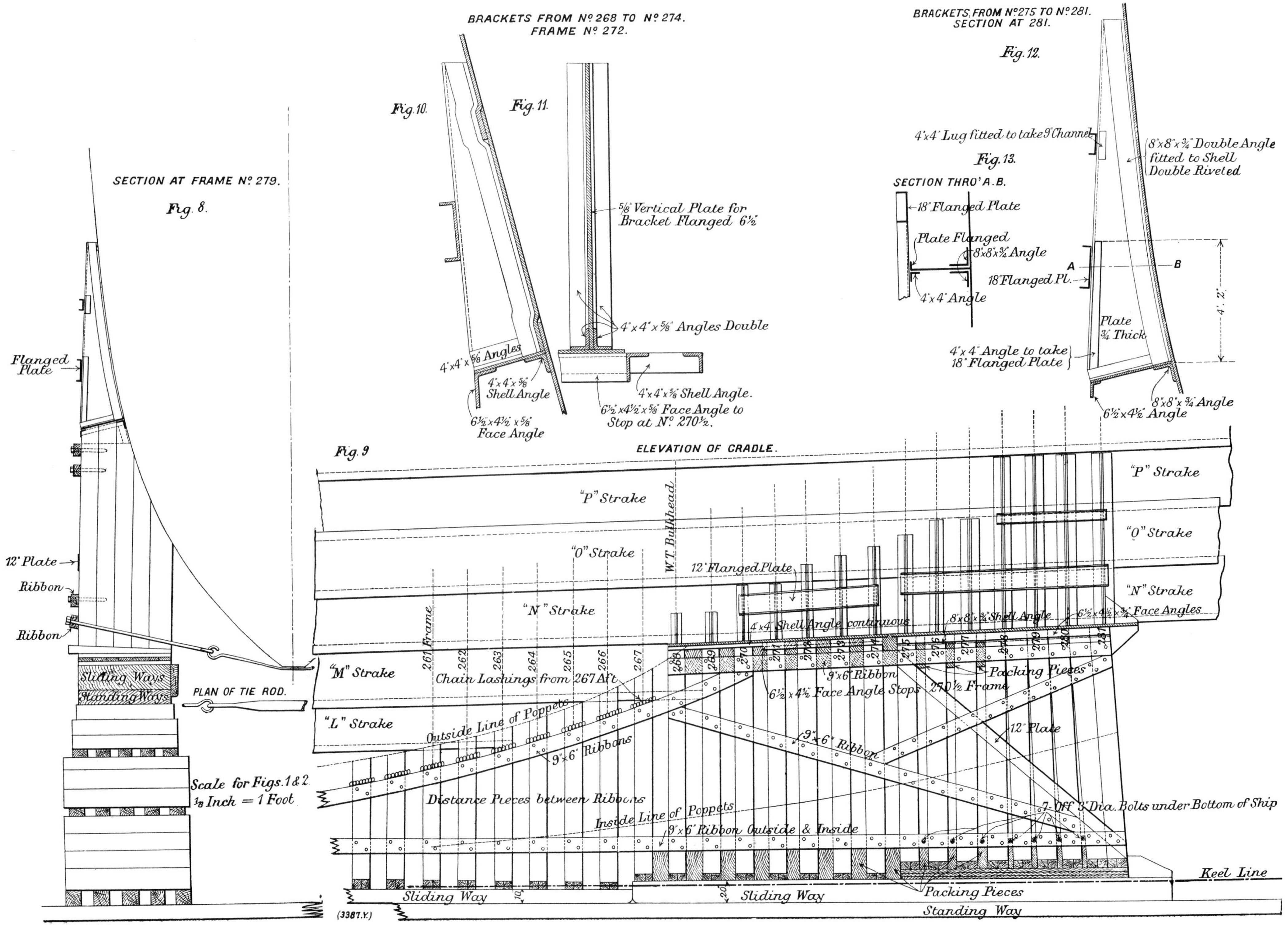

Fig. 12.

BRACKETS FROM Nº 275 TO Nº 281.
SECTION AT 281.

8"×8"×¾" Double Angle fitted to Shell Double Riveted

8"×8"×¾" Angle

6½"×4½" Angle

Plate ¾" Thick

Fig. 13.

SECTION THRO' A.B.

4"×4" Lug fitted to take 9"Channel
18" Flanged Plate
Plate Flanged
8"×8"×¾" Angle
18" Flanged Pl.
4"×4" Angle
4"×4" Angle to take 18" Flanged Plate

Fig. 11.

BRACKETS FROM Nº 268 TO Nº 274.
FRAME Nº 272.

5⁄8" Vertical Plate for Bracket Flanged 6½"
4"×4"×5⁄8" Angles Double
4"×4"×5⁄8" Shell Angle.
6½"×4½"×5⁄8" Face Angle to Stop at Nº 270½.

Fig. 10.

4"×4"×5⁄8" Shell Angle
6½"×4½"×5⁄8" Face Angle
4"×4"×5⁄8" Angles

Fig. 8.

SECTION AT FRAME Nº 279.

Flanged Plate
12" Plate
Ribbon
Ribbon

PLAN OF TIE ROD.

Scale for Figs. 1 & 2.
2⁄3 Inch = 1 Foot

Sliding Ways
Standing Ways

Fig. 9.

ELEVATION OF CRADLE.

"P" Strake
"O" Strake
"N" Strake
"M" Strake
"L" Strake

Keel Line

Packing Pieces

7"OF 3" Dia. Bolts under Bottom of Ship

Standing Way

Sliding Way

8"×8"×¾" Shell Angle
6½"×4½" Face Angles
12" Plate
9"×6" Ribbon
27½" Frame
6½"×4½" Face Angle Stops
4"×4" Shell Angle continuous
12" Flanged Plate
9"×6" Ribbon Outside & Inside
9"×6" Ribbon
W.T. Bulkhead
Inside Line of Poppets
Distance Pieces between Ribbons
9"×6" Ribbons
Outside Line of Poppets
Chain Lashings from 267 Aft

261 Frame 262 263 264 265 266 267 Aft 268 269 270 271 272 273 274 275 276 277 278 279 280 281

(3387.Y.)

THE FORWARD LAUNCHING CRADLE.

FIG. 14. THE BOW CRADLE.

Right Hon. Sydney Buxton, President of the Board of Trade, gave expression to this feeling in proposing the toast of success to these institutions, which was responded to by Sir Thomas Mason, the Chairman of the Clyde Trustees.

THE DEEPENING AND WIDENING OF THE RIVER CLYDE.

Improvements were made in the depth and width of the channel of the river, not only in anticipation of the launch, but for the navigation of the ship to the sea. This work was carried out by the Clyde Navigation Trustees. Much had been done prior to the completion of the Lusitania. Thus, in 1904, the Clyde Trustees obtained parliamentary powers for widening the river at the point at which the Clydebank ships are launched. The location of the yard was originally decided upon in the early 'seventies, because nearly opposite to it is the confluence of the rivers Cart and Clyde, and for the launch of the Lusitania about 2 acres were thrown into the water space on the east side of the mouth of the Cart, and $6\frac{1}{4}$ acres to the west of the Cart. There was therefore no need to add to the water area for the launch of the Aquitania, but special dredging had been done in the line of the launch from the berth to the mouth of the Cart, the depth reaching a maximum of $45\frac{1}{2}$ ft. below high water of ordinary spring tides.

Under contract with Messrs. John Brown and Co., Sir William Arrol and Co. lengthened the fitting-out basin by extending the head landwards into the works. This was done by the sinking of cast-iron cylinders with the help of grab-dredgers, in order to provide a foundation for the new wall. Alterations were also made at the entrance of the basin in order to facilitate the movement of the Aquitania into and out of the dock. The basin itself was dredged, so that the Aquitania was always afloat when lying alongside the 200-ton cranes available for putting machinery, &c., on board.

At the same time the river was further greatly widened by the Clyde Navigation Trustees, the builders of the Aquitania contributing 10.000*l.* towards the cost. The widening has been carried out on the south side of the river, where there exists an island known as Newshot Isle. This was arable land, and fully 13 acres were cut away and added to the water space. The part of the river from Clydebank to Dalmuir was thus increased to a uniform width of 600 ft., whereas formerly it varied from 460 ft. to 555 ft. At this place there was a bend in the river, which had proved awkward for heavy and long ships, and would have increased the difficulty of navigating the Aquitania to the sea. At the bend the width was increased from 630 ft. to 695 ft.; beyond this the increase in width was from 485 ft. to 610 ft. This work must be of lasting benefit to navigation. Further down the river a good deal of dredging had also to be done to Port Glasgow by the Clyde Navigation Trustees, and beyond that by the Clyde Lighthouse Trustees, the responsible authorities for the channel from Port Glasgow to the sea.

THE PASSAGE OF THE SHIP TO THE SEA.

Thus, when the Aquitania, completed with all her machinery, left the Clydebank Works on the 10th May, 1914, there was little need for anxiety as to her passage to the sea, notwithstanding her great size and the narrowness of the channel. Mr. W. M. Alston, M. Inst. C.E., the engineer-in-chief of the Clyde Trust, worked assiduously during the building of the ship for the completion of the works, and satisfied himself by soundings and other means, that all that could be done had been accomplished for the voyage of the ship to the sea. All that was necessary was a calm day. This was realised, and if the drizzling rain that fell was a discomfort to the 500,000 or 600,000 people who gathered along the banks of the river, the haze added a touch of the mystic to the slow, but continuously steady progress of the majestic ship, with her attendant tugs, preceded by the Clyde Trust Commodore steamer, and followed by a convoy of pleasure steamers. She came out of the mist in her great bulk, passed by the crowds gathered at each vantage point, and receded again in impressive stately silence into the vague obscurity. When she reached the Firth, however, the weather cleared and the sun shone, and a short spin at 8 or 9 knots was made, twelve boilers being alight. Finally, she anchored to coal up and prepare for her full-

THE "AQUITANIA" LEAVING THE BUILDERS' YARD.

FIG. 15.

power tests. Views are given on the present and opposite page of the vessel as she was swung out of the fitting-out basin at the Clydebank Works into the river ready for her passage to the sea.

THE STEAM TRIALS.

The trials of the Aquitania were of shorter duration than those prescribed in connection with the Lusitania and Mauretania. Several reasons account for this. It should be remembered that when the two earlier Cunard ships were ordered, the steam-turbine had only been tried in Channel steamers and torpedo - boat destroyers. Consequently it was decided, in order thoroughly to assure public opinion, that prolonged trials should take place under sea conditions. Thus it was arranged that each vessel should steam four times over a measured course 300 miles long, making a continuous trial of 1200 miles, in addition to various other severe manœuvring tests. The result was that both ships developed a speed of over 26 knots, covering the distance in less than 48 hours. The working of the machinery was most regular and without misadventure even of the slightest nature. In service the results have been equally favourable. There is also the fact that no firm in this country has had greater experience of high-power turbines than Messrs. John Brown and Co., of Clydebank, so that there was confidence not only in the details of the design evolved by the firm, but also in the efficiency and reliability of the workmanship. It was therefore decided that the trials of the Aquitania should be of short duration, espe-

cially as this afforded a greater period of time for the preparation of the ship to take up her station on the 30th May. As regards the attainment of the guaranteed speed, this has become almost a matter of precision, in view of the possibility of determining from models the power necessary to drive at a given rate of speed a ship of certain lines, and with the best propulsive efficiency. The proportions and lines of the Aquitania were determined by such model tests at the experimental tank at Clydebank, so that there was little doubt about the realisation of the speed on the trials or in service.

On May 11 the vessel took on board over 2000 tons of coal, and water-ballast to bring her down to the mean draught while on the Atlantic voyage. On the following day she left her anchorage for her trials, with the intention not so much of ascertaining her speed for the designed full power as to test the turbines and their manœuvring gear, and to ensure that all auxiliaries were in thoroughly satisfactory order, as also to get the engine-room staff fully acquainted with their duties. The turbines were therefore worked up gradually to full power, and opportunity was taken to make runs over the measured mile at Skelmorlie at progressive speeds, beginning at 12 knots. The data could not, however, be regarded as accurately determining the relation of power to speed, as the vessel had been in the tidal basin since her launch thirteen months ago, so that the immersed part of the hull was in a condition involving excessive skin resistance. A view is given on the frontispiece of the vessel during one of these runs. On Tuesday afternoon the

vessel proceeded into the outer estuary of the Clyde, where a greater seaway was available for manœuvring purposes, and the engineer had greater freedom for testing the valves when changing over from triple-series working to compound working, and for bringing the turbines on the port and starboard side of the ship into action for ahead and astern steaming. The valves and interlocking gear for this purpose will be described later, but here it need only be said that the aim of the designers was realised as regards surety and rapidity of operation under the various alternative systems of working.

Following upon this a series of high-power and full-power runs were made between Holy Isle and Ailsa Craig. The wind had steadily increased to force 5, and notwithstanding the unsatisfactory state of the immersed hull, the result was satisfactory, speeds of 24 knots being reached without any effort; there is accordingly every confidence of the guaranteed speed of 23 knots on the Atlantic being exceeded. The night was spent at sea, running under various conditions of working, by way, principally, of introducing the engineers of the ship to their work. On Wednesday again, there were further full-power runs, equally satisfactory. There was a pallograph on board, and diagrams were taken at all points where there was any possibility of vibration being disclosed, but in no case was any such movement indicated. This demonstrates the success of the special care taken in the direction of stiffening the ship, a matter to which reference will be made when we describe the structure of the ship. The

THE "AQUITANIA" ON HER WAY TO THE SEA.

Fig. 16.

bulkhead doors were also tested. In the Aquitania there are two separate circuits — one for the doors in the transverse bulkheads, and another for those in the longitudinal bulkheads; both are operated independently from the bridge. The main doors can be kept permanently closed, and the bunker doors can be closed from the bridge or at the doors themselves. Another feature is that the coal-bunkers in each boiler compartment can hold sufficient for the use of the boilers, so that each boiler-room is entirely within its own water-tight area at all times. Other corresponding tests were made, and it was established that in every case the experience and the solicitous care and enterprise exercised by Mr. Booth and the directors of the company, as well as by Messrs. John Brown and Co., Limited, have fully realised the anticipated results.

THE PERSONNEL OF THE SHIP.

The Aquitania is commanded by Captain Turner, formerly of the Lusitania and the Commodore of the Cunard fleet. He has had great experience in the management of the company's large liners, and the fullest reliance may be placed in his ability and caution. With him are two commanders, so that one will always be on the bridge. Nearly all the members of his staff of seven officers have captain's certificates. Equal care has been taken in the choice of the officers in charge of the powerful machinery in the ship. The chief engineer is Mr. Bryce, who has been thirty years in the service of the Cunard Company, his last ship having been the Lusitania. Moreover, he has all the qualities which heredity bring, as his father was forty years an engineer in the Cunard liners. His staff of thirty-four officers are all tried and qualified men, many of them with chief's certificates. Appended is a full list of the complement of the ship.

SHIP'S COMPLEMENT.

Captain and staff-captains		..	..	..	..		3
Officers	..	..	..	..	..		7
Engineers and chief	..	..	..	..			34
Refrigeration engineer	..	..	..	..			1
Seamen and boys	..	..	..	..			48
Quartermasters	..	..	..	..			6
Boatswain and mates	..	..	..	..			3
Carpenters and joiners	..	..	..	..			3
Lamp-trimmer and yeoman	..	..	..				2
Inspector and interpreter..	..	..	..				2
Bandsmen	..	..	..	..	..		8
Plumber	..	..	..	..	..		1
Baggage-master	..	..	..	..			1
Firemen	..	..	..	..	..		168

Trimmers	..	..	..	..	..	..	100
Leading firemen	..	..	..	..	..		16
Greasers	..	..	..	..	..		20
Doctors	..	..	..	..	..		2
Purser	..	..	..	..	..		1
Assistant pursers	..	..	..	..			2
Chief steward	..	..	..	..			1
Second stewards	..	..	..	..			2
Third steward	..	..	..	..			1
Second-class steward, chief	..	..	..				1
Chef	..	..	..	..	..		1
Barbers	..	..	..	..	..		3
Matron..	..	..	..	..	..		1
Nurse	..	..	..	..	..		1

Stewardesses..	..	..	..	..			20
Typists	..	..	..	..	..		2
Marconi operators	..	..	..	..			2
Leading stewards	..	..	..	..			16
Stewards	..	..	..	..	..		352
Assistant stewards	..	..	..	..			54
Butchers and bakers	..	..	..	..			10
Junior bakers	..	..	..	..			24
Leading cooks	..	..	..	..			24
Chief baker and confectioner	..	..					2
Cooks	..	..	..	..	..		28
							973

Having thus given a brief review of the evolution of the design, and of the progress of construction to completion ready for service, and the arrangements incidental thereto, we may now turn to a more detailed description of the ship and machinery, and to the method of carrying out the more important details.

THE STRUCTURAL DETAILS, PASSENGER ACCOMMODATION, AND

EQUIPMENT OF THE SHIP.

WE now propose to consider in detail the hull, its design, structural strength, provision against misadventure, and the suitability and comfort of the habitable quarters to attain the maximum of pleasure for the passengers. We leave for the next chapter a description of the propelling machinery of the ship, with the auxiliaries connected therewith. We shall then deal with the principal features embodied in the design to ensure the highest degree of economy, and those ingenious devices introduced to achieve rapidity and certainty, without possibility of confusion, in the control of the turbine machinery, great in power and mass, so that manœuvring orders will be promptly fulfilled. This detailed description of the hull may be regarded from the standpoints of strength, safety, comfort, easy handling from the bridge and economy in the management of the ship. Under these are embraced the scantlings, sub-division of the interior, fire prevention, lifeboats, the equipment of the ship as a floating hotel, navigating appliances, moorings, and such other mechanical apparatus as the baggage, mail and cargo-handling gear. In almost every one of these connections one finds evidence of that ingenuity and that teaching of experience to which reference was made in the first sentences of this book.

This detailed description may be preceded by the remark that every idea evolved or suggested by their experience has been carefully considered by the owners and builders, and these have been adopted without regard to cost, if there was any possibility of adding to strength, safety, or comfort. Reference has already been made to the many improvements effected in details, and in the course of our description these will be indicated. They affect almost every department in the ship. In the arrangement for instantaneously closing the water-tight doors from the bridge, for instance, two circuits have been fitted, one for controlling the doors in the main transverse bulkheads, and the other commanding the doors in the longitudinal bulkheads. Thus such doors in the latter as may have to be left open for the stoking of the boilers do not affect the rule that the main doors shall be kept closed at the will of the captain, while the other doors, although left to be normally controlled at the door, may be closed from the bridge instantaneously on emergency. Provision, too, has been made for isolating fire by the institution of special fire-proof bulkheads, and in nearly 100 compartments in the ship electric alarms have been fitted, so that the fusing of metal on a relatively small increase of temperature in any compartment may make an electrical contact and give alarm on the bridge, where an indicator shows the compartment affected. Immense pumping power is provided. Again, an instrument on the bridge shows when smoke mingles with air induced from the holds, and steam from the boilers can instantly be injected into such holds from the bridge. In the ventilation of the passenger quarters there is both a main supply and a main exhaust system, and the latter is so arranged that there is no possibility of the heated air or cooled air becoming short-circuited and entering the exhaust main instead of being diffused throughout each room. An ingenious method, too, has been introduced of increasing the number of rooms having natural light and ventilation, even though these rooms are far removed from the shell of the ship. Great success, again, has been achieved in overcoming vibration. The difficulty in most ships is not so much the movement within the moulded structure as on the superstructural decks and at the after end, and particularly above the level where the transverse bulkheads terminate. In the Aquitania there has been introduced above the top level of the bulkheads stiffening partitions athwart the ship, with very heavy web buttresses, which, while adding strength, provide also sheltered nooks in the promenade spaces. The superstructural decks are similarly stiffened up, and, as a necessary sequence, three breaks have been made on these decks to allow for the hogging and sagging of the ship on waves. There are many other details, in connection with the lighting and other appliances, and these will fall to be noted under the respective headings in our detailed description of the structure and equipment of the ship.

These several improvements, and others which will be described in due course, are the result of many conferences between the technical officers of the builders and the owners. In this connection it should be stated that the Cunard Company maintain a large designing staff, and advisedly, because these technical officers study with singleness of purpose the lessons of experience deduced from their own ships during their voyages.

TABLE III.—*Number of Steamers of Large Tonnage.*
(Compiled from Lloyd's Register Books published on July 1.)

Tonnage Range.	1891.	1896.	1901.	1906.	1911.	1912.	1913.
Over 30,000 ..	—	—	—	—	2	3	6
25,000 to 29,999 .	—	—	—	—	1	2	1
20,000 to 24,999 ..	—	—	—	7	8	9	9
15,000 to 19,999 ..	—	—	1	7	15	17	29
10,000 to 14,999 ..	2	6	50	83	110	147	173
7,000 to 9,999 ..	13	29	85	174	295	378	406
5,000 to 6,999 ..	53	148	376	601	875	1016	1157
4,000 to 4,999 ..	152	304	472	885	1298	1449	1577
3,000 to 3,999 ..	441	737	1199	1701	2108	2204	2640
2,000 to 2,999 ..	1464	1961	2095	2288	2308	2339	2340
Total number..	2125	3185	4278	5746	7020	7564	8338

Not only have the designers for the Cunard Company and Messrs. John Brown and Co. drawn upon their extensive and unique experience in all these respects, but they have availed themselves, in regard to scantlings, of the services of Lloyd's Registry of Shipping, who undertook the calculations which were advantageous in settling many details. This recognition of valuable service is only just to a public organisation which is doing so much to advance naval architecture generally. The effect of the influence of Lloyd's Registry in this respect may be demonstrated by giving some data as to the growth in dimensions and speeds of merchant steamers. Table III. shows the number of steamers in various tonnage-ranges. It will be seen that in the issue of 1891 the largest steamers were under 15,000 tons, and there were then only two over 10,000 tons—the American liners New York and Paris (now Philadelphia) built at the Clydebank Works. Five years later there were only six between 10,000 and 15,000 tons, including the Cunard liners Campania and Lucania, of 12,500 tons. Then came a full recognition of the advantage of great size, and by the beginning of the century the number exceeding 10,000 tons had gone up from six to fifty-one, one of the vessels being over 15,000 tons — the White Star liner Oceanic. Five years later, the number over 10,000 tons increased to ninety-seven, and of these, seven were over 15,000 tons, and seven more over 20,000 tons. The increasing popularity of the big liner was still more marked in the next quinquennial period, as in July, 1911, Lloyd's record showed 136 ships exceeding 10,000 tons, and of these fifteen were between 15,000 and 20,000 tons, eight were between 20,000 and 25,000 tons, one was between the latter figure and 30,000, and the Lusitania and Mauretania marked the highest point—31,550 tons. Then came the Olympic, of 45,000 tons. In Table II., on page 2, are particulars of the leviathans in service to-day. But in service there are now 218 vessels exceeding 10,000 tons, while twenty-three years ago there were only two. Equally illustrative of the present-day tendency is the growth in the same period of vessels from 7000 to 10,000—13 to 624.

Although it involves some digression, it is interesting, before returning to the description of the Aquitania, to glance at the contemporaneous advance in speed. The figures given in Table IV. have again been compiled from Lloyd's Register. It will be seen that twenty-two years ago there were only eight steamers which had a speed exceeding 20

TABLE IV.—*Number of Fast Merchant Steamers.*
(Compiled from Lloyd's Register Books published on July 1.)

Speed.	1890-1891.	1895-1896.	1900-1901.	1905-1906.	1910-1911.	1912-1913.	1913-1914.
20 knots and above	8	24	58	68	105	108	115*
19 and under 20 knots	8	29	34	34	42	49	48
18½ knots.. ..	1	7	8	11	24	24	26
18 ,, ..	13	31	39	41	60	68	68
17½ ,, ..	17	25	26	41	48	38	41
17 ,, ..	12	45	64	61	83	80	83
16½ ,, ..	4	19	24	31	45	45	45
16 ,, ..	15	51	70	95	126	144	152
15½ ,, ..	8	23	34	43	47	48	48
15 ,, ..	38	98	121	155	215	228	230
14½ ,, ..	37	56	56	72	85	92	97
14 ,, ..	58	148	141	189	276	325	320
13½ ,, ..	59	107	140	140	137	170	163
13 ,, ..	90	256	323	417	462	463	487
12½ ,, ..	62	152	185	189	206	220	2'4
12 ,, ..	121	391	488	662	732	748	773
Totals ..	551	1462	1811	2249	2693	2850	2920

* Of this number, 17 were of 23 knots and above.

knots, a number which had increased sevenfold to fifty-eight at the end of ten years, and about thirteen-fold at the end of twenty-two years to 108. Many of the vessels now steam over 23 knots, mostly steamers engaged in the Channel service and on other short-distance runs, the Lusitania and Mauretania being conspicuous examples of express ocean liners.

THE USE OF THE SHIP AS A MERCHANT CRUISER.

According to the agreement made with the Admiralty, the Aquitania is to be utilised at the will of the Admiralty for naval service, and, as has already been pointed out, her design, so far as the structural arrangement is concerned, particularly in regard to subdivision as a protection against the effects of gun attack or ramming, conforms to naval conditions. Provision has been made also for the carrying of a large number of quick-firing guns. On the plans of the bridge and shelter-decks, published on Plate III., there will be seen the positions on the decks specially strengthened for carrying the conical pedestal mountings of these quick-firing guns. Thus on port and starboard sides amidships on the bridge-deck, and aft on the poop, are two such gun positions, while on the forecastle head there are also two on each side of the ship, and aft on the same deck two such positions on each side, so that, in all, twelve guns are provided for.

THE HULL.

There are given on pages 12 to 23 a series of views illustrating the construction of the hull, while the cross-section, Fig. 17, on the present page, will further assist towards a complete appreciation of the great strength of the structure. The stiffening of the bulkheads and other divisional walls in the superstructure, already referred to, is also further illustrated by Fig. 42, on page 20.

From bow to stern there is a double bottom, which has a depth of 5 ft. 4 in., increased to 6 ft. 3 in. in the turbine-room. Illustrations on pages 12, 14, and 15 show the double bottom, which consists of longitudinal and transverse girders, some of them continuous to form water-tight compartments, and others having large man-holes to lighten the structure and to afford means of communication in the compartments which form ballast, reserve-feed, or condensed-water tanks. In all there are forty-one water-tight compartments in the double bottom, each of which can be pumped out or filled separately. Five of the fore and aft girders are solid or water-tight: the centre girder, the fifth girder from the centre on each side—about 30 ft. from the centre line—and the margin plates, from the last of which rise the side frames. There are further six longitudinal intercostal girders, composed of $\frac{12}{20}$-in. plates connected to the floor-plates and to the outer and inner bottom by strong angles. Transverse to these longitudinals are the "floors" or girders, with man-holes for communication between bottoms. The centre girder is built up of $\frac{24}{20}$-in. plates with double angles at top and bottom secured to a flat keel made up of three plates of a collective thickness of $3\frac{1}{2}$ in. The seven longitudinals on each side of this centre girder are $\frac{12}{20}$ in. thick, secured to the floor-plates and to the inner (or tank-top plating) and outer skin by angles. There are the usual forward and aft peaks, which serve as trimming-tanks.

At the after end, for a distance of about 60 ft. from the stern, the ship is cut away to give a clear run of water to the inner propellers, as shown in the longitudinal section of the ship (Fig. 50, on Plate II.). A strong heel casting is fitted to distribute the great stress which comes on the blocks at this part when the ship is being docked (Fig. 19 on page 12). From this heel-post, as seen in the views on page 13, there is a centre girder supporting the propeller brackets and the rudder-post. This girder, formed of double plates, is in continuation of the central keel, and is of great depth—from the keel to the steering flat. On each side of this girder the boss-framing is attached by strong angles, as illustrated in Fig. 24, on page 13. This framing, it will be understood, is for carrying the propellers for the inner shafts only; those for the outer shafts are further forward, with the framing bossed in the ordinary way. To the aft end of the girder and keel-plate is riveted the main casting of the stern frame to carry the rudder (Fig. 23, on page 13). Above the main casting of the stern frame there is a continuation of lighter structure which forms the outer line of the vessel aft (Fig. 25).

The stern frame, constructed by the Darlington Forge Company, is of "dished" section (Figs. 23 and 25), The weight of the stern frame and brackets is 130 tons, of which the main piece of the stern frame (which was cast in one piece) represents 50 tons, the after brackets 33 tons, and the forward brackets 35 tons. Two propellers are carried by the after brackets, which are connected with the foremost end of the stern-frame casting, and the other two are arranged 86 ft. further forward, and supported in similar brackets. These castings have the following dimensions :—Stern frame, extreme length, fore and aft, 44 ft.; extreme height, 42 ft.; and extreme width, 12 ft. 6 in.; forward brackets, centre of shafts, 57 ft.; diameter of bosses, 4 ft. 3 in.; after brackets, centre of shafts, 20 ft.; diameter of bosses, 4 ft. 3 in. The rudder is of the balanced type, and of solid cast steel, built in three sections. The stock is, however, of forged steel. The total weight of the rudder is 70 tons, the extreme width of blade 28 ft., and the diameter of the stock 25 in. The pintle, $18\frac{1}{2}$ in. in diameter, is arranged so that it can be readily unshipped. Upon the nut being removed, the pintle can be lowered into a cavity in the blade immediately below, and then drawn out through special doors, 4 ft. 3 in by 1 ft. 9 in., formed one on either side of the rudder blade. In casting the main piece of the stern frame 75 tons of molten metal were used, and as now completed its weight is 50 tons. The making of the mould in which the stern frame was cast represented two months' work, and the completion of the finished casting another five months.

The whole of the ship's floors, intercostal girders and continuous girders, tank-top plating, and outer bottom plating in the double bottom, and the whole of the stern structure, were riveted by hydraulic machines, the method of applying these to the work being shown on pages 14 and 15. It will be seen that in most cases each riveter was suspended to one end of a beam supported on a standard on a truck traversed on rails, there being a counterbalance weight in the form of a drum on the other end of the beam. In other cases, however, as shown in the view, the riveter was carried by an ordinary jib-crane.

Views on pages 14 and 15 show the full extent of the double-bottom framing with some of the tank-top plating in position. The margin-plate on both sides of the ship is well shown, and some idea can be formed of the great size of the ship as well as of the number of hydraulic riveters used in construction. It will be seen that the double bottom has been extended at its maximum depth to the turn of the bilge in order to accommodate the bed-plate girders carrying the wing turbines; consequently there is a quick change in the level of the margin-plate which would seem to suggest some alteration on the lines of the ship's form at this point. This is an optical illusion; the lines of the ship are not affected, but only the margin-plate.

Illustrations on pages 16 and 18 give a fair idea of the side framing which from the margin-plate of the double bottom upwards is formed of steel channels. Web-frames, 36 in. deep, are introduced at every third frame throughout the greater part of the length of the ship, but closer where required, notably in the machinery space. All these extend at least to the deck 9 ft. above the load water-line, and some to decks above this level. The web-frames, as well as the ordinary framing, are clearly seen in Figs. 28 and 34, on pages 15 and 18. The latter view is taken near the space now occupied by the turbine-room, and there are girders for carrying the bed-plates of the turbines, which extend from the top floor-plates shown at the bottom of the frames on the right and left of the view. On the frames to the left there will be seen also angles for supporting intercostal stringers, 36 in. wide, extending at two levels in the height of the frames right fore and aft. This view further shows the bracket-knees for the

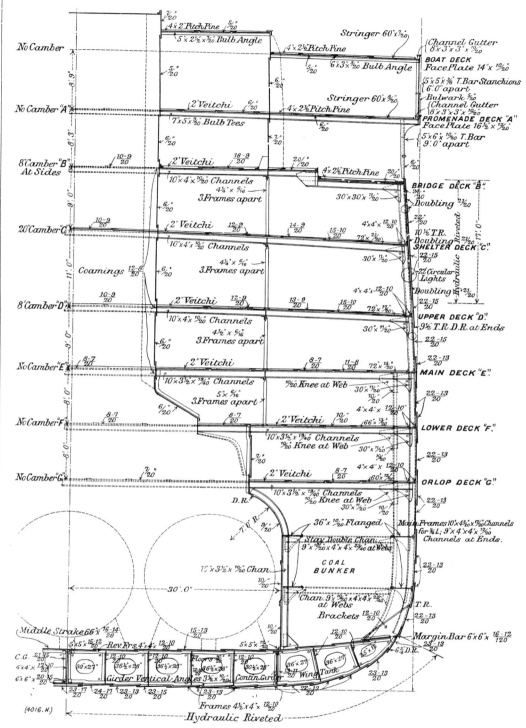

FIG. 17. HALF MID-SECTION OF SHIP.

THE QUADRUPLE-SCREW TURBINE-DRIVEN CUNARD LINER "AQUITANIA."

Fig. 19. View at Aft End, showing Steel Stern Casting and Aft Tank Floors.

Fig. 21. Aft Framing and Lower Orlop Deck,

Fig. 18. Framing of Double Bottom, looking Forward, with Longitudinals, Centre Girder, and Keel-Plates.

Fig. 20. General View of Centre Keel and Double-Bottom Framing Aft.

THE QUADRUPLE-SCREW TURBINE-DRIVEN CUNARD LINER "AQUITANIA."

Fig. 23. Lower Part of Stern Casting being Hoisted into Position.

Fig. 25. Stern Casting and Inner Propeller Brackets in Position.

Fig. 22. Cut-Away Aft, showing Longitudinal Girder and Steel Casting.

Fig. 24. Bossed Frames for Inner Propeller-Shaft on Starboard Side.

THE QUADRUPLE-SCREW TURBINE-DRIVEN CUNARD LINER "AQUITANIA."

Fig. 26. View of Double Bottom, showing Appliances for Hydraulic Riveting of Longitudinal and Transverse Members and Plating.

THE QUADRUPLE-SCREW TURBINE-DRIVEN CUNARD LINER "AQUITANIA."

FIG. 27. DOUBLE-BOTTOM FRAMING, WITH MARGIN-PLATES (LOOKING FORWARD).

FIG. 28. VIEW LOOKING AFT, SHOWING SIDE FRAMING TO "B" DECK, LONGITUDINALS, WATER-TIGHT BUNKER BULKHEADS FORMING INNER SKIN, WITH MAIN-DECK PLATING AFT.

beams for the various decks. Further details may be gleaned from the transverse section on page 11.

The shell-plating is $\frac{22}{20}$ in. thick amidships, the four sheer-strakes being doubled and riveted by hydraulic power (Fig. 37, on page 19). There are eight rows of rivets on the butt-straps.

As to the decks, assuming the ship to be a box-girder formed by the double bottom and the side framing and shell-plating, the top would be what is known as "B" deck, which is 73 ft. from the keel-plate, while the other decks and the columns

steel plating. An idea of the strength of these beams is afforded by the view, Fig. 36, on page 19, which illustrates the "D" deck two floors below the top of the structure. The opening in the foreground is for one of the boiler casings. The shores, of course, were only temporary, and were ultimately replaced by pillars, of which there are four rows in the width of the ship (Fig. 17). As these are between each deck and the next, they constitute a series of vertical stiffeners from the keel to the boat-deck. In the boiler-room the

structure, giving increased space for promenading, games, and stowage of boats.

THE SUB-DIVISION OF THE SHIP.

Having dealt with the ship from the point of view of strength, we may turn to the second desideratum in design—safety—and may refer first to the sub-division of the ship. Before describing the structural details of bulkheads and water-tight decks dividing the hull into separate compart-

FIG. 29. **DIAGRAM ILLUSTRATING EFFECT OF FLOODING FIVE CONSECUTIVE COMPARTMENTS FOR.**
VIZ:- PEAK AND CARGO HOLDS Nos 1, 2 & 3 AND No 1 BOILER ROOM.
"G" AND "H" DECKS ASSUMED WATERTIGHT WHERE SO CONSTRUCTED.
CORRECT ALLOWANCES MADE
DRAFT FOR. 57' 8"
" AFT 26' 0"

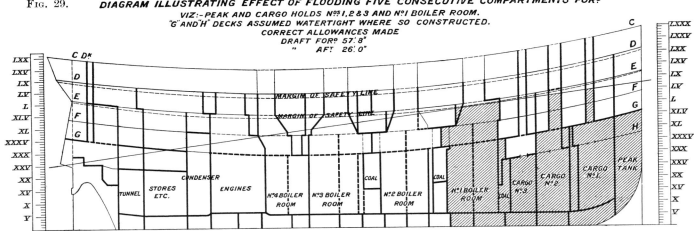

FIG. 30. **DIAGRAM ILLUSTRATING EFFECT OF FLOODING FIVE CONSECUTIVE COMPARTMENTS AFT.**
VIZ:- FROM ENGINE ROOM AFT INCLUSIVE
"G" AND "H" DECKS ASSUMED WATERTIGHT WHERE SO CONSTRUCTED
CORRECT ALLOWANCES MADE
DRAFT FOR. 25' 2"
" AFT 55' 10"

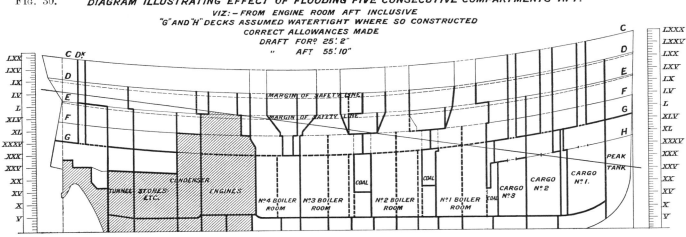

FIG. 31. **DIAGRAM ILLUSTRATING EFFECT OF FLOODING FIVE CONSECUTIVE COMPARTMENTS AFT.**
VIZ:- FROM ENGINE ROOM AFT INCLUSIVE
"G" DECK ASSUMED WATERTIGHT WHERE SO CONSTRUCTED
"H" " " TO BE DAMAGED.
CORRECT ALLOWANCES MADE
DRAFT FOR. 22' 7"
" AFT 60' 5"

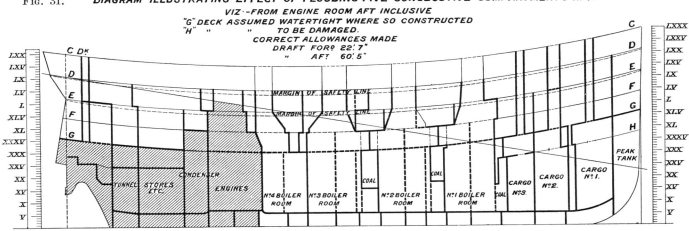

add greatly to the stiffness of the girder. This is well illustrated in the section on page 11. The deck-plating is doubled for a width of 12 ft. at the gunwale; for the remaining part of the girder "B" deck is single-plated. Below this level there are five complete decks extending fore and aft, the distance apart vertically being from 8 ft. to 11 ft., the greater height being on the deck where the first and second-class dining-saloons are located. Before and abaft the machinery spaces there is another, a partial, deck, making six within the moulded structure of the ship. These decks have beams at every frame, consisting of 10-in. channels, and these are completely covered with

columns are splayed as shown in the section to admit of a passage-way. The thickness of the deck-plating varies from $\frac{1}{2}$ in. to 1 in.

The view, Fig. 38, on page 19, shows special beams for the turbine compartments, in order to carry the gear for raising and lowering the upper part of each casing and the rotor for inspection purposes. Girders also serve the function of transverse ties in view of the great width of the engine-room casing.

Above the moulded structure of the ship there are two decks, designated the "A" deck and the boat-deck. As shown in Fig. 17, on page 11, these extend 2 ft. beyond each side of the moulded

ments, it may be stated that the whole scheme of the sub-division of the Aquitania was reviewed, in the light of full experience, when the designs were being worked out. An exhaustive mathematical investigation was outlined by the Cunard Company, and made with great care on their behalf by Messrs. John Brown and Co., the builders of the ship. Some of the actual results of Messrs. John Brown and Co.'s investigations, together with graphical sections showing the estimated trim and heel of the ship in certain conditions, were, by permission of the Cunard Company, included in a paper by Mr. L. Peskett, the naval architect of the company, read at the Institution of Naval Architects on April 3 last. These diagrams are reproduced in Figs. 29 to 33, on the present and opposite pages, and these should be compared with the longitudinal section of the ship (Fig. 50, on Plate II.).

In Fig. 29 the assumption is made that five compartments from the bow, including the peak tank, three cargo-holds, and the forward boiler-room, are flooded up to the water-tight flat, where such exists, and in other cases to as high a level as the trim of the ship in the flooded condition permits. In such event the ship would be considerably down by the head, the draught at the bow being 57 ft. 8 in. and at the stern 26 ft.; but there would be, even under these severe conditions, adequate reserve of buoyancy, as shown by the margin of safety load-line on the diagram. Even at the bow the actual draught is well within the margin of the safety line. In the

well as the Frahm anti-rolling tank, as shown in the longitudinal section and plan, the water-tight deck "G" marking the highest possible level of the water. The water capacity of the wing compartments, excluding the turbine and condenser-rooms, is 3060 tons without coal, and the angle of heel of the ship would be, with these flooded, 21 deg.; but with coal the additional weight due to flooding would be 1225 tons, and in such case the angle of heel would be 10 deg. The flooding of the wing turbine-room would add 1330 tons of water, and involve a heeling to the extent of 12 deg. more, while the flooding of the starboard or port condenser-room would involve 930 tons of water, the consequent angle being 4 deg. more. It will therefore be seen that with this great range of side compartments filled, taking 5320 tons of water, the result would be a heeling of the ship to the extent of 26 deg., which is

tudinal section of the vessel on page 20 (Fig. 40), extend up to 19 ft. above the load water-line, the few others to 9 ft. above the load water-line. The turbine-room is divided into three compartments by two longitudinal bulkheads, the machinery driving each wing shaft being isolated from the machinery driving the two inner shafts, which is in the central compartment. Similarly, the condensing plant is divided into two units by a centre-line bulkhead. In order that the damage by collision at the point of junction of the transverse bulkhead in the machinery space with the shell-plating should not affect two compartments within the skin of the ship a ∧-shaped connection has been made, as shown on the plans of the lower decks of the ship on Plate II., so that damage at that point may be localised to one compartment only. The tunnel aft of the condenser-room is

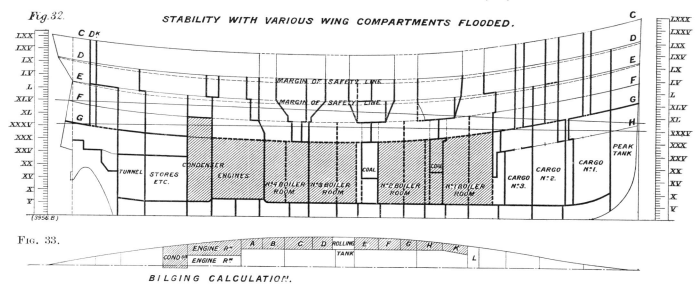

Fig. 32. STABILITY WITH VARIOUS WING COMPARTMENTS FLOODED.

Fig. 33. BILGING CALCULATION.

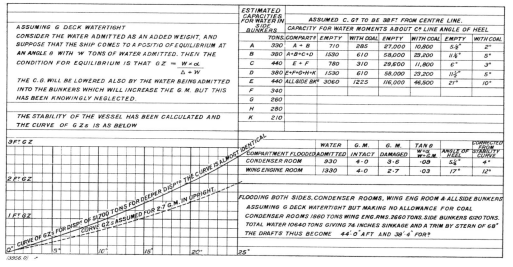

ASSUMING G DECK WATERTIGHT

CONSIDER THE WATER ADMITTED AS AN ADDED WEIGHT, AND SUPPOSE THAT THE SHIP COMES TO A POSITIO OF EQUILIBRIUM AT AN ANGLE θ WITH 'W' TONS OF WATER ADMITTED. THEN THE CONDITION FOR EQUILIBRIUM IS THAT $GZ = \dfrac{W \times \alpha}{\Delta + W}$

THE C.G. WILL BE LOWERED ALSO BY THE WATER BEING ADMITTED INTO THE BUNKERS WHICH WILL INCREASE THE G.M. BUT THIS HAS BEEN KNOWINGLY NEGLECTED.

THE STABILITY OF THE VESSEL HAS BEEN CALCULATED AND THE CURVE OF GZs IS AS BELOW

ESTIMATED CAPACITIES FOR WATER IN SIDE BUNKERS		ASSUMED C.G? TO BE 38 FT. FROM CENTRE LINE.						
	TONS	COMPART?	CAPACITY FOR WATER		MOMENTS ABOUT Cₑ LINE		ANGLE OF HEEL	
			EMPTY	WITH COAL	EMPTY	WITH COAL	EMPTY	WITH COAL
A	330	A + B	710	285	27,000	10,800	5½°	2°
B	380	A+B+C+D	1530	610	58,000	23,200	11½°	5°
C	440	E + F	780	310	29,500	11,800	6°	3°
D	380	E+F+G+H+K	1530	610	58,000	23,200	11½°	5°
E	440	ALL SIDE BKⁿ	3060	1225	116,000	46,500	21°	10°
F	340							
G	260							
H	280							
K	210							

COMPARTMENT FLOODED	WATER ADMITTED	G.M. INTACT	G.M. DAMAGED	TAN θ $\frac{W+\alpha}{W+G.M}$	ANGLE OF HEEL	CORRECTED FROM STABILITY CURVE
CONDENSER ROOM	930	4·0	3·6	·09	5½°	4°
WING ENGINE ROOM	1330	4·0	2·7	·03	17°	12°

FLOODING BOTH SIDES, CONDENSER ROOMS, WING ENG ROOM & ALL SIDE BUNKERS
ASSUMING G DECK WATERTIGHT BUT MAKING NO ALLOWANCE FOR COAL
CONDENSER ROOMS 1860 TONS WING ENG.RMS. 2660 TONS. SIDE BUNKERS 6120 TONS.
TOTAL WATER 10640 TONS GIVING 74 INCHES SINKAGE AND A TRIM BY STERN OF 68°
THE DRAFTS THUS BECOME 44' 0" AFT AND 38' 4" FORᵈ

9 Ft GZ
2 Ft GZ
1 Ft GZ
0° 5° 10° 15° 20° 25°
CURVE OF GZs FOR DISPT OF 51700 TONS FOR DEEPER DISPᵀˢ THE CURVE IS ALMOST IDENTICAL
CURVE GZs ASSUMED FOR 2·7 G.M. IN UPRIGHT

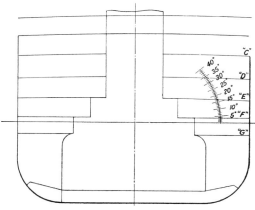

diagram, Fig. 30, the five aftermost compartments, up to and including the three turbine-rooms, are assumed to be flooded up to the water-tight decks, where these exist, and this obtains in all the cases excepting only in the turbine-room uptake. In this case the draught aft would be 55 ft. 10 in., and forward 25 ft. 2 in. This condition, it will be seen, is more severe than were damage done to the ship forward, but still there is a satisfactory margin of safety. The most severe condition possible would be with a similar flooding aft and damage to the water-tight deck "H" at the stern, as shown in the diagram, Fig. 31. Then the draught aft would become 60 ft. 5 in., and forward 22 ft. 7 in., but the water-line as shown would, except at the extreme after end, be within the margin of the safety line.

The question of longitudinal bulkheads, on which there is considerable difference of opinion, had also very full consideration before it was decided to adopt the system throughout the machinery compartments. The case of the Aquitania was dealt with entirely on its merits, and without reference to the general application. In Figs. 32 and 33 there are shown the results of the investigation of the extreme case, where all the wing compartments were flooded as

not in any way excessive, although the contingency of such flooding is so remote as to be declared almost impossible. To overcome the heel, the corresponding compartments on the other side of the ship might be flooded at will; then there would be 10,640 tons of water in the ship, no allowance being made for coal. The effect would be to increase the draught of the ship by 74 in., making it 44 ft. aft and 38 ft. 4 in. forward, and to give the ship a trim by the stern of 68 in. These conditions are well within the margin of safety.

It was therefore decided to adopt the system, the details of which had thus been investigated; and to fit, in addition to transverse bulkheads, a longitudinal bulkhead throughout the boiler-rooms on each side, 18 ft. from the skin of the ship, and to divide the space into separate water-tight coal-bunkers; and, further, to make three turbine-rooms and two condenser-rooms, as shown in the plan, Fig. 33, and in greater detail on the plan of the lower deck and hold on Plate II.

The hull is thus divided into eighty-four compartments, in addition to the forty-one in the double bottom. There are sixteen transverse bulkheads, most of which, as shown in the longi-

also divided up into several compartments by the fresh-water tanks.

The fore-and-aft bulkhead on each side of the space occupied by boilers extends for a distance of 450 ft., so that in this part of the ship, where the compartments are largest, and where, perhaps, there might be the greatest danger due to the ingress of sea-water, there is achieved the great desideratum of a "ship within a ship." The longitudinal bulkheads forming the inner walls of the bunkers are 18 ft. from the outer skin of the ship. The space within the inner walls, constituting the boiler-rooms, is thus 60 ft. wide. Fig. 28, on page 15, and Fig. 35, on the next page, show the longitudinal bulkhead which is curved at the top. The former view, being taken from a much higher level, shows clearly the great space between the longitudinal bulkhead and the skin-plating of the ship. In the intervening space forming the bunkers there are partial transverse bulkheads dividing these bunkers into ten water-tight cellular sections on each side, varying from 27 ft. to 33 ft. in length. These fore-and-aft bulkheads are connected to the shell by strong stays formed of double channels spaced 9 ft. apart.

D

THE QUADRUPLE-SCREW TURBINE-DRIVEN CUNARD LINER "AQUITANIA."

FIG. 34. SIDE FRAMING, CONNECTION TO TANK, TANK-TOP, AND FLOOR (LOOKING FORWARD).

FIG. 35. INNER LONGITUDINAL WATER-TIGHT BUNKER BULKHEADS IN BOILER SPACES.

THE QUADRUPLE-SCREW TURBINE-DRIVEN CUNARD LINER "AQUITANIA."

Fig. 37. Upper Structure; Hydraulic Riveting of Sheer Strakes.

Fig. 39. Pneumatic Tool Drilling the Upper Sidelights.

Fig. 36. Main Deck Plated.

Fig. 38. Special Beams and Longitudinal Girders in Turbine-Room.

In determining the distance apart of the main transverse bulkheads, consideration was had to the question of providing adequate coal-bunker capacity in each boiler-room to run all the boilers within the compartment throughout the voyage. Thus there will be no need during the trip to convey coal through the transverse bulkhead-doors, each boiler-room being self-contained. As a consequence the doors in the main transverse bulkheads can always be kept closed at the will of the captain. Should at any time these doors require to be opened for the convenience of the officers working the ship, such officers must in passing through hold the valve

duced vertical web-stiffeners 3 ft. deep, formed of $\frac{10}{20}$-in. plates and double angles. In line with the two intercostal girders between the web-frames at two points in the height of these vertical members, already mentioned, there are horizontal girders carried across the bulkheads at a level between the double bottom and the "G" deck. It will thus be recognised that the construction is strong enough to resist any head of water due to one compartment being flooded while the other adjacent to it is empty.

All the doors below and adjacent to the load-line are of the sliding pattern. In the event of collision

to the underside of the bulkhead-deck their function is to provide water-tight sub-division, and, of course, transverse strength ; above this deck the strength is continued by webs and buttresses, but a light bulkhead is preserved, being fitted with fire-proof doors. Finally, in the form of webs and buttresses, these diaphragms are made to support and stiffen the superstructure and upper works. To this continuity of transverse members the Cunard Company have come to attach great importance, and the whole subject of the design of framework of the ship is made to take precedence, if necessary, of the minor conveniences

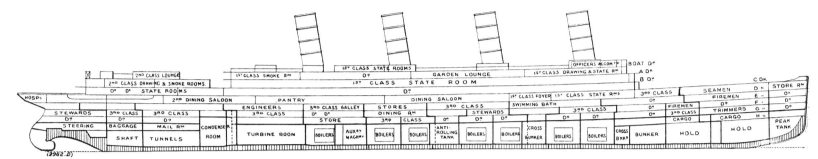

FIG. 40. LONGITUDINAL SECTION SHOWING BULKHEADS.

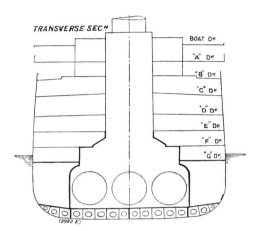

TRANSVERSE SEC.^N

*FIG. 41. CROSS-SECTION SHOWING BULKHEADS.

open, as the door otherwise automatically closes, according to the principle of the Stone-Lloyd bulkhead-door-closing system. This permanent closing of the doors was rendered possible by the novel and very wise provision of arranging that the mechanism for automatically closing the doors in the transverse bulkheads from the navigating-bridge should be entirely separate from the corresponding appliances controlling the doors in the longitudinal bulkheads. Many of these latter are bunker-doors, and, consequently, it was desirable that under ordinary circumstances these should be retained in the open position. It will be understood, of course, that with the usual Stone-Lloyd system each door may be closed or opened separately, while in emergency the captain on the bridge can close the whole of the doors simultaneously. In such case each door may be opened temporarily, as has already been intimated in connection with the doors on the transverse bulkhead, but the valve lever must be held so long as the door requires to be open. Upon the release of the valve lever, the door closed in from 9 to 15 seconds during the test made on the steam trials of the Aquitania, but this period may be altered as desired.

The hatches to the cargo-holds are trunked and made water-tight to the weather-deck. The engine and boiler-casings are extra well stiffened by webs and made water-tight to 20 ft. above the load water-line. Thus water entering any of the cargo, engine, or boiler compartments cannot flow into any adjacent compartment, but is confined within the trunk hatches or casings. This, in conjunction with the making of the decks water-tight, will localise the space which may, owing to accident, be flooded with sea-water.

The main transverse bulkheads are formed of $\frac{10}{20}$-in. plating stiffened by 12-in. channels spaced 2 ft. 6 in. apart, and at intervals there are intro-

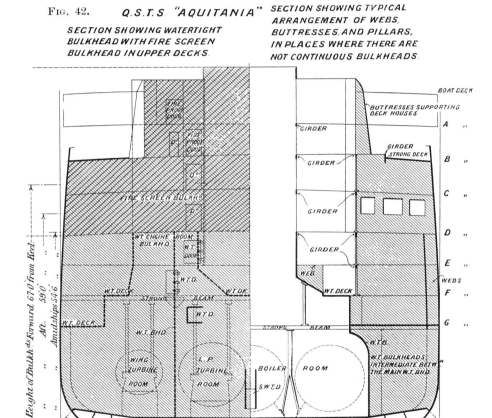

FIG. 42. Q.S.T.S "AQUITANIA" SECTION SHOWING TYPICAL ARRANGEMENT OF WEBS, BUTTRESSES, AND PILLARS, IN PLACES WHERE THERE ARE NOT CONTINUOUS BULKHEADS.

SECTION SHOWING WATERTIGHT BULKHEAD WITH FIRE SCREEN BULKHEAD IN UPPER DECKS.

or an accident which would cause flooding of any part of the vessel, the officer on the bridge can close all the doors immediately. An electrically-operated indicator on the navigating bridge shows the position of all the water-tight-doors throughout the vessel, and whether these are open or closed. The pumps and gear for this installation were supplied by Messrs. Stone, and the builders fitted the installation in the ship. The doors are by Messrs. Mechan, Scotstoun.

FIRE DETECTION AND PREVENTION.

Great care has been bestowed on this subject, and the interior of the ship has been divided up into a series of fire-proof compartments. Thus the transverse water-tight bulkheads are continued as diaphragms throughout the entire structure from keel to boat-deck, being made to fulfil various functions in several parts of the ship. Up

of general arrangements. It has been in cases where discontinuity was the salient feature that the company have experienced the greatest expense in structural upkeep. Two typical sections of the Aquitania are given in Fig. 42, and some explanatory notes have been added to the drawing to indicate the arrangement of these comprehensive division walls from keel to boat-deck.

In these fire-proof compartments there are fitted up a large number of electrical instruments wherein the circuit is kept open only by a metal connection which fuses at a comparatively low temperature, so that any high temperature within the compartment will make contact, with the result that a powerful electric bell is rung on the bridge of the ship, and the instrument affected is indicated by a dial on the bridge. Thus warning is at once given of any outbreak of fire, and the organisation of the *personnel* is of such a nature that the outbreak can be promptly combated through the very extensive

THE QUADRUPLE-SCREW TURBINE-DRIVEN CUNARD LINER "AQUITANIA."

Fig. 43. General View of Vessel in Frame, with R.M.S. "Niagara" of 13,500 Tons Alongside, and H.M.S. "Southampton" in Dock.

THE QUADRUPLE-SCREW TURBINE-DRIVEN CUNARD LINER "AQUITANIA."

Fig. 44.   Stern View of the Vessel on the Stocks.

THE QUADRUPLE-SCREW TURBINE-DRIVEN CUNARD LINER "AQUITANIA."

FIG. 45. BOW VIEW OF THE VESSEL ON THE STOCKS.

THE QUADRUPLE-SCREW TURBINE-DRIVEN CUNARD LINER "AQUITANIA."

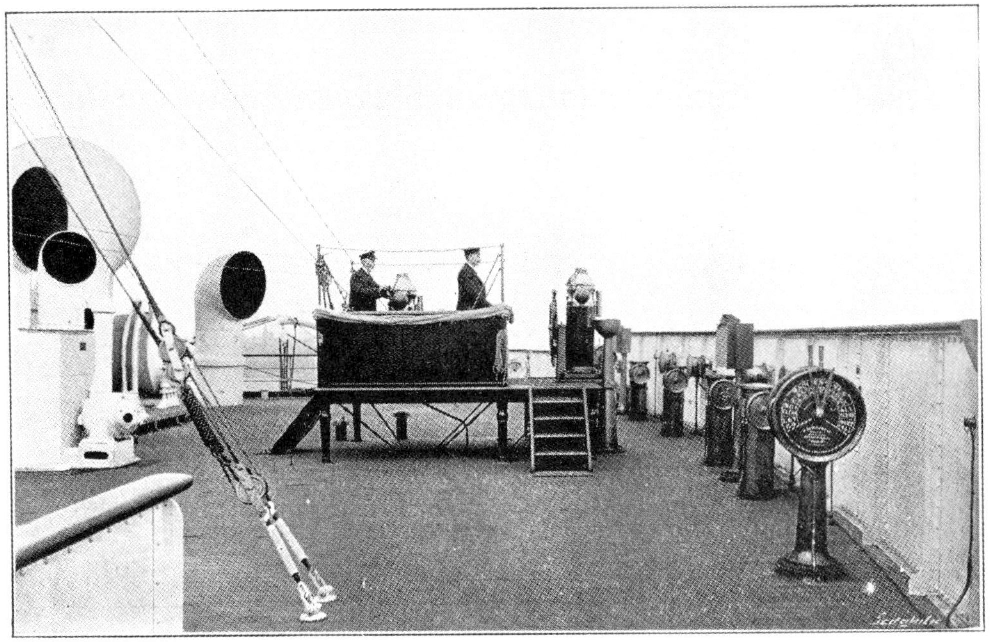

FIG. 47. THE UPPER NAVIGATION BRIDGE.

FIG. 49. VIEW FROM DECK-HOUSE ON POOP, LOOKING FORWARD.

FIG. 46. VIEW OF "TERRACED" ("B") DECK.

FIG. 48. VIEW FROM UPPER NAVIGATION BRIDGE, LOOKING AFT.

system of water-mains and fire-hydrants provided in the ship. The pressure in these mains can be maintained not only by the use of the very powerful fire and bilge-pumps in the engine-room, but by pumps fitted for other duties being utilised for fire service.

As regards the holds, the method adopted is different, but equally effective. Rich's indicator is located on the bridge. This apparatus, which is now very widely applied, consists in a trunk communication being made from the bridge to each separate hold, the terminal of the trunk on the bridge having over it a powerful exhaust-fan, which is intermittently worked by clock mechanism, and thus any smoke generated in a hold will at once disclose itself by the condition of the air exhausted from the trunks. Alongside the indicator are fitted couplings to the steam-pipes directly connected with the main steam-boiler supply, so that on the first evidence of smoke issuing from any hold, steam may be injected into the hold through the trunk, in order to quench the fire.

MARCONI WIRELESS TELEGRAPH INSTALLATION.

The general consideration of the element of safety involves the subject of the Marconi installation, and here the Cunard Company have had unexampled experience, because of the power of the installations in both the Lusitania and Mauretania. In these two vessels communication with the land has been only interrupted for about three hours in mid-ocean, but in the case of the Aquitania there will be an appreciable period of time on the voyage when telegraphic connection can be maintained with both sides. The generating set is of 5 kw. capacity, and the potentiality of the current, it is anticipated, will attain about 80,000 volts. The location of the Marconi installation, with the public post-office, will be seen from the plan of the boat-deck, Fig. 53, on Plate III., and a notable feature is that there is a specially enclosed noise-proof room for the reception of long-distance messages.

THE ANTI-ROLLING TANKS.

Turning now to the subject of comfort, reference may be made to the provision to ensure steadiness in a seaway, without which the landsman cannot be comfortable, however luxurious the arrangement of the ship. The great size and beam of the Aquitania are in themselves some guarantee; but, as is shown in the plan of the hold and the boiler-rooms, Frahm anti-rolling-tanks have been fitted in place of one of the coal-bunkers on each side of the ship, and it is of some significance that, after experience with the system in the Laconia, the Cunard Company are for the present dispensing with bilge-keels, although these can be fitted at any time should the tanks fail to prevent rolling in a seaway. The system has already been illustrated in ENGINEERING in connection with the Cunard steamer Laconia.* A striking feature is the relatively small space required for the tank in which the water flows from side to side in order to counteract the rolling of the ship. Regarding the system Mr. Peskitt, in the paper from which quotation has already been made, said that "the Cunard Company have experimented with Herr Frahm's tanks on the Laconia, and it has been shown without question that in that particular instance they have resulted in a reduction in the amplitude of rolling amounting to an average of 60 per cent. In the case of ships of the proportions of the Aquitania, rolling is a feature to be avoided by every possible means. The great beam of such vessels increases the actual amount by which passengers berthed near the shell of the ship are alternately raised and lowered as rolling takes place."

LIFE-BOAT EQUIPMENT.

We pass now to a consideration of the equipment of life-boats, which provides, in the last, an exceedingly improbable, contingency, the final element of safety. From the inception of the design the Cunard Company made provision for life-boats to take off every soul on board. This early decision on the question was necessary in order that the carrying of this great load on the boat-deck, so high above the load-line, would be allowed for in determining the proportions of the ship from the standpoint of stability. There are on the ship, as shown on the plan of the boat-deck, Fig. 53, on Plate III., ninety boats of the largest size, including two powerful motor-boats, each under its own davits, and with plenty of passenger assembly space behind the boats. In addition there are thirty cellular boats under the davits, arranged three in a tier, while other boats are arranged on deck-houses athwart the ship, so that they may be skidded over to the davits.

The view of the boats taken from the navigating-bridge (Fig. 48, on page 24) shows the general arrangement of the boats and davits. Each boat is under its own davit, and the davits are operated by long-approved worm-and-pinion gear. In several cases there is a double tier of boats, including the ordinary boat and the collapsible boat. On the deck-house on the poop, as shown in Fig. 49, on the same page, there are eight double tiers of boats, and in this case the Welin appliance for moving the boats rapidly across the ship to the ordinary davits is utilised.

Messrs. Thornycroft built the two motor-boats, which embody many features likely to be standardised. Most of the recommendations made by the Board of Trade Departmental Committee on Ships' Boats and Davits are embodied in the construction of these boats. The dimensions are:—Length, 30 ft.; breadth, 9 ft. 6 in.; depth, 4 ft. 6 in.; and each boat is fitted with a Thornycroft paraffin-motor, developing 30 brake horse-power. These motors are arranged to start on petrol until the vapouriser is sufficiently heated, and then are turned over to paraffin. The design of these boats is a distinct departure from the usual type of ship's boat, their primary function being to tow the ordinary rowing life-boats. Each of the two boats would be able to tow a considerable number of boats. The wide beam and specially designed lines make them excellent sea-boats. A cabin is fitted amidships housing the motor. The forward end is divided off by a sound-proof bulkhead, forming a room for Marconi wireless apparatus. These compartments are lighted by eight port-holes, and ventilated from the roof by mushroom ventilators. Wells are placed fore and aft of the cabin, each being fitted with large relieving-valves. This arrangement, specified by the owners, is found to be very satisfactory for handling purposes, when the water drains off very quickly from the floors (which are placed well above the water-line). In addition to the functions of towing, each boat is fitted with accommodation for medical chests, blankets, and food supplies; thus, in time of emergency, the comfort of the passengers in the smaller boats is, to some extent, arranged for. An important feature with this type of craft is the wireless installation already referred to, by means of which the boats can be kept in touch with other vessels in the line of shipping. The receiving range for these sets is about 300 miles. The aerial wires are carried on two 25-ft. bamboo masts, which may be lowered on to chocks when not in use. On official trials the speed obtained by the two motor-boats was 9 miles per hour.

THE ARRANGEMENT OF THE DECKS.

There are nine decks in the Aquitania, in addition to the hold, and a plan of each is given, along with a longitudinal section of the ship, on Plates II., III. and IV. There is one more deck than in the Lusitania. Of these decks seven are in the main structure of the ship. Above these there are two superstructure decks, beginning about 200 ft. from the bow of the ship, and the first extending for about 624 ft., and the second, or boat-deck, to about 464 ft. in length. Further aft the deck-house for the second-class quarters is utilised for the carrying of additional boats on the same level as the boat-deck proper. The total height from the keel to the boat-deck level is 94 ft. The question of having another deck in the superstructure of the ship was carefully considered by the Cunard Company; but, although it would have added to the passenger accommodation, such an addition was dispensed with in the interests of stability. The consequence is that no difficulty has been experienced in arranging on the boat-deck level, where there is no obstruction possible, for life-boat accommodation for everyone on board.

Figs. 51 and 52, which are given along with the longitudinal section, show the holds and machinery spaces, but as the boilers, turbines, condensers, &c., will be fully described later, these drawings do not call for description now. The plans show the location of the steering-engine compartment, holds, refrigerating machinery, the electric power-station, baggage-rooms, &c., as well as the location of the Frahm anti-rolling tanks and coal-bunkers.

On the boat-deck (Fig. 53, on Plate III.) accommodation is found for the officers' quarters, immediately abaft the wheel-house and lower navigating-bridge. Amidships is a deck-house with chauffeurs' or other male servants' sleeping and mess-rooms, as well as the Marconi wireless telegraph offices. The deck-house on this level covers in the skylights or the domes over the important public rooms on the deck below. The ceilings of these public rooms are at a much greater height than is usually the case, a special arrangement of structural work being introduced to give vertical and lateral strength; while the coamings are made particularly heavy to make up for the larger openings in the decks.

On the next deck, designated the "A" deck (Fig. 54), the principal apartments are the first-class drawing-room, the lounge and the smoking-room, with a second-class lounge further aft. Later we shall deal with the decorative features of the public rooms. Forward are a number of large special cabins, and abaft these is the drawing-room forward of the main staircase. The first-class lounge, which is in the Georgian style, is 74 ft. long by 54 ft. wide, and 11 ft. 6 in. high. A novel arrangement has been introduced in the provision of a winter garden lounge. A considerable length of the promenade-deck on each side of the deck-house amidships is enclosed by sliding plate-glass windows, forming an extension of the bulwarks, with a vestibule at the forward and after ends, and this constitutes a winter garden, 126 ft. long and 21 ft. wide, on each side of the ship. By means of trellis-work in natural teak on walls treated to represent stone, there has been achieved the semblance of an old garden. The lounge and these conservatories on the port and starboard sides occupy a space of about 10,000 sq. ft. The smoking-room aft is 76 ft. by 52 ft., and has a height corresponding to that of the lounge. These two rooms are connected by the "Long Gallery," 132 ft. long by 15 ft. wide—a great width for ship's corridors. This forms a shelter promenade, with a complete sea-view, as it is at the side of the deck-house, which is here entirely glazed. It is being arranged, on one side, also as an art gallery, to be decorated with engravings and etchings. In the deck-house adjoining are the hairdressers' department, a deck-service pantry, typists' office, and access to an elevator to the decks below. The panels admitting light to these departments are glazed, with metal relief-work. The first-class smoking-room, at the after end of this gallery, is divided into two compartments, as shown on the plan, with a multiplicity of nooks and corners, and the ceiling is of great height. On the poop is a deck-house, with the second-class lounge, and on this deck-house are 8 double tiers of life-boats with Welin's traversing gear, already referred to. Abaft this house is the emergency dynamo-room, the equipment of which will be described later. This poop-deck is one deck higher than the Lusitania, and this greatly adds to the appearance of the vessel aft.

On the "B" deck, Fig. 55, there are 126 special state-rooms, with one and two berths in each. The deck-house containing these rooms is over 450 ft. long by 54 ft. wide, and of more than the usual height (8 ft. 6 in.). The promenade extends all round this deck-house, and is screened amidships on both sides for a length of 135 ft. by extending the bulwarks up to the "A" deck, and fitting large sliding plate-glass windows. There will thus be formed a shelter promenade. Entrance to these sheltered promenades, as in the case of the winter garden on the level above, is through vestibules.

Another important feature of this shelter promenade is that on the inboard side is a terrace, as illustrated in Fig. 46, on page 24. This is raised about 2 ft. from the height of the deck proper, and is reached by steps at various points. The object of having this terrace is, primarily, to enable those resting in deck-chairs to have a clear view seaward, unobstructed by passengers promenading, but it has other and more important advantages. The face-plate of the terrace constitutes in itself a strong, stiffening, fore-and-aft girder, and at various points in the length

* See ENGINEERING, vol. xcii., page 803.

the web of the girder is pierced to accommodate windows and ventilating louvres for a row of inner rooms on the deck below ("C" deck), as shown in Fig. 46. The coaming-plate of the deck-house to the rear of this terrace is similarly pierced, for windows and ventilating louvres, to a third row of cabins on the "C" deck, as is also shown on Fig. 46. At each end of the terrace, on both port and starboard sides, there is a secluded veranda in communication with special suites of rooms on this level.

On this "B" deck there are many such suites, several of which have been given the names of artists, and their decoration has been devised to conform to the spirit of the respective work of those artists, while engravings of historical pictures by the artists adorn the walls—Gainsborough, Reynolds, Romney, Raeburn, Holbein, Rembrandt, Vandyke, and Velasquez. It may further be said that these rooms, like all the principal state-rooms in the ship, are decorated to conform more to the bed-rooms in our latest hotels. Thus the walls, of special canvas and composition, are papered, while the furniture is in all cases the antithesis of the old-type cabin fittings. The bedsteads are of decorative wood or metal-work. The wardrobes are separate, and the corners are fitted with cupboards, in some cases of antique design; while the washstands, to which hot and cold water are supplied, have in most cases roll-top covers. In most instances, also, a bath-room and other conveniences are associated with each room, and the communication between the cabins is so arranged that almost any number of rooms can be allotted to parties, and still be absolutely self-contained. Even in less expensive quarters the principle has been adopted of making a door between two adjoining cabins to accommodate two members of a family who desire separate and yet contiguous and communicating rooms. It will be noted, too, that on the "B" deck there is a maids' dining-room, and adjacent to it a number of state-rooms are set apart for such domestic servants as accompany passengers.

On the after end of "B" deck there is a large house, 142 ft. by 52 ft., containing the second-class drawing and smoking-rooms, outside of which there is extensive promenading space.

The "C" deck, Fig. 56, which forms the top of the moulded structure of the ship, and is about 66 ft. from the keel, is almost entirely given over to sleeping quarters. The first-class accommodation on this deck, and generally on all decks, extends from a point 190 ft. from the bow to about 320 ft. from the stern, thus occupying about 400 ft. of the central part of the ship from above the water-line to the boat-deck. On the "C" deck there are 168 first-class rooms, 60 rooms which can be thrown either into the first-class or the second-class quarters, 98 rooms for the second-class passengers, and 48 rooms which may be used for either second-class or third-class passengers. As already described, a unique and ingenious arrangement has been made to ensure a higher degree of comfort by providing natural light and ventilation in the inner state-rooms than is obtainable even in some of the recent large passenger ships.

At the forward end of this "C" deck is the forecastle, with head capstans, cargo-hatches and cargo-winches, and a house enclosing the entrance to the third-class quarters on the decks below. The forward part of the deck also affords a promenade for the third-class passengers in fine weather. At the after end of the ship also there is space for working the ship by the necessary winches, capstan, and gear, to which reference will be made later.

The first deck within the moulded structure, named the "D" deck (Fig. 57), is given over in large measure to the cuisine department of this immense floating hotel. In order to add to comfort and simplify ventilation, the height between this and the deck above is 11 ft. The first-class dining-saloon, which is almost amidships, is 138 ft. long and the full width of the ship, and is decorated according to the Louis XVI. period. The square effect, however, is removed not only by the handsomely-treated casing around the funnel uptakes at the forward and after end, but by the well in the centre of the ceiling, which is effectively decorated. Along the sides, again, there are formed alcoves. A foyer for the first-class passengers, forward of the first-class dining-saloon, occupies over 50 ft. of the length of the ship, and will be a suitable rendezvous for those who are to dine together. Further aft, on the starboard side, with entrance

for the main dining-saloon, as well as from a companion-way and lift from the decks above and below, is a grill-room, with electric-grills and pantry immediately alongside. The second-class dining-saloon is further aft still, and is over 100 ft. long, being similarly treated with well and alcoves as the first-class dining-saloon. Between the two, and occupying about 150 ft. of the length of the ship, is the kitchen, equipped with all that pertains to the culinary arts.

In addition to the public rooms, there is a large compartment forward accommodating 44 state-rooms. At the extreme after end of this deck there is a third-class smoking-room and entrance to third-class quarters, with an extensive promenade under the poop, but with open bulwarks on all sides. In order primarily to stiffen the ship at this point, steel partitions have been put in as an extension to the deck-houses above the water-tight bulkheads below, and these are further strengthened by deep web-plates in the form of buttresses. These walls serve the further purpose of forming sheltered nooks for the passengers. At the forward end of this deck there is a large third-class non-smoking compartment. It will be understood that the third-class passengers are accommodated in two divisions forward and aft, and in each case separate public rooms and all other conveniences are provided.

The "E" deck (Fig. 58) has a height of 9 ft., and is regarded as the "working deck" of the ship. Thus there is found upon it accommodation for stores and a great variety of other departments. Indeed, to the manager of a liner, the arrangement of this deck should form a most interesting study. On it great experience has been concentrated, and the result will be exceptionally favourable to economy in service and promptitude in carrying out the functions of ship-manager. The engineers are accommodated on this deck close to the engine-room. There are three large spaces forward, aft, and amidships, for third-class promenades and for handling mails and baggage. Six large double water-tight gangway-doors through the shell-plating of the ship on each side give entrance to this space, in addition to smaller doors affording coaling facilities to each boiler compartment. Between the promenades for third-class passengers there is a passage 8 ft. wide for the use of third-class passengers, so that they have plenty of opportunity for exercise. At the after end of the deck there are 93 cabins for second-class passenger accommodation, and, in addition, room is found for hospitals, third-class galley, &c.

In an isolated part of this deck, on the starboard side of the ship, is the swimming-bath and the gymnasium adjoining. Access for the first-class passengers is provided by the elevators or the grand companion-way.

On "F" deck (Fig. 59) there are three large dining-saloons, collectively extending to 183 ft. of the length of the ship and its full width, for the accommodation of the third-class passengers. Aft there are a large number of single and double-berth rooms, which may be used either for second or third-class passengers, in addition to 178 rooms for third-class passengers.

The next deck, "G" (Fig. 60), is entirely reserved for third-class passengers' cabins. Under this deck, forward and aft of the machinery space, is a hold for cargo, baggage, and mails, while at the extreme after end of the ship is the steering-gear immediately in contact with the rudder-head.

The seamen, firemen, and trimmers are accommodated at the extreme bow of the ship on several decks, while the stewards have their sleeping quarters at the extreme after ends of the various levels.

STATE-ROOMS FOR PASSENGERS.

The arrangements we have described provide for the accommodation of a population of over 4000 persons, as follow :—

First-class	...	...	...	...	618
Second-class	...	...	...	...	614
Third-class	...	...	...	...	1998
Officers and crew	...	...	...	972
					4202

There are, however, some rooms which can alternatively be used as first or second-class rooms, and others as second or third-class rooms, so that the number of passengers of the respective classes, and even the total of all classes, is variable under

certain conditions. A great extent of the passenger accommodation is above the load water-line, which, under normal conditions, is a little above the "G" deck. The arrangement of the state-rooms is approximately as given in the appended table :—

State-Rooms in the "Aquitania."

	1st Class.	Interchangeable 1st or 2nd Class	2nd Class.	Interchangeable 2nd or 3rd Class.	3rd Class.	Stewards, Maids, and Chauffeurs.	Total
1-berth rooms	179	—	—	4	—	—	183
2-berth ,,	208	12	141	34	103	—	498
3-berth ,,	5	—	—	—	2	—	7
4-berth ,,	2	48	50	10	318	5	433
6-berth ,,	—	—	—	—	46	11	57
8-berth ,,	—	—	—	—	1	—	1
Total	394	60	191	48	470	16	1179
Passengers	618	216	482	112	1768	42	3238

THE DECORATIVE FEATURES OF THE PASSENGER ROOMS.

Some brief reference may be made to the decoration of the more important rooms of the ship. The first-class lounge on "A" deck is undoubtedly the most notable room in the ship from this point of view. The colour scheme is wine red and grey, and the treatment reminiscent of Sir Christopher Wren's work. The central part of the room, which is 18 ft. in height, has, as its central panel, an original canvas by Van Cuygen, and the spandrels at the ends of the room on each side of the arches are after Jean Baptiste Van Lee's panels of the elements—Fire, Earth, Water, and Heaven. At one end of the room is a fireplace with niches on each side, and at the other a semicircular stage with a coffered vault, under which is a reproduction of the Mortlake tapestry representing the battle of Solebay. The floor is of oak.

For inspiration in designing the smoking-room the artist has gone to Greenwich Hospital, and on all sides there are carved trophies and coats of arms, in the earlier manner of Grinling Gibbons. From a main central portion are some half-dozen nooks—almost separate rooms—with oak-beamed ceilings and window treatment suggestive of the stern of the old three-deckers. In sharp contrast is the lofty white panelled ceiling of the central part, and the paintings on the side-walls—"The Embarkation of St. Ursula" and a seaport, with figures.

The drawing-room is a fine interpretation of the Adams period of decoration, particularly the oval dome, with lunettes and lead mouldings. The chimney-piece is of statuary carved in marble.

The salons, or writing-rooms, adjoining the lounge are in the Louis XVI. style, recalling some of the features of an old French chateau. The prominent paintings are reproductions of works of Hubert Roberts, and the furniture is after models of Bergères. As in most of the public rooms, the lighting is reflected from the ceiling by means of cut-glass dish-lights. The main entrance, with its great dome and broad stairway with hammered iron rail, has an original decorative painting by Panini, and a carved bas-relief in the style of Clodian.

The dining-saloon is in the Louis XVI. style, and in panelled mahogany. The well which pierces the deck above is the principal feature. The ceiling has a decorative painting of "The Triumph of Flora," and the balustrade is of wrought iron with panels. Pilasters and columns throughout the saloon, with decorative paintings, mostly of the eighteenth century, with large canvases over the console tables at each end, give a handsome effect.

Probably enough has been said to indicate the degree of originality and variety and comeliness of the decorative work, which was designed by Mr. Arthur Davies.

COMPANION-WAYS AND PASSENGER-LIFTS.

In a great ship it is becoming more and more difficult to afford adequate means of communication, and, further, to adopt a scheme which will enable the landsman readily to find his way to the various departments of the vessel. It is because of this that the decks are now always lettered, instead of being given, as in the old days, the names evolved in constructional plans. The Cunard Company have been liberal in their indications as to the location of

THE QUADRUPLE-SCREW TURBINE-DRIVEN CUNARD LINER "AQUITANIA."

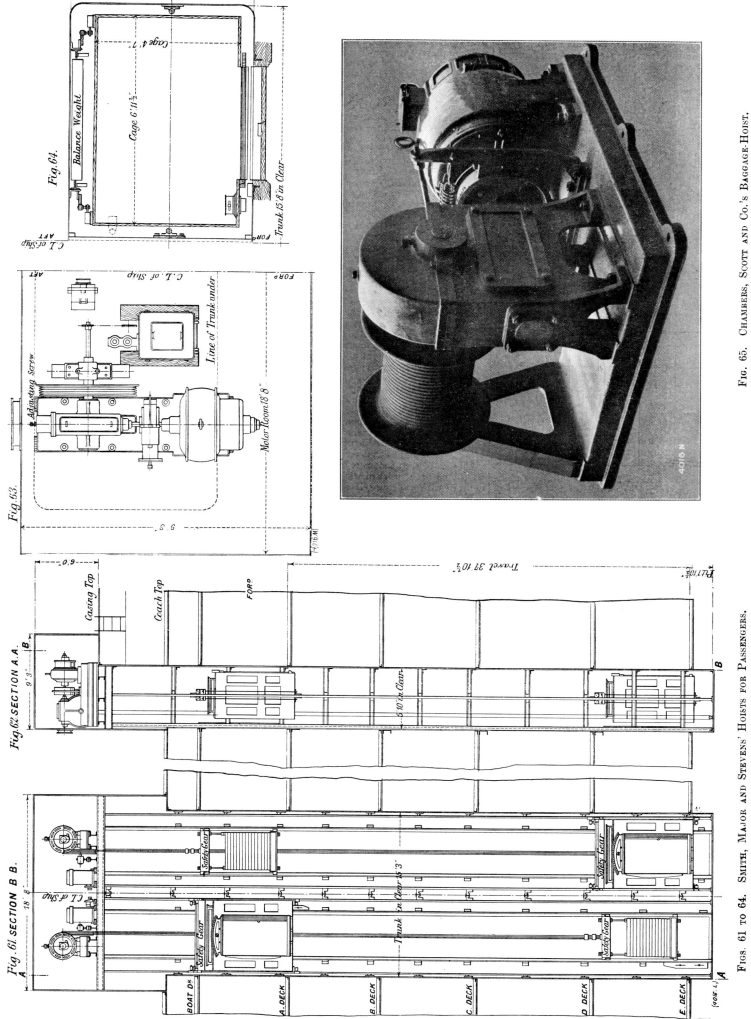

Fig. 64.

Trunk 5'10" Clear
Balance Weight
Cage 4'1"
Cage 6'11½"
Trunk 15'8" in Clear
C.L. of Ship
AFT
FOR'D

Fig. 63.

AFT
C.L. of Ship
FOR'D
Adjusting Screw
Line of Trunk under
Motor Room 18'8"
9'3"

Fig. 62 SECTION A.A.
Casting Top
Coach Top
FOR'D
Travel 37'10½"
PLATFORM.
5'10" in Clear
B
B
9'3"

Fig. 61 SECTION B.B.
A
A
18'8"
Safety Gear
C.L. of Ship
Trunk in Clear 15'3"
Safety Gear
BOAT D.K
A. DECK
B. DECK
C. DECK
D. DECK
E. DECK

FIG. 65. CHAMBERS, SCOTT AND CO.'S BAGGAGE-HOIST.

FIGS. 61 TO 64. SMITH, MAJOR AND STEVENS' HOISTS FOR PASSENGERS.

the cabins. With the multiplicity of promenades and alleyways the question arises whether these should not, on the respective decks, have some designation or name. On one point, however, every praise is due, and that is in the width of these highways, where people are most likely to congregate. The first-class passengers have a great, broad companion-way extending from the swimming-bath (which is on "E" deck) through the great reception-room adjacent to the main dining-saloon, and up, through the "C" and "B," to "A" deck, while from this level there is a broad enclosed stairway to the boat-deck. Opposite to the main stairway are two elevators. Further aft, and extending from "D" deck to the boat-deck, is a supplementary stairway along with an elevator; its position has been determined amidships in order to give communication from each deck to the grill-room, and also entirely under cover to the Marconi room on the boat-deck. The second-class passengers have also a wide companion-way, and here also the stairway has a central double handrail, so that there are four independent supports for passengers ascending or descending. This is a great advantage if the ship is in a seaway, and is just one of those little details the conception of which is highly creditable, although when accomplished they seem obvious.

The lifts are by Smith, Major and Stevens. In all there are three first-class passenger-lifts, two second-class, and five baggage, stores, and service lifts, of capacities as follow:—

No.	—	Load.	Cage Speed.	Height of Travel.		Decks Served.
			ft. per min.	ft.	in.	
2	First-class passenger ..	1800 lb.	150	37	6	E to A (5).
1	First-class passenger ..	1200 lb.	150	46	0	E to boat-deck (6).
2	Second-class passenger ..	1200 lb.	150	45	6	F to A deck (6).
2	Baggage ..	2 tons	100	44	0	H to C deck (6).
2	Stores	1 ton	100	25	0	G to D deck (4).
				16	0	G to E deck (3).
1	Service	1200 lb.	150	45	3	E to boat-deck (6).

As the technical details of all the lifts are generally similar, a brief description of the design of one of the passenger-machines may be taken as typical of the others. It is illustrated on page 27, Figs. 61 to 64. The supply to both motor and control circuit is direct current at 220 volts. The motor is of the multi-polar completely-enclosed type, and fitted with commutating poles, designed for a six hours' continuous test-bed run at full load, without the temperature rise exceeding 70 deg. Fahr. The motor is also designed to carry an overload of 50 per cent. for one hour without injury. Shunt winding is adopted, so as to give approximately constant running speed, but especially heavy series windings are also fitted for starting and accelerating. The series winding is shunted out of circuit on the last few steps of the rheostat.

The armature-shaft is directly coupled to the worm-shaft by a special form of concentric grip cone coupling, which entirely dispenses with all keys, and greatly facilitates the assembling or dismounting of the armature or worm-shaft when necessary. The brake-wheel is formed on the muff portion of the coupling, and is acted upon by a magnetically-controlled brake of the balanced type, thus avoiding any cross stresses on the worm-shaft. The worm gearing is of the self-sustaining type, specially designed to give the highest safe running efficiency, whilst ensuring the self-sustaining property under all conditions of cage load. The magnetic brake referred to is therefore only used for bringing the moving parts smoothly to rest after current is cut off, and is not in any way relied upon for sustaining the cage and its load. The worm gearing is completely enclosed in a dust-proof gear-case, forming an oil-bath, the worm being turned from a solid-shaft forging, and the wheel from close-grained hard cast iron, the teeth being cut from the solid blank. The unusually large bearing surfaces provided in the worm gear form an important feature of the design, the aim being to ensure the retention of an oil film between the working surfaces under all possible conditions of load.

A special method has been adopted for the automatic lubrication of all the worm-gear bearings from the oil-bath. The wheel teeth are cut in a bucket form, so that the worm is always dipping into new oil-pockets; the worm then throws off the oil centrifugally into a gallery cast round the inspection-cover at the top of the cage, whence it flows by gravity in a stream to the worm-shaft bearings and thrust-box. In this way a continuous circulation of oil is ensured. The worm-thrust is taken by a special multiple-disc bearing, arranged with steel and gun-metal discs alternating. These run completely immersed in oil, and each disc is formed so as to act as a centrifugal pump, maintaining a constant circulation of oil between the main reservoir and the thrust-chamber. The accessibility of the thrust-bearing will be noted in Fig. 63, and also the external adjusting-screw which enables any wear on the thrust-discs to be compensated.

The cage and counterweight are each suspended from four steel-wire lifting-ropes, and motion is imparted to them by means of the makers' well-known arrangement of **V**-wheel drive. This device affords a safeguard against accidental over-winding of the cage or counterweight under all conditions. It has the further advantage that should either cage or counterweight be stopped in descent, as by the action of the safety-gear, no slack cable can be paid out, as winding ceases immediately the tension on the ropes on either side of the **V**-wheel is relieved. The slack-cable safety device, which is a necessary adjunct and complication to the drum system of winding, is thus eliminated. The smaller space occupied by the **V**-wheel system of drive has enabled all the winding-engines for the passenger-lifts to be placed immediately over each lift-trunk, thus giving the best possible efficiency and rope-life. Each cage is guided on two 2-in. diameter round polished-steel guides, and the counterweights on **T**-iron section. The cage is fitted with a gravity-type safety-gear, which grips the cage to the guides upon the undue stretching of any of the four lifting-ropes; this gives warning of approaching failure of the ropes before they break. This safety-gear is actuated solely by the weight of the cage and its load, and does not rely upon springs. The counterweight, arranged to overbalance the cage by half the maximum load, is also fitted with a safety-gear of similar design to that on the cage.

The control in the cage is by means of a three-position switch, worked with a removable key, and is fitted with a spring self-centring device, so that current is automatically cut off and the lift stopped unless the switch be held over in the "up" or "down" running position by the operator. Automatic stopping of the cage and counterweight at either extreme of travel is provided for in three separate and distinct ways, operating in the following order:—Firstly, by incline planes engaging "limit" switches in the control circuit; secondly, should the first by chance fail, by the emergency switch wired in the main circuit, and opened by positive means by the cage, should it overtravel a few inches; thirdly, should the counterweight or cage land on its buffer-stops, the drive between the **V**-wheel and lifting-ropes immediately ceases, even though the motor may continue to run.

The controller embodied in the illustrations, Figs. 61 and 62, is completely worked by only two magnets, one for each direction of travel. Each magnet, through the intervention of timing-cams, operates both the circuit-breaker and the reversing-switch, and also provides the necessary clutch pressure for working the mechanical chain-drive to the rheostat. The circuit-breaker is fitted with self-cleaning finger-brushes, which are so arranged that the circuit is opened simultaneously at twelve points in series with one another, and this produces an exceptionally rapid breaking of the arc and dispenses with magnetic blow-out devices. The reversing-switch is so arranged that the shunt-field of the motor is left in parallel with the armature when the circuit-breaker opens, thus avoiding the use of kicking-coils. The movement of the reversing-switch for the opposite direction of travel is automatically delayed until after the armature has come to rest.

The chain-drive from the main hauling-shaft (shown in Fig. 63), working through the friction-clutch already mentioned, operates the rheostat until the motor has attained its full speed. At stopping, the clutch pressure is released, and a spring returns the rheostat-rod to the "all resistance in" position. A separate switch is fitted on the rheostat-rod, so as to prevent the closing of the circuit-breaker until all resistance has first been inserted in the armature circuit.

The entrance to the cage is protected by a collapsible gate, fitted with electrical contacts, so that the operator is compelled to close the gate before the lift can be worked. A patented form of self-contained electric lock is also fitted to the trunk-doors on each deck. This lock ensures that the lift cannot be worked until every door is closed, nor can any door be opened unless the cage is at the corresponding floor-level. In the case of the passenger-lifts, all cages are constructed of mahogany, the baggage and stores lift-cages being framed in wrought iron, with sheet-steel lining. Throughout the entire installation the aim has been perfect safety in working, the greatest attainable simplicity in design, and reduction of working parts.

THE KITCHEN APPLIANCES.

As can readily be understood, the provisioning of a ship with a population of over 4000 requires not only extensive appliances to ensure promptitude in service, but labour-economising apparatus of a high order. As we have said, the kitchens, pantries, &c., for the first and second-class passengers alone occupy a space 150 ft. by 97 ft., and they have been equipped by Messrs. Wilson, of Liverpool. The ranges, of which there are three in the first-class kitchen, have a total frontage of approximately 85 ft., and are provided with a total of 18 ovens. At one end of each range there is a bain-marie, in which tureens for keeping food hot are placed. Under the bain-maries are hot presses. The hot presses and bain-maries are all steam-heated by copper coils. In addition to the hot-plate boiling spaces on the top of the ranges, the kitchen is furnished with several large steam-jacketed stockpots. The larger ones are of 40 gallons capacity, the smaller ones of about 20 gallons. Two of the larger pans are provided with worm and wheel gear for tilting in order to facilitate the emptying of them. These two pans are provided with tinned-copper liners. The rigid boilers have tinned-copper, and the smaller vegetable pans pure-nickel, liners. In the kitchen there are also roasters and charcoal grills, appliances absolutely essential where Englishmen are to be catered for. The roasters provide for the cooking of meat in the old-fashioned English way, in front of a red fire, and are turned by electric-motors. From the point of view of novelty, the most interesting pieces of apparatus in this department are to be found in the grill-room. We refer to the two electric grills. So far as we are aware, larger electric grills have never been made. The grilling surfaces measure approximately 8 sq. ft., the grids being heavily nickel-plated. The finish of the apparatus is in planished steel and white metal, giving a handsome appearance, which is essential, as the grills are in view of the passengers taking meals in the grill-room.

Turning to the first-class pantry, extraordinary care has been taken to ensure rapid and convenient service of food. The carving-tables are of ample capacity, and are provided with bain-maries at the ends, and with hot presses under them. In the still-room there are installed coffee apparatus of the latest type, electric toasters and hot-plates, automatic egg-boilers, &c., all of which apparatus are essential to the production of the "little things" which are so very important in practice.

In addition to the first-class kitchens and pantries proper there are provided many sub-divisions, such as bakeries, confectioner's shop, vegetable-room, butchers' shops, silver-rooms, sculleries, bars, &c., and also full provision of kitchen and pantry space for the second and third-class passengers. In all these places there are machines and devices of the latest type for the saving of labour and the improvement of the catering. In the bakery the dough is, of course, mixed by machinery, after which it is proved, and then baked in the latest Wilson-Werner water-tube type of oven. The water-tubes are fixed so that one end dips into the furnace, while the body of the tube lies under the oven. This method of heating the baking-chamber leads to an equable temperature in practice, and as the oven bottom is tiled, and means provided for "spraying" the bread, the product is as good as anything produced ashore. The ovens are lighted by electric lamps and provided with inspection-windows. In the confectioners' and other shops, &c., there are many machines, mostly electrically driven, such as triturators, meat and bread-slicers, dish-washers, potato-peelers, knife and boot-polishers, mincing-machines, &c. The confectioner has an electrically-heated hot-plate for making cakes.

THE REFRIGERATING PLANT.

The refrigerating plant installed is entirely for the preservation of the ship's provisions, and has

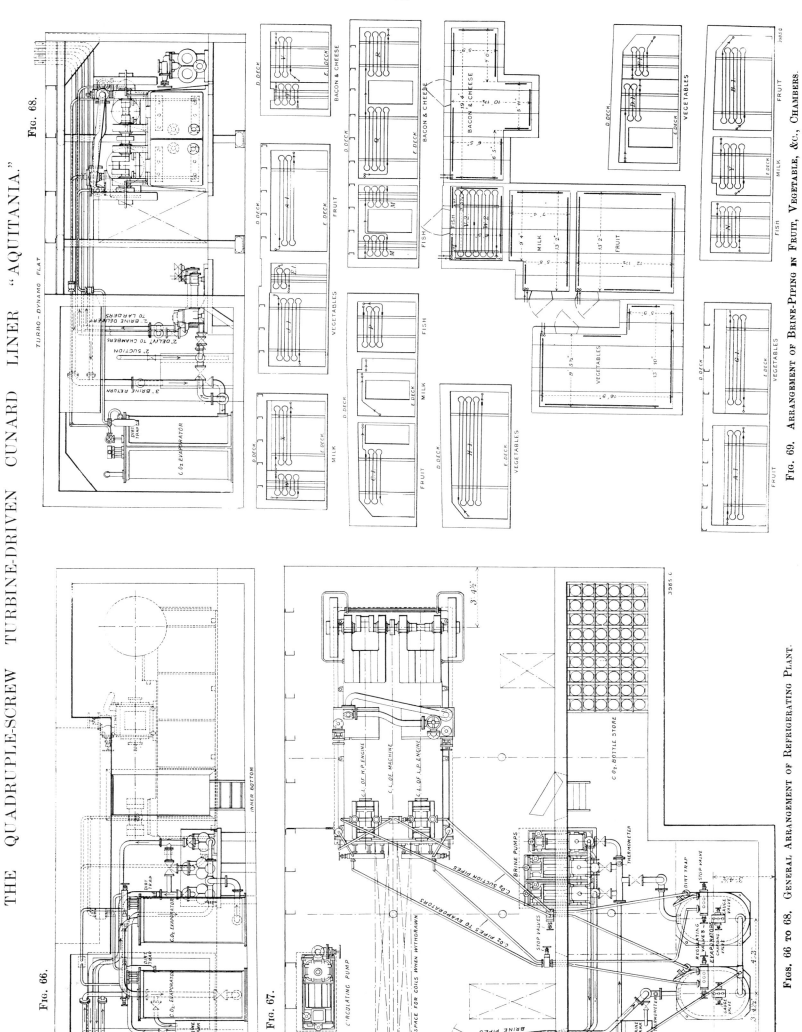

THE QUADRUPLE-SCREW TURBINE-DRIVEN CUNARD LINER "AQUITANIA."

FIG. 68.

TURBO-DYNAMO FLAT

FIG. 66.

FIG. 67.

FIGS. 66 TO 68. GENERAL ARRANGEMENT OF REFRIGERATING PLANT.

FIG. 69. ARRANGEMENT OF BRINE-PIPING IN FRUIT, VEGETABLE, &c., CHAMBERS.

THE QUADRUPLE-SCREW TURBINE-DRIVEN CUNARD LINER "AQUITANIA."

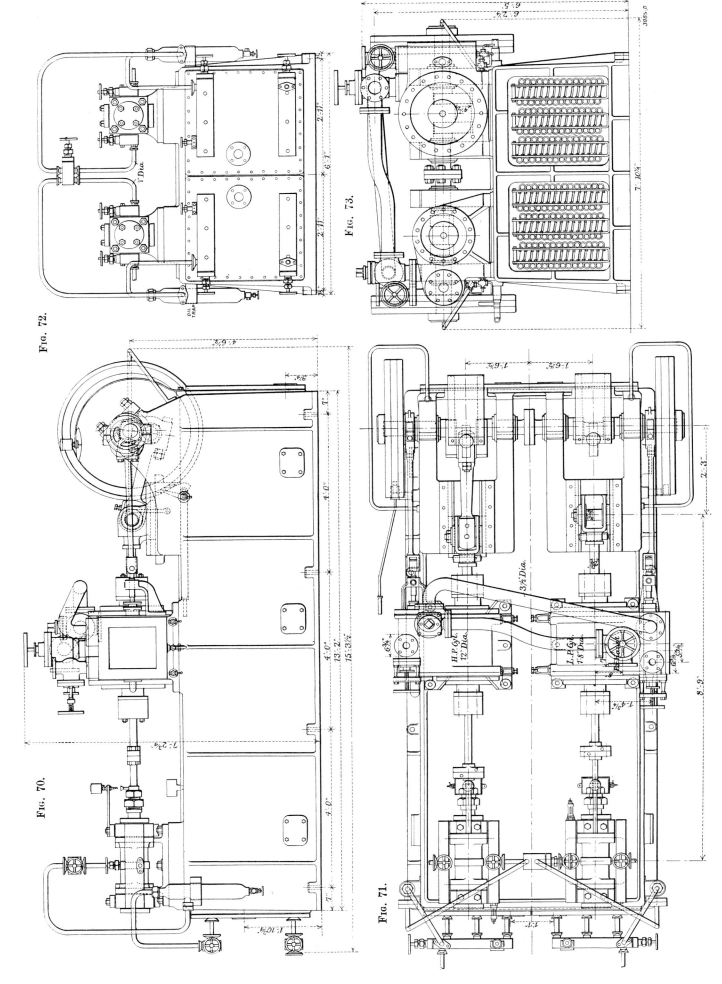

Fig. 72.

Fig. 73.

Fig. 70.

Fig. 71.

Figs. 70 to 73. Horizontal Compound Duplex Refrigerating-Machine; The Liverpool Refrigeration Company, Limited.

THE QUADRUPLE-SCREW TURBINE-DRIVEN CUNARD LINER "AQUITANIA."

FIG. 74. HORIZONTAL COMPOUND DUPLEX REFRIGERATING-MACHINE.

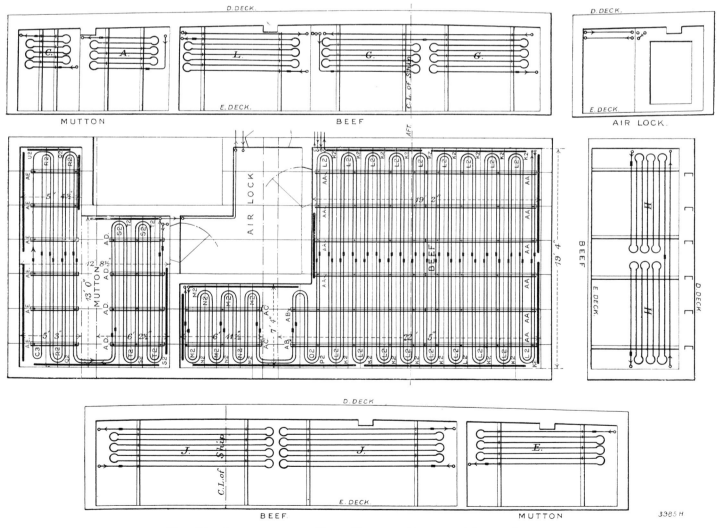

FIG. 75. ARRANGEMENT OF BRINE-PIPING IN BEEF AND MUTTON STORES.

been manufactured by the Liverpool Refrigeration Company, Limited, Liverpool. Of it detailed drawings are given on pages 29 to 31, and on the present page. It is located in a specially-constructed engine-room on the deck shown in Fig. 52, on Plate II. It is one of the largest ever fitted for this purpose, and embodies the refrigerators, wine and beer-coolers, cold pantries, &c., in various parts of the vessel, which are used as auxiliaries to the main cold chambers, for daily supplies, &c. All these are refrigerated direct by cold brine supplied from the refrigerating machinery through an extensive system of wrought-iron pipes, which are heavily lagged, and have the Fig. 74, on page 31, shows an engine of the same type as that in the Aquitania, but in the latter the condenser-coils are withdrawn from the end of the tank base, whereas in the engine illustrated side doors are fitted. The refrigerant used is carbonic anhydride. Two horizontal double-acting CO_2 compressors, illustrated by the sections, Figs.

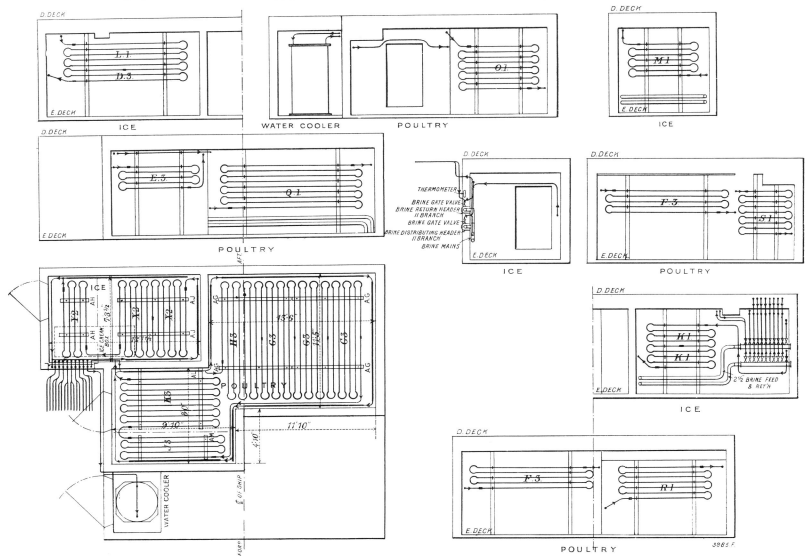

FIG. 76. ARRANGEMENT OF BRINE-PIPING IN POULTRY STORES.

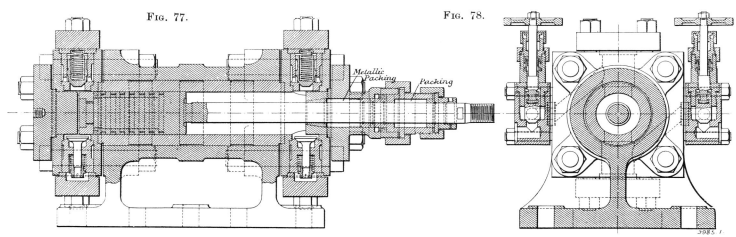

FIGS. 77 AND 78. SECTION OF DOUBLE-ACTING CO_2 COMPRESSOR.

latest practice. There are twelve insulated compartments fitted up for the storage of beef, mutton, poultry, ice, fish, dairy produce, vegetables and fruit, wines, beer, &c., and of several of these details of the cold-brine piping are given in Fig. 69, page 29, Fig. 75, page 31, and Fig. 76, above. Each class of goods has its own separate chamber or compartment, the temperature of which can be independently regulated. There are also nearly twenty cold cupboards, bar- necessary control-valves. A large central water-cooler, controlled by the machine, is also installed near the main provision-chambers, and a system of iced-water pipes is provided and fitted with numerous draw-off valves for the use of passengers and in the pantries.

The general arrangement of the plant is shown in Figs. 66 to 68, on page 29. The horizontal compound duplex refrigerating-machine is illustrated on page 30. The perspective view, Fig. 77 and 78, above, are driven from the tail-rods respectively of a high and of a low-pressure steam-cylinder. The crank-shaft is in two portions, coupled in the centre, and runs in four main bearings. Two fly-wheels are fitted, one at the outer end of each shaft. A complete system of steam-valves and cross-over pipes is provided, and fitted so that the engine can work compound, by uncoupling the crank-shaft, or as two separate engines, each steam-cylinder driving its own compressor independently. In the tank base upon which the machine is mounted are two independent CO_2 gas-condensers, one connected to each compressor. The machine is the full equivalent of two independent machines, which may be worked together or separately. Either half of the machine is capable of providing the whole of the refrigeration necessary. The compressors are of the makers' special design, and for which they claim several advantages. An outer cast-steel casing, having flanged feet, by which it is securely bolted down to the tank base, is fitted with an inner liner readily removable and forming the working bore. Two wrought-steel heads are bolted, one to the front and one to the rear end, and in these are fitted hard-steel suction and delivery valves and cages. The front head carries the stuffing-box. Wrought-steel breeches pieces connect the heads together. All covers are bolted on, no screw-plugs being used. The piston has metallic packing, having a series of fine cast-iron rings alternating with bull rings or carriers, the

stand-by. The brine-distributing arrangements are specially designed and arranged for the maximum convenience, and to ensure perfect control in every part.

The chambers, illustrated by Figs. 69, 75, and 76, are cooled direct by brine-piping arranged round the sides, ends, and overhead in the various compartments. Each compartment is absolutely independent. The whole of the piping is galvanised externally, and is of 1½-in. bore, lap-welded wrought-iron tube, bent by special hydraulic machinery and electrically welded into continuous grids of dimensions to suit the various chambers so fitted. The brine is circulated in entirely-closed circuits. There are no open tanks. There is consequently little or no loss of brine and no aeration. The system, once solidly full, remains so. All the cooling surface is efficient and the circulation free. A small tank is provided for mixing the calcium-chloride brine for charging. All piping, where passing through water-tight bulkheads, is fitted with stuffing-boxes, which make water-tight joints

revenue, to have a series of cabins on each side of the ship, is that only one cabin—the outer—can have natural light and ventilation. We have already indicated the ingenious method devised by Mr. Booth to afford this advantage to three rows of cabins on each side of "C" deck, but the application was necessarily limited to the rooms immediately under the promenade-deck. Where there was more than one room on each side of the ship, other methods had to be adopted. The difficulty of a general treatment is that the passenger occupying an outer room desires highly-heated air, whereas those in inner rooms generally need a supply of air at a less temperature. It was decided to provide a heated-air supply to the inner first and second-class state-rooms only; the outer state-rooms have each a steam-radiator; and thus the air supplied to the inner rooms may be of a temperature considerably less than that which can be attained by the steam-radiators (60 deg.).

Again, an independent series of trunks exhaust air from central positions, principally in the alley-

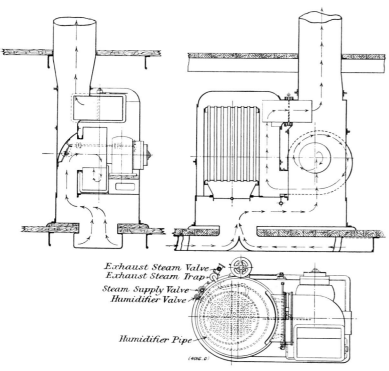

FIG. 79. THERMO-TANK UNIT WITH VALVES SET FOR
EXHAUSTING AIR.

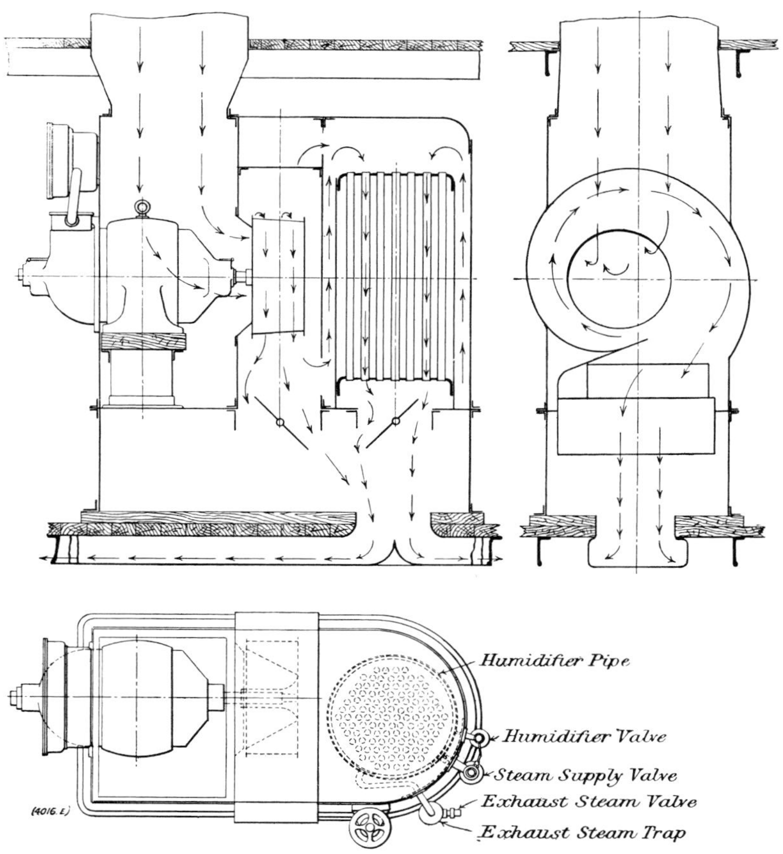

FIG. 80. THERMO-TANK UNIT FOR SUPPLYING HEATED AIR.

whole being kept in place by a patent junk-ring head, which it is impossible to slack back so long as the piston is in the bore of the cylinder. The compressor glands are packed with a metallic packing, no pressure lubricators being fitted, but instead a simple drop-feed oil-cup. With this arrangement much less oil is used. Wrought-steel traps are provided to prevent any oil passing into the condenser. The condenser coils are of solid-drawn tube withdrawable from the end of the tank base The headers are of forged steel, and the shut-off or stop-valves are arranged as far as possible in the headers. Cross-connections are provided, so that either compressor can deliver into both condensers and draw from both evaporators. The engine normally is supplied with steam at reduced pressure—about 120 lb. per sq. in., but the steam-cylinders are of sufficient strength and of suitable construction to work with full boiler pressure if necessary. The steam-glands are packed with United States metallic packing.

The water supply for the CO_2 condensers is circulated by a horizontal duplex pump fitted in the refrigerating engine-room; an auxiliary supply is arranged from the ship's fire-main. Two independent CO_2 evaporators of the vertical type are fitted in an insulated chamber partitioned off from the refrigerating engine-room. Three horizontal duplex brine-circulating pumps are provided. These are interchangeably connected, but in ordinary work one of the pumps is used for circulating the brine in connection with the main provision-chambers; a second one circulates the brine supply to the cold cupboards, bar-refrigerators, water-cooler, and auxiliary coolers generally; the third pump is a

while allowing the pipe slight freedom to move. Several of the main provision-rooms are fitted with beef-rails and hooks for hanging meat, and a complete outfit of shelving and other usual fittings is provided. The cold chambers have been insulated by the shipbuilders, Messrs. John Brown and Co., Limited, the insulating material used being granulated cork, and the latest construction followed. The net cubic capacity inside insulation of the cold chambers is over 18,000 cub. ft., and in addition there are the various auxiliary refrigerators, many of which are of large capacity. The machine has a refrigerating power of 30 tons of ice per twenty-four hours.

VENTILATION AND HEATING.

For dealing with the provisions made for the comfort of those who go down to the sea in the Aquitania, we may begin with the all-important question of the ventilation and heating of the habitable quarters of the ship. The success achieved in the Lusitania and Mauretania has only been looked upon as an incentive to further improvement in this respect. The thermo-tank system has here also been adopted, but important developments have followed a careful observation of results on the earlier ships. One of the difficulties in large steamships, where, owing to the great beam, it is necessary, in the interests of

ways, instead of exhaust-connections being made to each cabin. Experience has shown that when this latter system is adopted there is a possibility of the supply being short-circuited and entering the exhaust-trunk without adequate circulation in the room. Under the new conditions there is induced through the rooms a diffused current to the exhaust outlet in the alleyways, and at the same time each passenger has control over the volume of air entering through the supply-pipes. In summer the supply air is cooled, and in winter it is heated, in thermo-tank units. In the earlier ships these were placed on the boat-deck, but it was felt that in severe weather this position was inconvenient; as at the very time when everything was shut down and favourable ventilating conditions demanded, there was possibility of the plant not receiving the requisite attention. The apparatus for cooling and heating the air was therefore placed in a more accessible position. Fig. 79 is a section of a thermo-tank heating unit, with the valves set for exhausting air; while Fig. 80 shows a thermo-tank ventilating unit used for supplying moderately heated air. Other units are designed for a moderate degree of heating with a high rate of change of air. Normally, the aim is to change the air at the rate of from six to ten times per hour, according to the character and location of the compartment ventilated.

The installation consists of nearly 100 units,

which are of standard size, being interchangeable as far as possible. The various units are designed to give the necessary heat when using exhaust steam, circulation being provided by a connection to the auxiliary condenser to ensure that all the drain-taps will be kept free of condensed water. An auxiliary supply of steam at a pressure of 30 lb. per sq. in. is provided when exhaust steam is not obtainable. In the third-class quarters the practice has been to deliver the warm or cold air generally throughout the accommodation, and not into each room, and this has been found quite satisfactory. In some parts of the ship, for instance, in the lower-deck space adjoining the boiler-room, the cold air distribution only is applied, as, even in the winter, the normal temperature there does not require any artificial heating. In addition to the warm or cold air supply from the thermo-tank units, independent fans are provided for exhausting air from all lavatories and bath-rooms in the vicinity of the

is of a storage capacity of 400 gallons. The casing is of mild steel, galvanised, and it is fitted with a battery of tubes capable of raising 2500 gallons of water per hour from 70 deg. to 170 deg. Fahr., using exhaust steam at 15 lb. pressure. The other two have a somewhat smaller storage capacity. They are illustrated in Figs. 81 to 86, below. Of these, Figs. 81 and 82 relate directly to an apparatus having a storage capacity of about 200 gallons, and having heating surface in the form of Row indented tubes, sufficient to raise 2500 gallons of water per hour from 50 deg. to 160 deg. Fahr., employing exhaust steam at only 5 lb. pressure per sq. in. Fig. 86 shows a longitudinal section of the third calorifier, which is similar to the preceding, except that the battery of heating tubes is smaller, its duty being 2500 gallons per hour raised from 50 deg. to 160 deg. Fahr., with, in this case, live steam at 180 lb. pressure.

The main dimensions of these two calorifiers are

THE ELECTRICAL EQUIPMENT.

Electricity is very extensively utilised on board the ship for a great variety of purposes, and the electric generating station located on deck between two of the boiler-rooms, as shown in Fig. 51, on Plate II., has a total capacity of 1600 kw. The general arrangement of the station is shown in Figs. 87 and 88, on page 35, while an emergency station, with a Diesel-oil-engine driven generator is fitted on the promenade ("A") deck, as shown in Fig. 54, on Plate III. The general arrangement of this latter installation, with oil-tanks, compressed-air bottles, &c., is shown in Figs. 93 to 95, on page 37. It will be seen that this emergency set is entirely self-contained.

The main generating plant, of the British Westinghouse type, consists of four 400-kw., 1500 revolutions per minute, 225-volt direct-current turbogenerator sets, with slip-rings and static-balancers

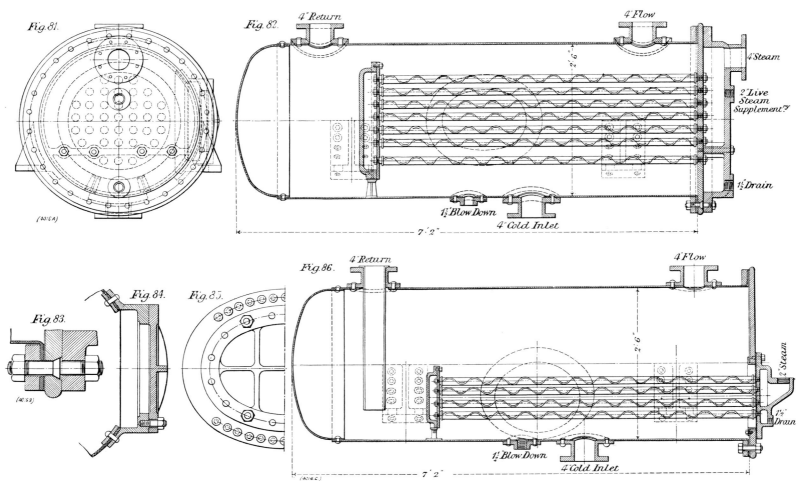

FIGS. 81 TO 86. ROYLE'S CALORIFIERS FOR PROVIDING HOT WATER FOR DOMESTIC PURPOSES.

habitable quarters of the ship, the change of air in these spaces being based upon the volume of the passenger accommodation in their vicinity. Special care has also been taken to arrange that the entering air should be kept well away from boiler, engine, and galley-casings, where the air is liable to be heated by radiation from these places. The main trunks are carried down special vertical trunks built into the hull of the ship. On the other hand, the exhaust-trunks are, in most cases, led up the boiler-casings, where any heating is not detrimental to the system.

SANITATION.

The question of sanitation has had equally careful treatment, but the only point to which reference need here be made is to the supply of hot water for domestic purposes. The hot water is laid on to all the principal first-class state-rooms. The water is provided by three Royle's calorifiers, fitted with Row's indented tubes, and from these passes to the supply-tanks (fitted with the necessary valves) on the boat-deck, being distributed thence through a series of mains and drainage pipes. One of the calorifiers

identical. The details shown in Figs. 83, 84, and 85 are common to both. They both have casings of copper, and these, together with that first described, were all tested under hydraulic pressure of 100 lb. per sq. in. before installation. All three calorifiers are fitted with Royle's automatic temperature control, regulating the supply of steam so that a constant water temperature is maintained. This control is effected by the movement of a bent rod or "bow-string" bar fixed at its extremities to the body of the calorifier. It will be evident that the expansion or contraction of the calorifier body, under any alteration of water temperature, will materially alter the deflection of a bent bar fixed in this way. This change is utilised to operate a steam control-valve. Expansion of the body straightens out the rod and depresses the stem of the control-valve, closing the supply in proportion to the temperature reached by the water. On the other hand, a contraction of the calorifier body, due to the presence of a large amount of cold water, increases the deflection of the bar. This relieves the steam-valve, which opens, supplying a greater quantity of steam. This control has proved very sensitive, and the steam supply is regulated with such nicety when properly set that the water temperature is maintained practically constant.

for three-wire distribution. The static-balancers have been designed to deal with an out-of-balance current in the middle wire equal to 12 per cent. of the full-load current of the machines. A perspective view of one of the sets is shown in Fig. 92, on page 36, and other views of turbine and generator are given in Figs. 89 to 91, on the same page. Each set has three bearings and is mounted on its own bed-plate, which contains an oil-pumping and cooling system for supplying oil to all the moving parts. The turbine is capable of dealing with all loads up to 25 per cent. overload when supplied with steam at 150 lb. per sq. in. and exhausting against a back pressure of 20 lb. per sq. in. absolute. The turbines are of the Westinghouse Company's standard impulse type, having three rotating wheels, each carrying two rows of blades. The impulse type of turbine is very short, consequently the rotating element is absolutely rigid. The clearances, too, between rotating and stationary parts are large, and this construction, coupled with the fact that the cylinder is not subjected to high pressures and temperatures, with their consequent distortion, makes this type of machine reliable. Each turbine is complete with its own speed and emergency or "runaway" governor, which is arranged to cut off the steam supply should the speed rise more than

10 per cent. above the normal. The generators are fitted with the Westinghouse Company's well-known radial commutator and ventilated brush-gear. This type of commutator, in addition to providing more cooling surface, decreases the length of the machine, and as the brushes bear on radial surfaces, all tendencies towards chattering or vibration of the brushes on the commutator faces, are entirely eliminated. The slip-rings for the middle-wire connection are situated at the

supply air to the brush-gear. Each generator is fitted with fans capable of forcing a sufficient quantity of air through the machine to keep the temperature of all the parts within the specified rise—namely, not more than 40 deg. Cent. above the surrounding atmosphere.

The emergency set, located at the after end of "A" deck, consists of a 45-brake-horse-power Diesel engine by Messrs. Mirrlees, Bickerton and Day, coupled to a Westinghouse 30-kw. generator.

flange on the end of the shaft. This arrangement would enable other types of air-compressors to be used if necessary. The air-compressor used, and shown in the illustrations, is of the Mirrlees design and manufacture.

The cam-shaft is carried along the top of the cylinders, and is driven by a vertical shaft or skew-gear from the crank-shaft. The valves are carried in the cylinder heads, as illustrated to a large scale in Fig. 99. This arrangement allows of

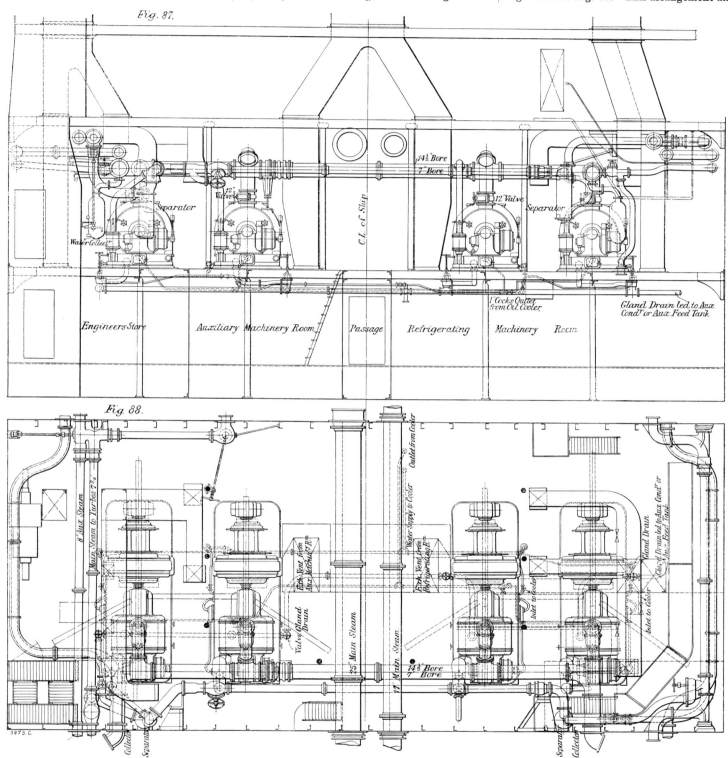

FIGS. 87 AND 88. GENERAL ARRANGEMENT OF ELECTRIC POWER-STATION.

turbine end of the generator. From these slip-rings connections are made to static-balancing transformers, the middle point of each transformer being connected to the middle-wire bus-bar. As shown on the elevation of the power-station, Fig. 87, a complete ventilating installation has been provided by the shipbuilders for ventilating these generators, the air being conveyed from the top deck in sheet-steel ducts, which are laid below the bed-plates of the generators, special in-take pipes being provided at the turbine ends of the generators to supply air to the armature and field, and at the outboard end of the generator to

The engine, which is illustrated in Figs. 96 to 100, on page 38, has three cylinders, 8 in. in diameter by 9 in. stroke, and runs at 450 revolutions per minute. It is of the standard Mirrless enclosed type, and the general lines of its construction will be easily followed from our illustrations. Messrs. Mirrlees build up all their engines from standard parts, and each cylinder, piston, upper portion of the crank-case or other part in the engine is inter-changeable with its fellows. Even crank-shafts are standardised, and it will be noted that the air-compressor shown at the left-hand end of the engine in Figs. 96 and 98 is driven from a crank bolted on to a

very fine clearances. The inlet and exhaust-valves are of nickel steel, and have renewable seatings. This arrangement has the conveniences that the valve-seats may be made of hard material which would not be suitable for the cylinder heads, and at the same time allows all grinding-in to be done at leisure by removing a worn seat and re-placing it by a new one, so that the engine has not to be stopped while the grinding is being carried out. The fuel-valve is of the ordinary needle type, and is shown between the inlet and exhaust-valves in Fig. 99. The fuel injection is varied in terms of the load by controlling the length of time

THE QUADRUPLE-SCREW TURBINE-DRIVEN CUNARD LINER "AQUITANIA."

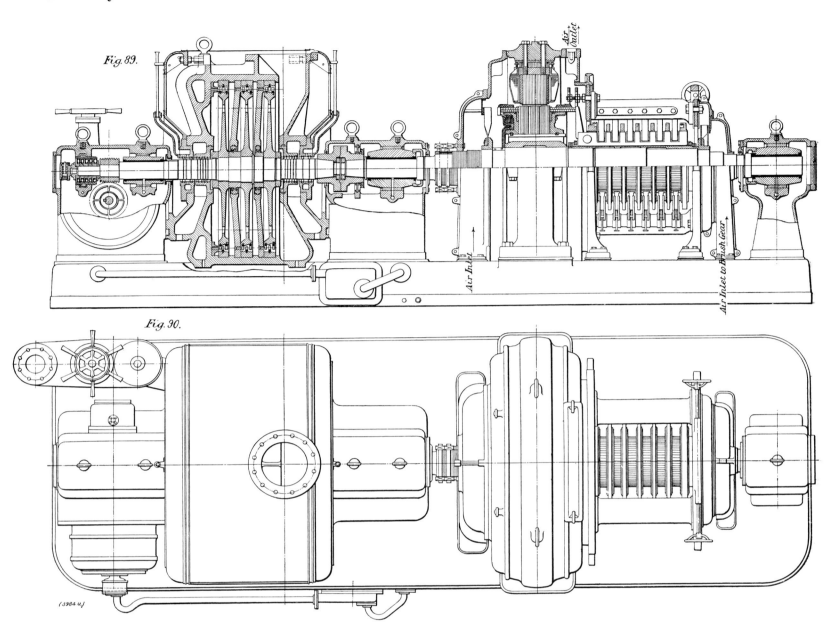

Fig. 89.

Fig. 90.

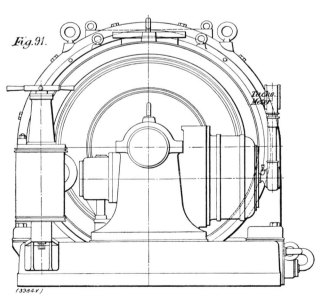

Fig. 91.

Fig. 92.

FIGS. 89 TO 92.   BRITISH WESTINGHOUSE 400-KW. TURBO-GENERATORS.

during which the pump-delivery valve is open, by means of the governor. The stroke of the pump does not alter. The air-compressor, as we have already said, is of the firm's own manufacture. It can be seen in section in Fig. 96. It is of the two-stage type with an intercooler between the stages. The valves are divided up into a number of small units. The engine cylinders are, of course, furnished with the usual starting-valves. Forced lubrication is used. The type of connecting-rods used and other details will be seen from the illustrations, one of the pistons being detailed to a large scale in Fig. 100.

The main switchboard, which measures 43 ft. 8 in.

wire system. The main cables are divided into port and starboard circuits, and are carried on porcelain insulators, protected by wood casing, along "G" deck. Ten pairs of cables carry current to auxiliary switchboards, from which the lighting, ship-ventilating fans, and other power-consuming devices are supplied. Separate mains are run to each fan-flat for supplying power to the fourteen forced-draught fans, also to the engine-room for ventilating-fans, turbine turning and lifting-gear motors, motors for boat-davits, galley machinery, &c.

The total number of motors fitted throughout the ship is close upon 180, and these range in size

turbine-casings; four motors are employed for driving lathes, shaping-machine, and radial drills in the workshop, and a 27-horse-power motor is employed for driving a centrifugal pump for supplying water to the sanitary tanks. For the ventilation of the engine-room and fan-flats there are twenty-six motor-driven Keith Blackman fans. Electrically-driven passenger and stores lifts to the number of ten in all have been fitted. Five of these lifts are for the use of passengers, two for baggage, and three for stores and serving pantries. On the boat-deck aft is fitted an installation of Welin davit boat-control gear, operated by two specially geared 30-horse-power motors. Two

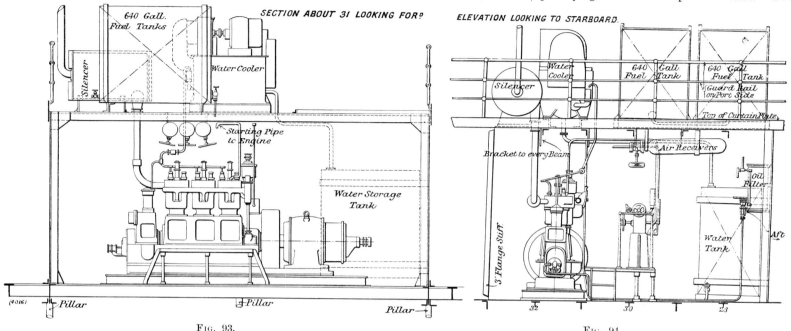

Fig. 93.   Fig. 94.

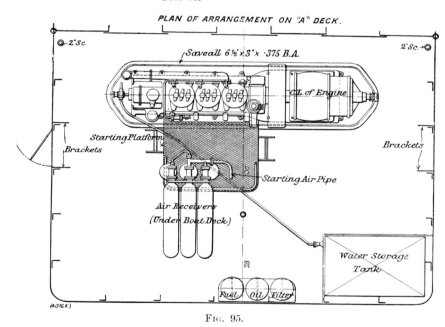

Fig. 95.

Figs. 93 to 95. General Arrangement of Emergency Electric Generating Station on Promenade Deck ("A").

in length, is placed on the same platform as the main turbo-generators, immediately in front of them. It is provided with electrically and hand-operated overload and reverse-current circuit-breakers for the dynamos, and double-pole overload circuit-breakers for each of the twenty-four feeder-circuits, all having time-limit adjusting devices. In addition to these protecting devices, a full range of ammeters, paralleling and bus-bar volt-meters, mid-wire and out-of-balance ammeters, earth testing lamps, and other necessary apparatus for operating the dynamos in parallel and controlling the circuits supplied by them, is provided on this board.

The installation, which is by Messrs. Martin, Glasgow, is, as already mentioned, on the three-

from 50 brake horse-power for the boiler-room forced-draught fans down to ½ horse-power for knife-cleaners, ice-cream machines, and such-like apparatus in use in the galleys. The total horse-power in motors aggregates slightly over 2000. With one or two exceptions all motors are wound for 220 volts, and are connected to the outers of the three-wire system, while lighting circuits are supplied with current at 110 volts, the load taken by these circuits being as nearly as possible balanced on either side of the middle wire and outers of the system.

Among the more important electrically-driven machinery may be mentioned the following:—In the engine-room, motors of 30 and 40 horse-power are employed for turbine-rotor turning and raising

turret-cranes for lifting baggage on board, operated through "Crypto" gear by 18-horse-power motors, are situated one on each side of the ship, in the vicinity of the second-class quarters. Electrically-driven thermo-tanks, cold-air supply, and exhaust-fans to the number of 88, and aggregating 387 horse-power, are provided for ventilating and heating all quarters of the ship.

As already stated, the bulkhead doors are operated by hydraulic power from the bridge, but information as to whether each door is open or closed is automatically registered on two indicators, consisting of small electric lamps showing through openings on a framed plan of the ship, one on the lower bridge, and the other above the engine-room starting-platform.

The whistles are electrically controlled on the Willett-Bruce principle. The position of the rudder is indicated on the bridge by an Evershed electric helm-indicator. The sounding-machine, by Kelvin, Bottomley and Baird, is operated by an electric motor.

Submarine signalling apparatus is fitted, the receivers being placed in a small telephone cabinet on the captain's bridge. Electric clocks, on Gent's pulsynetic system, and supplied by Messrs. Edward and Sons, are fitted throughout the ship, all the dials being controlled by a master-clock placed in the chart-room. Loud-speaking telephones are employed for communication between the bridge, engine-room, crow's-nest, poop, forecastle, turbo-generator room, pump-room, and steering gear, while intercommunication telephones are installed for the use of the captain, chief engineer, chief steward, purser, doctor, and other officers.

It need hardly be mentioned that the installation of wireless telegraphy by the Marconi Company is of their latest and most powerful type. The internal lighting of the ship is almost entirely by metal-filament lamps, carbon-filament lamps being only employed where rough handling is to be expected, such as for portable lamps in engine-rooms, coaling reflectors, and such-like. Special lighting is provided on the boat-deck for illuminating the boats. This is, of course, connected to the emergency lighting-circuits. The total number of lamps fitted is close upon 10,000.

An extensive system of automatic and hand-operated fire-alarms, consisting of fifty-eight sta-

THE QUADRUPLE-SCREW TURBINE-DRIVEN CUNARD LINER "AQUITANIA."

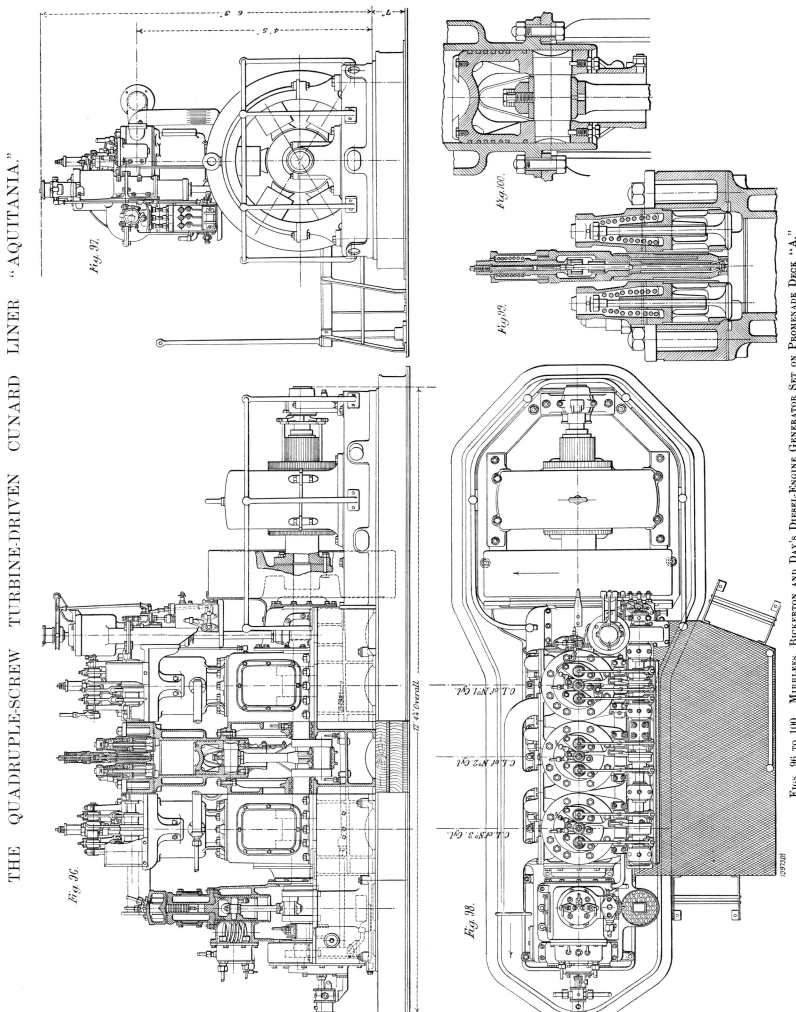

Fig. 97.

Fig. 96.

Fig. 100.

Fig. 99.

Fig. 98.

12 4 5 Overall

C.L of N° 1 Cyl.

C.L of N° 2 Cyl.

C.L of N° 3 Cyl.

(39720)

FIGS. 96 TO 100. MIRRLEES, BICKERTON AND DAY'S DIESEL-ENGINE GENERATOR SET ON PROMENADE DECK "A."

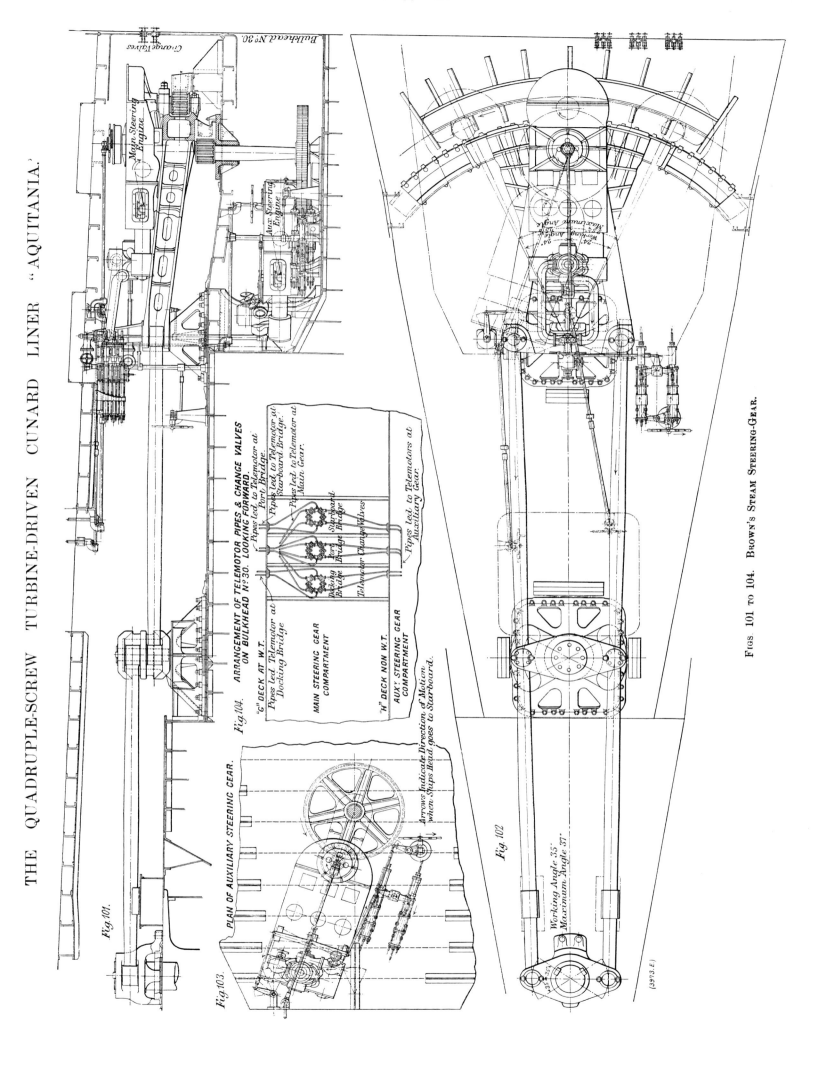

THE QUADRUPLE-SCREW TURBINE-DRIVEN CUNARD LINER "AQUITANIA."

Fig. 101.

Main Steering Engine

Aux. Steering Engine

Garage Valves

Bulkhead No. 30.

Fig. 104. ARRANGEMENT OF TELEMOTOR PIPES & CHANGE VALVES ON BULKHEAD No. 30. LOOKING FORWARD.

Pipes led to Telemotor at Port. Bridge.

Pipes led to Telemotor at Starboard Bridge.

Pipes led to Telemotor at Main. Gear.

"G" DECK AT W.T.

Pipes led. Telemotor at Docking Bridge

Docking Bridge   Port Bridge   Starboard Bridge

Telemotor Change Valves

MAIN STEERING GEAR COMPARTMENT

Pipes led to Telemotors at Auxiliary Gear.

"H" DECK NON W.T.

AUX. STEERING GEAR COMPARTMENT

Arrows indicate Direction of Motion when Ships Head goes to Starboard.

PLAN OF AUXILIARY STEERING GEAR.

Fig. 103.

Working Angle 35°. Maximum Angle 37°.

Fig. 102.

(3973.E.)

FIGS. 101 TO 104. BROWN'S STEAM STEERING-GEAR.

tions with indicator and key-plan fitted in a case on the captain's bridge, has been installed.

Electricity is much in evidence in the galleys and pantries for grills, hot-plates, dough-mixers, dish-washers, toasters, egg-whisks, potato-peelers, and such-like culinary apparatus.

As regards the cabin bells, an interesting feature is the arrangement for notifying stewards and stewardesses during the night of the calls of the passengers without disturbing anyone. For this purpose a special signal is provided for notifying the steward in his own cabin, while opposite each indicator-board in the alleyway is a three-sided light, which is illumined instead of the bell being rung to direct attention to any one of the indicators on the board. One of the three lights is white, and shines only on the indicator-board; the other two, looking forward and aft, are red, and these apprize the steward or stewardess of the indicator which is affected by the call of the passenger.

THE NAVIGATION OF THE SHIP.

Every provision has been made to bring the navigating officer into touch with every event which

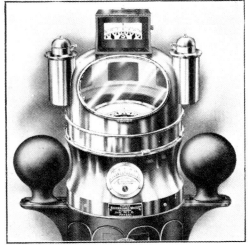

KELVIN'S VERTICAL CARD COMPASS.

may transpire in the course of the navigation of the ship. The navigation bridge is practically on the same level as the "A" deck, and on it there are

power-station and other parts, as already described in connection with the use of electricity.

An interesting development has been made in the design of all the compasses in the introduction of Kelvin's "vertical card compass," shown in the illustration annexed. This consists of an optical device contained within the hood of the binnacle, and by a lens and mirror an image of the compass card is thrown upon a screen so as to appear vertical, the size of the picture being approximately 6 in. by 4 in. There is thus obtained a much larger image of the card. The image is not inverted, as is the case with the steering-prisms. The device, being entirely in the hood of the binnacle, is totally removed when the hood is removed for

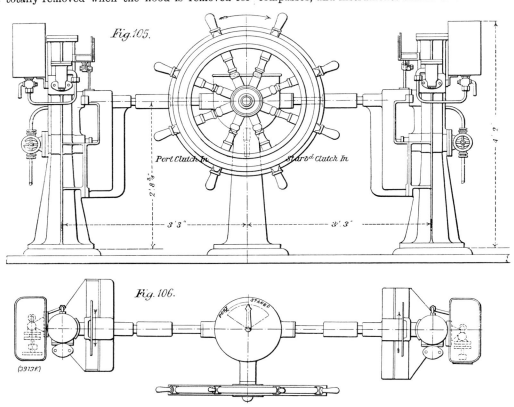

FIGS. 105 AND 106. BROWN'S TELEMOTOR GEAR.

of the ship under the water-line. The whistle is electrically operated, and the fog-horn has gear for bringing it into use at the will of the captain or at required periods of time during a continued fog. Before dealing with the main navigation-bridge, it may be said that there is a counterpart of this upper bridge right aft, principally for docking and undocking the ship, and both bridges are in communication by telephone and mechanical telegraph.

The lower bridge is, of course, the more important, as here, one might say, the captain has his finger on the pulse of every one of the organisms of the ship. This also is a very spacious bridge, and in the large wheel-house there are a telemotor gear, compasses, and instruments similar to those on the

FIGS. 107 AND 108. THE BUOY PENDANT AND MOORING ANCHOR.

the wheel-house, the chart-house, and abaft that the officers' quarters. There is, however, an upper bridge which is above the boat-deck level, extending the full width of the ship and of very ample area, as is indicated by the perspective view of it in Fig. 47, page 24. As will be seen, on this bridge are the telegraphs to each of the turbine-rooms (with instruments showing the direction and rate of revolution of each of the turbines), and to the capstans and windlass-gear stations, while telephones are provided to the look-out on the bow and foremast as well as to the engine-rooms, electric

the purpose of taking an azimuth bearing. This leaves the bowl with an absolutely clear surface, so that it can be used with an azimuth mirror. Owing to the larger size of the image, the steersman can get the complete orientation of his card from the magnified image. The steersman obtains a full view of his entire card through the ordinary aperture at the same time that he is obtaining the magnified image in the vertical plane.

On a slightly raised platform is a steering-wheel, with the telemotor gear for actuating the main steering-engine, situated at the extreme after end

bridge above; and, again, here the captain has under his control and observation the opening or closing of the bulkhead doors. There are sections and plans of the ship with each door marked, and discs show the position of the door. As already explained, there are two circuits, which ensure a larger measure of safety without interfering with the working of the ship. The captain has, moreover, under full observation the mechanism for communicating any outbreak of fire, as well as the command of the means of combatting such outbreak. There is also a cabinet to listen for sub-

THE QUADRUPLE-SCREW TURBINE-DRIVEN CUNARD LINER "AQUITANIA."

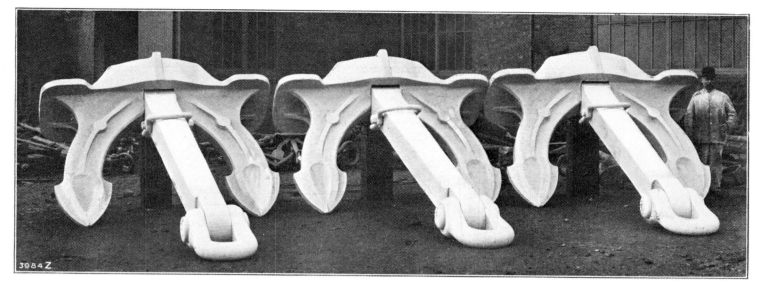

FIG. 109. THE ANCHORS.

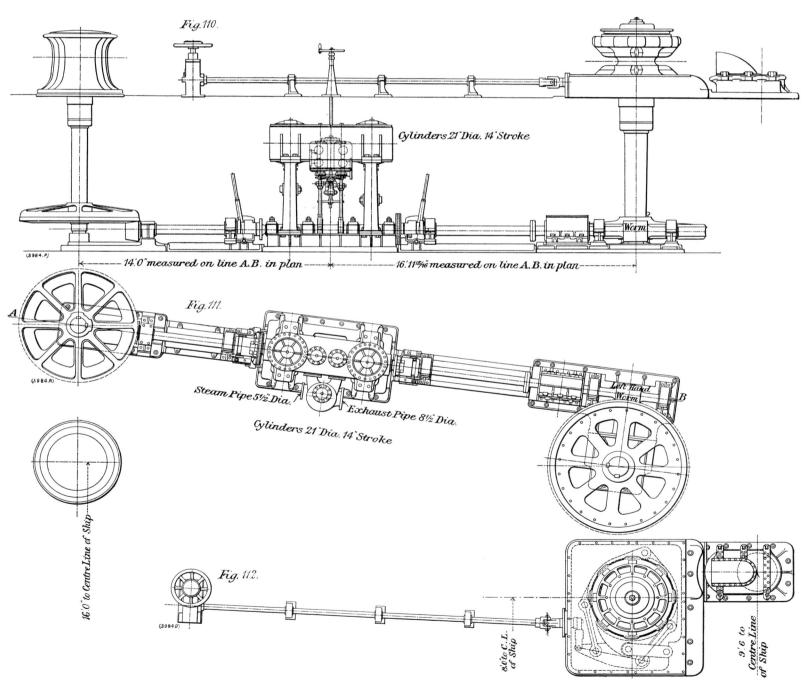

FIGS. 110 TO 112. NAPIER'S MAIN WINDLASS AND CAPSTAN GEAR.

THE QUADRUPLE-SCREW TURBINE-DRIVEN CUNARD LINER "AQUITANIA."

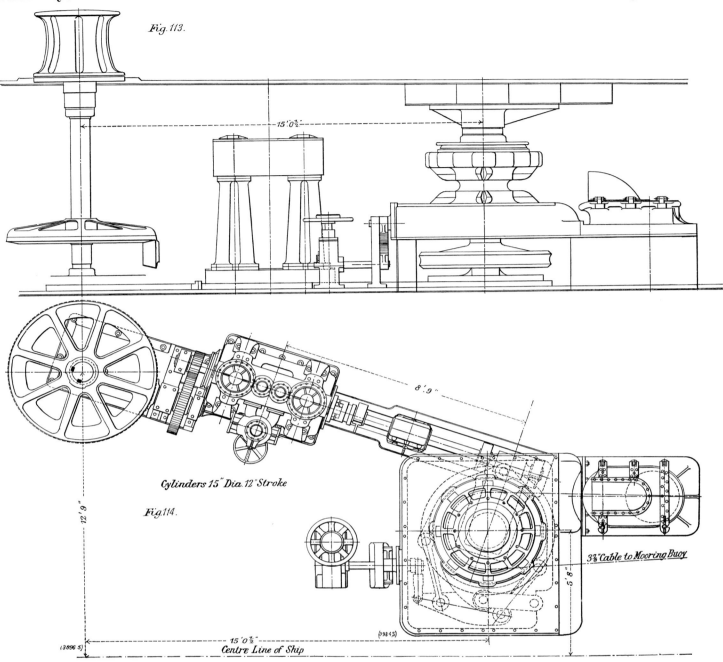

Fig. 113.

Fig. 114.

Cylinders 15″ Dia. 12″ Stroke

12′ 9″

15′ 0½″

(3896 5)   (39845)

Centre Line of Ship

3¾″ Cable to Mooring Buoy

5′ 8″

8′ 9″

15′ 0½″

FIGS. 113 AND 114. NAPIER'S MOORING WINDLASS AND CAPSTAN GEAR.

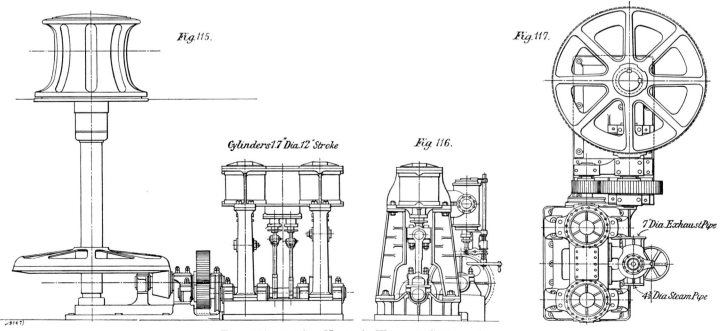

Fig. 115.

Fig. 117.

Cylinders 17″ Dia. 12″ Stroke

Fig. 116.

7″ Dia. Exhaust Pipe

4½″ Dia. Steam Pipe

(3147)

FIGS. 115 TO 117. NAPIER'S WARPING CAPSTAN AFT.

— 43 —

THE QUADRUPLE-SCREW TURBINE-DRIVEN CUNARD LINER "AQUITANIA."

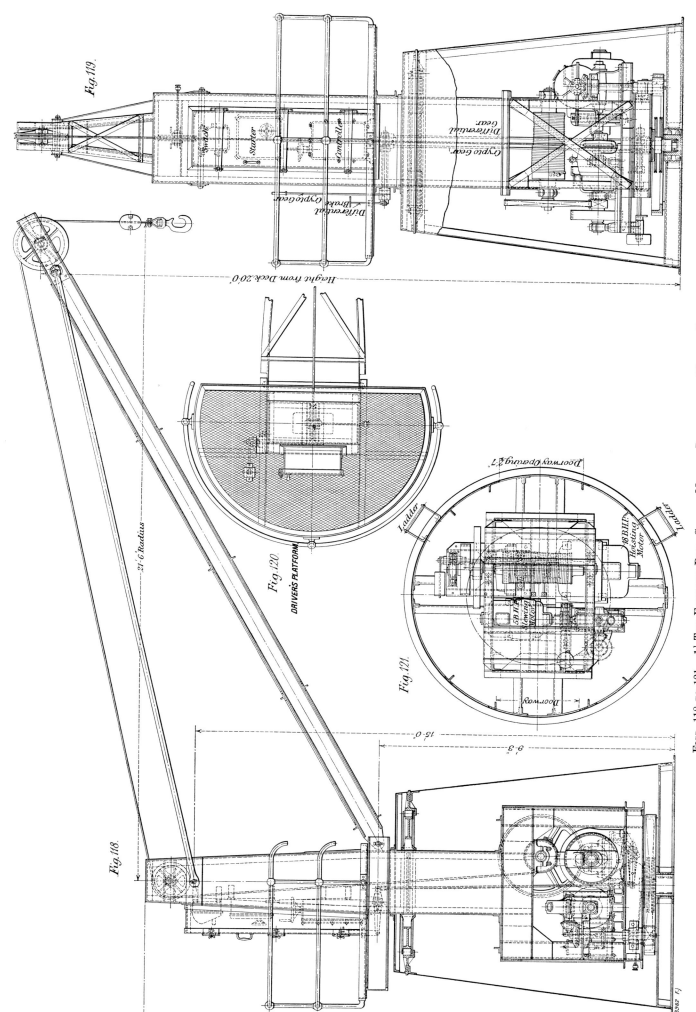

Fig. 119.

Fig. 120.
DRIVER'S PLATFORM.

Fig. 121.

Fig. 118.

FIGS. 118 TO 121. 1½-TON ELECTRIC DECK-CRANE; MESSRS. BABCOCK AND WILCOX, LIMITED.

marine signals. An indicator, too, shows the actual movements of the rudder in response to the turning of the wheel. Thus the officer in charge is in control of the whole of the movements of the ship.

The steering-engines are controlled from the navigating-bridge and also from the docking-bridge aft by a complete telemotor installation, shown on page 40, Figs. 105 and 106. The navigating-bridge is provided with two telemotor transmitters, arranged so that either may be clutched to the steering-wheel fitted on a pedestal adjacent to the compass, or to a steering-wheel fitted on a pedestal on the flying-bridge. On the docking-bridge aft there is placed a third telemotor transmitter. Each transmitter has an independent lead of piping to a group of change-valves in the main steering compartment, these change-valves permitting the connection of each transmitter to the motor cylinder at the main or auxiliary steering-engines.

The steering-gear has been designed and manufactured by Messrs. Brown Brothers and Co., Limited, of Edinburgh, and the main gear is of their well-known steam-tiller type, modified and arranged to suit the exceptional dimensions and requirements of the ship. It is illustrated on page 39. The whole of the gear is placed well below the water-line, the position being shown on the deck plan, Fig. 51, on Plate II. Owing to the very fine lines of the ship it has been necessary to place the tiller on a dummy-post (some 47 ft. forward of the rudder cross-head), and to use an intermediate dummy-post and crosshead to carry the rods which connect the tiller to the rudder crosshead.

The tiller, which is a steel casting, is triangular in plan, and is surmounted by the main steering-engine, which is of the makers' enclosed type, having forced lubrication and water-cooled oil service-tank. The main engine has cylinders of 14 in. diameter by 14 in. stroke, and is fitted with the makers' improved economic valve, patent differential valve-gear, &c. It is capable of developing 750 brake horse-power and exerting a torsion effort on the rudder-stock of 1200 ft.-tons. The rudder can be moved from hard-over to hard-over in 30 seconds. The auxiliary steering-gear is placed in a compartment directly below the main gear, access being obtained through a water-tight hatch in the deck. The engine is similar to the main engine, all parts being interchangeable with the similar parts of the main engine.

The drive from the auxiliary engine to the rudder is through massive cast-steel gearing to a vertical shaft, which passes through the deck to the main steering compartment; the pinion on this shaft engages with a cast-steel toothed sector, which is bolted on to the under side of the tiller. This arrangement provides large bearing surfaces, and gives great rigidity to the combined gears, the auxiliary gear being equal to the main gear both in power and speed. The engaging gears for the main and auxiliary steering engines are the makers' special design of expanding clutches, and can be operated from either steering compartment or from the steering-gear trunk at the level of the upper deck. Clutches and control-gears are arranged to allow the change over from main to auxiliary gear, or vice versâ, to be performed independent of the position of the steering-gear, and the change over can be made with the ship in a heavy sea with ease and absolute safety. Control and clutch connections are designed to permit the change from main steering engine to auxiliary steering engine, or vice versâ, being effected without any one entering either steering-engine compartment, thus allowing the gear to be operated though either compartment were flooded, or otherwise inaccessible, a method unobtainable in any other vessel, excepting the Mauretania and Lusitania, which are fitted with similar control and clutch mechanism. Mechanically-operated control gear is also fitted in each steering-engine compartment.

MOORING AND ANCHOR GEAR.

The question of supplying suitable cables, anchors, and harbour moorings for a vessel of this size and weight was a serious problem and entailed careful consideration. The firms who could be relied upon to make cables of the size and quality necessary being limited, it was eventually decided to entrust the manufacture of the cables to Messrs. Brown, Lenox and Co., Limited, who made the first ship's cables for the Admiralty about a hundred years ago. More recently they have completed some specially heavy harbour moorings for the Admiralty, the tests of which gave remarkable results; each of a large number of samples, cut from the cables for the destruction test, withstood the limit strain of the testing-machine, 350 tons, and consequently could not be broken.

The total length of ship's cable made for the Aquitania is 330 fathoms, and the weight 125 tons. The links vary in size from 3⅞ in. nominally, but are actually 4 in. to 4⅝ in. in diameter. The iron for the cables was ordered from Messrs. Hingley and Sons, and is of their highest Admiralty quality. The anchors selected were Hall's latest improved type, and were manufactured by Messrs. Hingley. Fig. 109, on page 41, shows three of the anchors, each of 11 tons.

As this great ship has to be moored periodically in the Mersey, the buoy moorings were of immense importance, as on the strength and reliability of her moorings and cables depended the security of the ship. Messrs. Brown, Lenox, who have made a speciality of buoy moorings, and who have recently manufactured (by an entirely new process, rendered necessary by the increased size) specially large moorings for the British Admiralty, were called in to inspect, and, where necessary, alter and strengthen their buoy moorings for the Lusitania and Mauretania, and described in ENGINEERING, November 8, 1907. This was done, and it may be mentioned that the new buoy pendant they have recently supplied (which is illustrated in Fig. 107, on page 40) is the largest chain ever manufactured, as it is beyond doubt the most important; the iron in the links for the most part is 5⅜ in. in diameter, and the swivel in the centre weighs 10 cwt. The mooring anchor, Fig. 108, on page 40, by the same firm, weighing over 12 tons, is connected to the buoy pendant by Admiralty-pattern square mooring chain.

The anchor and warping-gears, by Messrs. Napier, are illustrated on pages 41 and 42; but in the plans of the general arrangement only one-half is shown, usually for the port side; the arrangement on the starboard side is exactly the same. The position of the gear on board is shown on the deck plans (Fig. 56, on Plate III.). The anchor gears, which are of the well-known Napier type, consist of two cable-holders, suitable for working 3⅞-in. diameter stud-link chain cable, which are mounted on the forecastle head, and are driven from the deck below by two 21-in. by 14-in. double-cylindered engines through worm gearing, and are capable of heaving both anchors at a speed of 50 ft. per minute. These are clearly shown on page 41, the plan showing only the port half of the gear. The forward warping-gear consists of four capstans mounted on the forecastle head. Two of these are driven through bevel gearing from the windlass engines, and are each capable of lifting 30 tons at full speed. The other two are driven by independent 15-in. by 12-in. double-cylinder engines through spur and bevel gearing from the deck below, and are each capable of lifting 25 tons at full speed.

In addition to the above, there is a special mooring gear consisting of two cable-holders for the 3⅞-in. cables, placed forward of the independent warping capstan engines, and driven by them through worm gearing. This gear is for use when the vessel is moored in the Mersey, or other confined waters, and is shown in Figs. 113 and 114, on page 42. Each of the forward anchor and mooring-gear cable-holders is fitted with powerful Napier patent differential self-holding brakes, which are unexcelled for their holding power where heavy loads have to be dealt with in a limited space, their special virtue being that it is the load which governs the grip, so that once a brake is put in gear it can be safely left alone, no matter how severe the weather may get, as the greater the stress on the cable the tighter it is held.

The amidships warping-gear consists of two capstans fitted on the shelter-deck, and driven from the deck below by independent 15-in. by 12-in. double-cylinder engines through spur and bevel gearing, and each capstan is capable of lifting 25 tons at full speed. The aft warping-gear (Figs. 115 to 117) consists of two capstans on the shelter-deck, driven from the deck below by independent 17-in. by 12-in. double-cylinder engines through spur and bevel gearing, and each capstan is capable of lifting 30 tons at full speed. The gears throughout are so designed as to ensure an ample margin of strength, and are the result of Messrs. Napier's experience extending over half a century. Cast steel is used wherever possible, and the worm-wheel rims are of gun-metal. All the gear-wheels are machine-cut, as has been the firm's practice for the last thirty years.

CARGO AND BAGGAGE CRANES AND HOISTS.

As shown on the deck plans on Plates III. and IV., there are three cargo holds forward, and in connection with these are six cargo and warping-winches of the silent type, by Messrs. Wilson, of Liverpool, placed on the "C" deck. The mail and baggage-rooms are aft. The cranes resemble those fitted in earlier Cunard liners, and have been illustrated and described in earlier volumes of ENGINEERING.

On page 43 there is illustrated one of two Babcock and Wilcox cranes fitted aft on "B" deck for handling baggage, light goods, and mails. They are capable of dealing with loads up to 30 cwt., lifting at a speed of 120 ft. per minute, and slewing at 300 ft. per minute. The main structure for carrying the column consists of a conical mild-steel casing, in which is fitted all the machinery and electrical appliances. The column is built of steel, carrying a light channel-steel jib at a fixed radius of 21 ft. 6 in. The casing is fixed directly on to the deck, and has fitted in the top of it a race-path and live ring of rollers for supporting the column; the foot of the column being carried on a ball-race at the bottom of the casing. The casing is fitted with large hinged water-tight doors, so that the machinery is always accessible for inspection and repairs. The general design enables the cranes to be very easily fitted to a ship, as they are entirely self-contained and the weight is distributed over a large area of the deck. The hoisting-gear is of the well-known Babcock and Wilcox patent type, consisting of a compound motor, operating the hoisting-barrel through "Crypto" gear and the mechanical self-sustaining brake. This combination enables the cranes to be handled by inexperienced operators with the least possible chance of causing damage, either to the goods or cranes. The cranes are operated from a small platform attached to the side of the column, so that the operator is always facing the load he is lifting.

In addition to those already described, Messrs. Chambers, Scott and Co., have supplied electrically-driven hoists, one of which is illustrated in Fig. 65, on page 27. The operating gear is mounted on a bulkhead close by the hatchway, and the load is carried by a special non-rotating wire rope, with safety-hook, working over a derrick-block. The gear consists of a specially-grooved drum, driven through worm reduction-gearing by an enclosed motor on a bed-plate, and operated by a reversing drum-controller. A self-sustaining electro-mechanical brake is provided, electrically interlocked with the controller, so that it is entirely automatic in action, and is capable of holding the maximum load under all conditions. The gearing runs in an oil-casing, fitted with gun-metal and ball bearings. The wheel has a phosphor-bronze rim, a worm of forged steel, and the teeth are machine-cut from solid metal. Provision is made for access to all the parts. The motor is totally enclosed, series wound, to give automatic speed variation, and is equipped with self-oiling bearings and compensating carbon-brush gear, with covers over the commutator. A starting, reversing, and speed-regulating drum-controller, with crank-handle, is employed for lifting and lowering, and this is equipped with renewable contacts and non-corrosive grids giving a wide series of speeds and full control at all loads. All bearings are fitted with gun-metal bushes and lubricators, and a safety ironclad switch and fuse are provided for the protection of the gear.

THE PROPELLING MACHINERY OF THE SHIP.

WE turn now to the machinery of the ship, which, as has already been explained, is of the Parsons turbine type, arranged to work in treble series, the high-pressure turbine on the port-wing shaft exhausting into the intermediate-pressure turbine on the starboard-wing shaft, which in turn passes its steam to two low-pressure turbines, one on each of the two inner shafts. As will readily be understood, the adoption of the treble series lengthens the range of expansion, and is consequently conducive to high thermal efficiency. For driving astern, there are turbines on all four shafts. On the port shaft is a high-pressure turbine separate from the ahead turbine and exhausting into a low-pressure astern turbine on the port inner shaft. This low-pressure astern turbine is incorporated in the same casing as the low-pressure ahead turbine; while on the starboard outer shaft there is also a separate high-pressure turbine exhausting into a low-pressure astern turbine in the starboard inner shaft.

The adoption of the treble-series system for ahead working has required the exercise of considerable ingenuity to ensure that the turbines can be worked independently of any one which may be thrown out of action; and it may be said here that with one turbine thrown out of gear there will be no difficulty in maintaining practically full speed. Later we shall deal fully with the alternative systems of working the turbines, but here it may be said that it is possible to change over from triple-series working to compound working, in which case the high-pressure turbine would exhaust into the adjoining low-pressure turbine, while the intermediate-pressure turbine, taking steam direct from the boilers, would exhaust into the low-pressure turbine on the same side of the ship. Similarly the intermediate-pressure turbine can be cut out of action, and the high-pressure turbine exhaust to both low-pressure turbines, or the high-pressure turbine can be cut out of action, and the intermediate-pressure turbine, taking steam from the boilers, would become the high-pressure turbine exhausting to both of the low-pressure turbines. Either of the low-pressure turbines may also be disconnected from the system. The arrangement of valves for these various systems of working will be described later.

The weight of the machinery is about 9000 tons, which is 10 per cent. less than in the case of the Lusitania. The designed power at 165 revolutions is 60,000 horse-power for an ocean speed of 23 knots, whereas in the Lusitania the power, at 180 revolutions, is 68,000 horse-power for an ocean speed of 25 knots. The weight of machinery in the new ship thus works out at 6.6 shaft horse-power per ton, which is exceedingly satisfactory in view of the great margin provided in the boilers, where the heating surface per horse-power is 2.3 sq. ft., but it should be remembered that a considerable amount of steam is required for auxiliaries that are not associated with the propelling machinery.

THE GENERAL ARRANGEMENT OF THE MACHINERY.

On page 46 there are given a longitudinal section and plan (Figs. 1 and 2) of the machinery compartments from the forward boiler-room bulkhead, which is about 200 ft. from the bow, showing the four boiler-rooms, the turbine-rooms, the condenser compartment, and the shafts and propellers. The cross-section, Fig. 3, shows how the boiler-rooms are enclosed by longitudinal bulkheads, the space

between these and the skin of the ship being utilised as coal-bunkers, while the section, Fig. 4, shows how the turbines are located in three separate compartments formed by longitudinal bulkheads.

The boiler-rooms, cross-bunkers, and auxiliary machinery rooms in connection therewith occupy a space 369 ft. long. There are four boiler-rooms. Six boilers are arranged in each of the three forward boiler-rooms, while in the after boiler-room there are three, making a total of twenty-one boilers in all. All the boilers are alike, of the cylindrical type, double-ended, with eight furnaces in each, and they will be illustrated later. The boilers are arranged three abreast, each room being 60 ft. wide, the remaining width of the ship being utilised as bunker space. The after boiler-room is 42 ft. long, and the others are 78 ft. long. A large elliptical funnel, the outer casing of which is 24 ft. on the major axis by 17 ft. on the minor axis, serves each boiler compartment. The forward funnel is 154 ft. 9 in. high above the firegrate of the centre furnaces and 59 ft. above the casing top. The inner casing of the after funnel is necessarily much smaller than the others, although the outer casings are similar, the additional air space being utilised as an upcast vent from the centre turbine-room. Cross-bunkers are arranged between boiler-rooms 1 and 2 and 2 and 3. Between boiler-rooms 3 and 4 at "H" deck level the turbo-generating plant is situated. Beneath this plant, at the stokehold level, a large auxiliary-machinery compartment is arranged.

For dealing with ashes there are seven Stone's ash-expellers fitted in large recesses in each boiler-room, into which, after cleaning fires, all ashes can be stowed, to be expelled at will, thus facilitating the work of the stokers by having a clear firing-platform at all times. In addition to these expellers, eight ash-hoists are distributed throughout the boiler-rooms. In a recess in the cross-bunker, between the boiler-rooms 1 and 2, there are a bilge-pump, a ballast-pump, and an assistant feed-pump. There are also an assistant feed-pump and a ballast-pump in the auxiliary-machinery room beneath the turbo-generators.

The turbines in the three separate engine-rooms athwart the ship are arranged to work on the triple system, as has been done on some of the most recent liners. Under normal working conditions, the high-pressure ahead turbine, which, along with a high-pressure astern turbine, occupies a separate compartment on the port-wing turbine-room, receives boiler steam direct, which is passed in turn to the intermediate-pressure turbine, occupying, along with a high-pressure astern turbine, a similar compartment on the starboard wing. The two low-pressure ahead turbines on the two inner shafts receive their steam from the intermediate-pressure turbine. These low-pressure turbines are placed in the central compartment. Abaft the turbine-rooms are the two main condensers in separate rooms, each with its circulating and air-pumps.

The condensers are of the "Uniflux" type. In each of the two condenser compartments there are two centrifugal pumps. Two 30-in. diameter discharge-pipes from these pumps supply the circulating water to each condenser. In each compartment there are two air-pumps of the "Dual" type, which discharge into hot-well tanks, one in each compartment, fitted with float-control gear. Four hot-well pumps draw from these tanks, and discharge through four filters to two "Uniflux" surface heaters and two direct-contact heaters—also fitted with float-control gear. Six pairs of feed-pumps

draw from the heaters or direct from the hot-well tanks, and discharge to the boilers through an independent line of piping to each boiler compartment. In each wing engine-room there is an auxiliary condenser, with a circulating and air-pump in connection therewith. There are four water-service pumps and one sanitary and one wash-deck pump in the centre engine-room. There is also a motor-driven sanitary pump in the port-wing engine-room. In the centre engine-room are placed three pumps in connection with the water-tight doors. There are four bilge-pumps. There is also a hot-salt-water pump, drawing from the condenser waterways for supplying baths. In the port-wing engine-room there are two fresh and condensed-water pumps, discharging to service tanks on deck. There are six main forced-lubrication pumps in the centre engine-room, and in connection with these there are the necessary strainers and oil-coolers. All the tunnel-blocks have forced-lubrication connection, and the drain from these blocks flows into two tanks in the after part of the ship. From these tanks a pump, with float control, discharges the oil to the main-drain tanks to facilitate the natural flow of the oil back to the main tanks.

There are two evaporators, each of 75 tons capacity per 24 hours. In connection therewith there are a feed-pump, two condensers, and two filters for drinking and washing purposes, and a duplex pump for circulating purposes.

The section and plan, Figs. 1 and 2, page 46, also show the arrangement of the shafting and propellers. The inner shafts are 10 ft. from the centre line of the ship—i.e., 20 ft. apart. All shafts are parallel to the centre line of the ship, while the vertical rake is approximately $\frac{3}{16}$ in. per foot in the case of the inner, and $\frac{1}{4}$ in. per foot in the case of the outer shafts, being downward in the aft direction. The outer shafts are 28 ft. 6 in. from the centre line of the ship—i.e., 57 ft. apart and 18 ft. 6 in. from the inner shafts.

The intermediate shafting is $19\frac{3}{4}$ in. in diameter and with a $9\frac{3}{4}$-in. hole, while the tunnel shafting is 21 in. outside diameter with a $9\frac{3}{4}$-in. hole, and has continuous gun-metal liners, the diameter over the liner being $23\frac{1}{2}$ in. The liners are in one piece, and are shrunk on to the shafts. The stern tubes are about $19\frac{1}{2}$ ft. long over all, and are of the ordinary merchant type. They are made of cast iron, fitted at each end with gun-metal bushes, lined with lignum vitæ strips. All the shafting was made at the Atlas Works, Sheffield, of Messrs. John Brown and Co.

The four propellers have been manufactured of the Manganese Bronze and Brass Company's "turbadium" alloy. The weight of the four working propellers is approximately 65 tons, representing an outlay of nearly 10,000l. The propellers are balanced so that they can be made to revolve simply by pressure of the hand. The essential point to be borne in mind in the manufacture of such propellers is the obtaining, as far as possible, of a perfect Beta structure, in order to secure the maximum resistance to erosion. The difficulty in realising this aim will be understood when it is stated that for each propeller there had to be melted about 30 tons of bronze in three separate furnaces, and that the whole quantity had to be in a certain specified condition in regard to composition at the moment of tapping. If this had not been carried out successfully the propellers would have been subject to active erosion during service. The tensile strength also has been raised from about 33 tons per sq. in. to 42 tons per sq. in., with an elastic limit of about 18 to 19 tons per sq. in., and

THE CUNARD LINER "AQUITANIA;" GENERAL ARRANGEMENT OF PROPELLING MACHINERY.

Fig. 1.

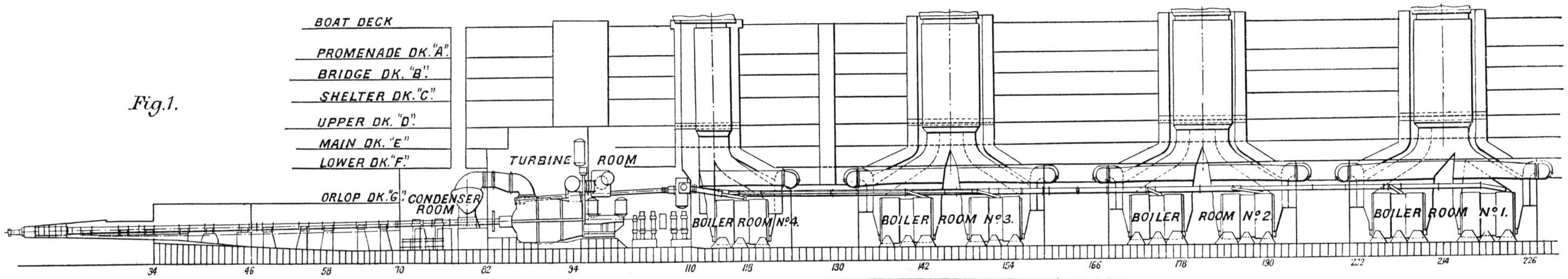

Fig. 2.

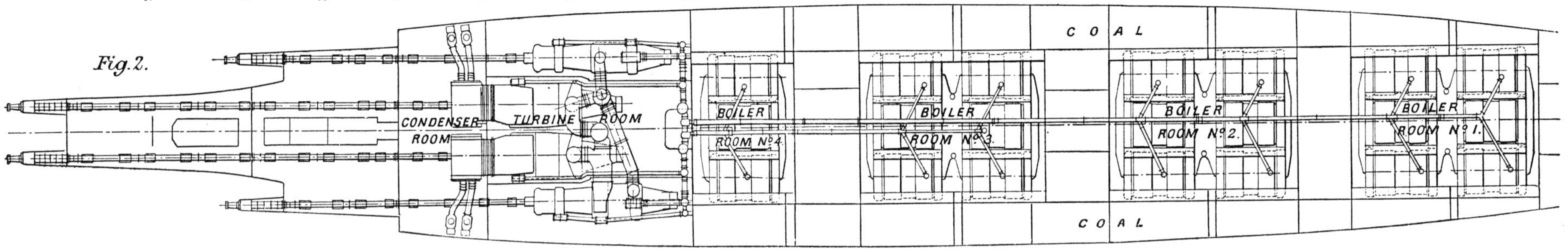

a reasonable elongation. The makers are continuing their research work.

THE MAIN TURBINES.

In describing the machinery in detail, we begin with the main turbines. There are two turbines, one ahead and one astern, on each line of shafting. On the outer shafts these turbines are entirely separate; but on the inner shafts, on which are mounted the low-pressure turbines, the ahead and astern units are incorporated in one casing. On Plate V. there is given (Fig. 5) a section of the high-pressure ahead and astern turbine on the port-wing shaft. On the same plate (Fig. 6) is a section of the intermediate-pressure ahead and of the high-pressure astern turbine working the starboard-wing propeller. The astern turbines on these shafts are alike in every respect. A section of one of the low-pressure ahead and astern turbines is given on Plate VI., on which also are several details of the thrust-block and its adjusting gear common generally to all the turbines. Perspective views of the turbines in various stages of construction are given on pages 53 to 60.

It can readily be understood that for a ship of this size and speed the turbines must be of massive construction. The high-pressure ahead turbine from the aft coupling to the forward end is 40 ft. 2 in. long over all, and the total weight is 240 tons. The main bearings are 25 ft. $4\frac{1}{4}$ in. between centres. The journals on the rotor spindle at these bearings are 2 ft. 6 in. in diameter and 3 ft. $8\frac{1}{4}$ in. long, while the spindle in way of the cast-steel discs forming the drum-ends is 2 ft. 11 in. in diameter. The spindles are hollow, the hole varying from 11 in. to 23 in. in diameter. The high-pressure ahead rotor drum is 9 ft. 2 in. in diameter, and in its finished form has a weight of about 80 tons. It was made at the works of Messrs. Thomas Firth and Co., Limited, Sheffield. The drum is in two portions, with a massive junction-wheel connecting the two. This, as in the case of the Lusitania, was necessary, owing to the great length and diameter of the rotor. Provision was made at the forward end of the spindle for steam heating the interior of the spindle, in order to ensure equal expansion during running. The casing of the turbine is of cast iron, heavily ribbed circumferentially as well as longitudinally. There are four stages of expansion; the blades—on the rosary system—vary from $3\frac{3}{8}$ in. to 7 in. long.

Fig. 3.

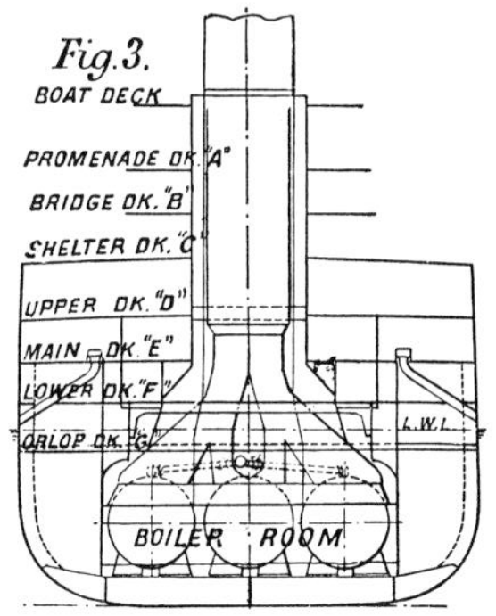

Fig. 4.

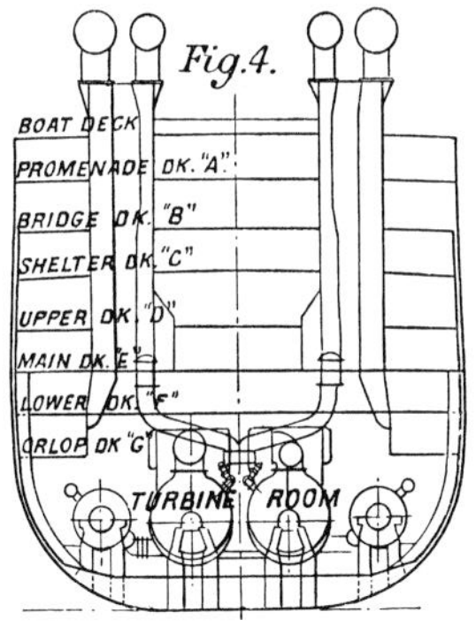

It will be seen from the section that in this and also in the intermediate-pressure turbine the thrust-collars are turned on to the end of the spindle, and are not a separate forging, as in the case of the low-pressure turbine, the great length of the latter making the fitting of a separate thrust prudent. The rotor-journals run in gun-metal bushes, with provision for water-cooling. The keeps of the bearings are of cast iron, with provision for water-cooling. They also form the top half of the bushes. The main bearing-bushes are supported on massive cast-iron stools, entirely separate from the turbine-casing, and securely bolted to the latter. The thrust-block at the forward end is also a separate casting, and is similarly bolted to the bearing-block. The bearing-block at the after end is also a separate casting, and is bolted to the turbine-casing at its forward end, while at the after end it is bolted to the forward bearing of the high-pressure astern turbine. The turbine is fixed to the ship at the after bearing, and provision is made at the forward end for expansion. The feet of the forward bearing-block and thrust-block slide on cast-iron stools, securely bolted to the structure of the ship. Great attention was paid to the seating to ensure rigidity in the structure of the ship in the way of the turbines. Into the forward end of the spindle there is screwed a short length of shafting, so as to provide a journal for running in a bearing at this point, in order to steady the spindle itself and to carry the spiral wheel for driving the governor and the revolution-counting gear. The usual type of labyrinth glands with Ramsbottom rings is fitted.

The high-pressure astern turbine, which is fitted abaft the high-pressure ahead turbine, is 22 ft. 11 in. over the couplings, and weighs 120 tons, the bearing centres being 17 ft. $7\frac{1}{2}$ in. The journals are 2 ft. in diameter and 2 ft. $7\frac{3}{4}$ long. There are four expansion stages, the blades in the first stage being $1\frac{1}{2}$ in. long, increasing to 3 in. long in the third and fourth stages, the final stage being arranged for by the "winging" of the blades. The high-pressure astern rotor-drum is 7 ft. 10 in. in diameter. The rotor is similar in general construction to the rotor of the high-pressure ahead turbine, but the dimensions differ, the weight being a little over 40 tons. The drum, being of smaller proportions, is all in one piece. The casing is of cast iron, heavily ribbed, as in the case of the ahead turbine, but the top and bottom halves are each in one piece. The bearing-blocks are separate castings, and rigidly connected to the ship through the high-pressure ahead turbine, as already indicated. Provision is made at the after block for expansion. The after coupling of the astern turbine carries a turning-wheel, which is solid, of cast steel, and not in halves, as is the more frequent practice. The high-pressure ahead and high-pressure astern turbines make a total length of 63 ft. 1 in.

The construction of the intermediate-pressure turbine, as will be seen from the section, Fig. 6, Plate V., is almost identical with the h.p. turbine, but the dimensions differ, the weight of the rotor in this case being about 90 tons. The main bearings of the intermediate-pressure turbine are 26 ft. $0\frac{1}{2}$ in. between centres, and the journals are 4 ft. $4\frac{1}{2}$ in. long, this increase in length of $8\frac{1}{4}$ in. over the high-pressure journals being due to the greater weight of the intermediate-pressure rotor. The rotor spindle is of the same diameter as that of the high-pressure ahead turbine. The over-all length of this turbine is 41 ft. $6\frac{1}{2}$ in. from the aft coupling to the forward end, $16\frac{1}{2}$ in. more than that of the high-pressure turbine. As in the high-pressure turbine, there are four expansion stages, the blades varying from $6\frac{3}{4}$ in. long to 14 in. long. The rotor-drum is 10 ft. 4 in. in diameter. In the case of the high-pressure astern turbine working on the same shaft as the inter-

— 47 —

THE CUNARD LINER "AQUITANIA;" FORWARD BEARING-BLOCK OF LOW-PRESSURE TURBINE.

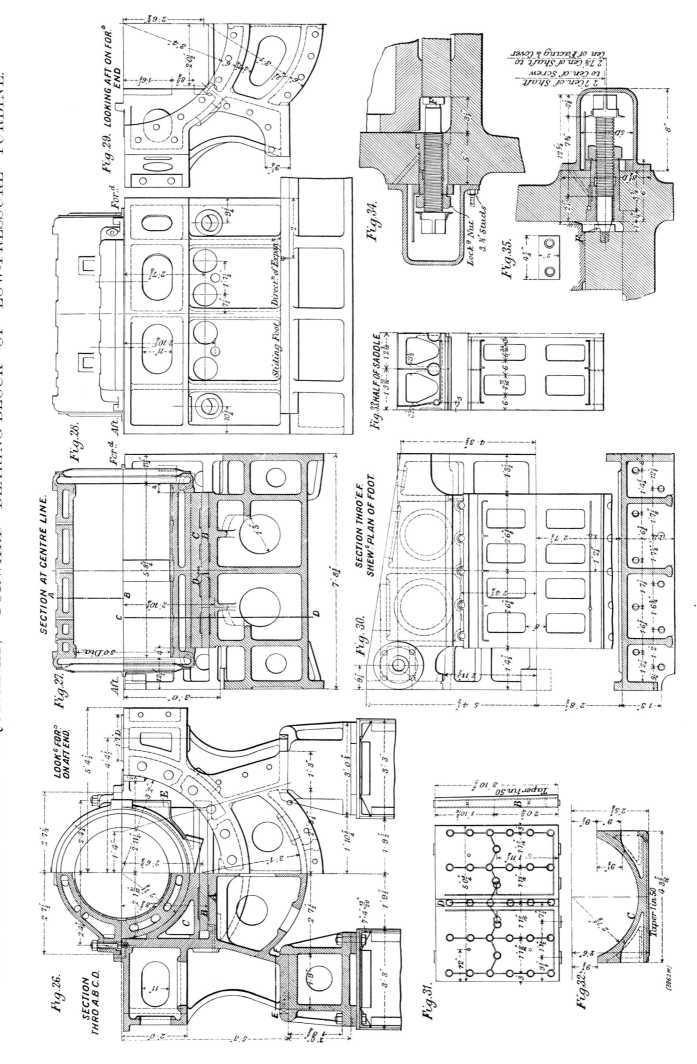

mediate-pressure turbine, the design and dimensions are exactly the same as the astern turbine on the same shaft as the high-pressure turbine, but it rotates in the opposite direction.

The low-pressure ahead and astern turbines, Fig. 7, on Plate VI., as already mentioned, are contained in one casing, with common eduction to the condenser. An idea of the enormous size of these turbines can be got on reference to the perspective views published on the several pages numbered 53 to 60. The total weight of this low-pressure ahead and astern turbine is 445 tons.

Firstly, as regards dimensions, the rotor-drums are 12 ft. and 10 ft. in diameter respectively. The turbine is 54 ft. 3 in. long over all from the forward end to the aft coupling. The main bearings are 35 ft. $1\frac{1}{8}$ in. between centres, and the journals are 3 ft. in diameter by 5 ft. $9\frac{3}{4}$ in. long. In way of the discs the rotor-spindle is 3 ft. 2 in. in diameter. There are nine expansion stages in the ahead turbine, and four in the astern turbine. In the former the blades vary from 7 in. to 20 in. long, and in the latter from 5 in. to 7 in. The thrust-blocks and adjusting-gear are situated at the forward end of each line of shafting. Powerful motor-driven turning-gear is fitted on the couplings immediately aft of each pair of turbines. The overhauling gear for the main bearings is very efficient, ample provision being made by means of beams and travellers for lifting, tilting, and stowing the massive covers and bushes. To deal with such weights as the low-pressure turbine-casing or rotor a lifting arrangement of no mean order was required. This is shown in Fig. 47 on page 51, and Fig. 50 on page 52. This gear, motor-driven, is arranged over each turbine on heavy beams built into the ship. The guide-columns at both ends of the turbines are extended to these lifting-beams, and afford efficient supports when overhauling. The lifting-motors, of 30 brake horse-power, operate the lifting-screws through worm-gearing. The low-pressure lifting-screws are $7\frac{3}{4}$ in. in diameter. This arrangement will be separately illustrated and described later.

Secondly, as regards the constructional details of the low-pressure turbine, the rotors differ from those of the high-pressure and intermediate-pressure turbines. The ahead and astern drums are connected by a cast-steel ring, while the ahead drum, which is in two portions, has a junction-wheel of cast steel, similar in design to that used in the high-pressure and intermediate-pressure turbines, but the forward and aft wheels connecting these drums to their spindles are each made up of two conical discs, as shown in Fig. 7. This type of wheel was decided upon as a result of the great experience of the firm in the construction of turbines of great dimensions, and as a direct outcome of experiments made with a view of obtaining stiffness when dealing with rotors of very large diameter and weight. The low-pressure ahead rotor-drum has a diameter of 12 ft., with a total weight of rotor complete of 140 tons. To have transmitted this weight to the spindle through the same type of wheel as is adopted in the high-pressure and intermediate-pressure turbine, with rotors respectively of about 80 and 90 tons, would have called for a disproportionately heavier disc for equal strength. By the adoption of the double sections for the disc, disposed as shown in the section of the turbine, Fig. 7, there was gained a great increase in strength for a given weight. Thus each double disc in the low-pressure rotor is of about 20 tons weight, as compared with 14 tons in the case of each disc for the high-pressure rotor and 18 tons in the case of the intermediate-pressure rotor, notwithstanding that the first-named turbine is so much heavier.

THRUST-BLOCKS AND THEIR ADJUSTMENT.

In the case of the low-pressure turbines, the thrust-collars are turned on a separate forging, which is bolted to the forward end of the spindle, instead of being turned on the spindle itself, as in the case of the high-pressure and intermediate-pressure turbines. A bearing is provided in this case also. In the case of the low-pressure turbines, the rigid attachment to the ship is made at the after bearing-block, which is securely bolted to the ship's structure, provision being made for expansion at the forward block, as in the case of the other two turbines. In an intermediate position in way of the exhaust-belt additional support is provided in the form of a foot, which assists to carry the weight of the casing, but is free to move under the influence of expansion.

The thrust-blocks are illustrated on Plate VI., while on page 53 are perspective views. Figs. 8 to 14, on Plate VI., show the blocks of one of the turbines, which is typical of the lot, and Figs. 15 to 17 illustrate the liners. They are, of course, situated at the forward end of each turbine, and in each case there are seventeen collars for both ahead and astern operation, the collective thrust surface in each direction being 1860 sq. in. The diameter of the shaft is $21\frac{1}{4}$ in. between the collars, and 29 in. over the collars. There is a hole bored through the centre 11 in. in diameter. The thrust-block is of the ordinary Parsons type, the bottom halves of the rings being arranged to take the ahead thrust, and the top halves the astern thrust. The rings are of phosphor-bronze, lined with white metal on the working surface, and fitted into a cast-steel liner, which is housed in a cast-iron block.

Particular attention has been given to the means provided for the movement of the block fore and aft in order to adjust the dummy clearances when the turbines are running. The top half of the steel liner carrying the rings has horns at each side, shown at A in Figs. 9, 16, and 17. On the bottom half are corresponding horns B. The top and bottom portions are bolted together in the proper relation one to the other by means of the bolt C, a distance-piece D being introduced to simplify the setting up (see also Fig. 10). With the rotor in its correct position, the dummies having their proper clearance, the white-metal surfaces of the rings on the bottom half bear hard up against the forward sides of the collars on the thrust-shaft. The white-metal surfaces on the top half are then clear of the after sides of the collars on the thrust-shaft by an amount approximating to $\frac{15}{1000}$ in., this amount being termed the "oil-film clearance." This relation is determined by the thickness of the liner D, which is adjusted in the shop when setting up the turbines. It will be obvious that if the top halves of the white-metal surfaces had been brought hard up against the collars, as was done with the bottom halves, there would naturally be no room for the oil-film; hence the need for the $\frac{15}{1000}$-in. clearance mentioned. This, it should be added, however, is the usual practice in setting thrust-blocks of this type. The halves of the thrust-block top and bottom, having been bolted together as explained, any movement of the liner as a whole cannot affect the relation of the top and bottom surfaces—*i.e.*, the oil-film clearance is always maintained provided no wear has taken place, and even in such case the setting of the block itself may be modified by means of the liner D to give any desired clearance.

Turning now to the means for adjusting the thrust-block as a whole, it will be seen in Fig. 10 that each of the horns forms the extension of a larger horn which is cast on the bottom half, as will be clearly seen in Fig. 8. These larger horns form sockets, into which adjusting-rods are fitted, as shown at E, in Figs. 8 to 10. These adjusting-rods extend forward, and are slotted to receive adjusting-wedges, marked F and G, in Figs. 9, 13, and 14. The rods and the wedges are shown separately in detail in Figs. 18 and 19. The wedge F is utilised for increasing, and the wedge G for reducing, the dummy clearance. These wedges are of specially hard steel, and the working surface in each case bears against gibs of tempered steel. The operation of moving these wedges is as follows:— Each wedge extends through the block transversely, and is so arranged that the wedging action applies in opposite directions—*e.g.*, on the port turbine, as illustrated in Fig. 9—wedge F is inserted with its large head to the starboard side, and wedge G with its large head to the port side. Any transverse movement of wedge F towards the port side results in the thrust liner being bodily moved aft; whereas any movement of the wedge G towards the starboard side will give a movement of the thrust liner forward. To effect these respective movements both ends of the wedges are threaded, as shown in Fig. 19, and are fitted with nuts (see Fig. 54, page 53). Those adjacent to the thin end of the wedge are arranged to form worm-wheels, driven by a worm, because the load comes upon the thin end in the process of adjustment; while, on the other screw-thread, ordinary nuts are fitted, as they are only used to follow up any movement and to lock the wedges. This arrangement is shown in Fig. 13, and a detail of the worm-gear for pulling the wedges is shown in Figs. 20 and 21. By this means the operation of adjusting the dummy clearances when running becomes a very simple matter, and index-plates are fitted, which record movements in $\frac{1}{1000}$ in.

From Fig. 11 will also be seen the means provided for adjusting the wedges of the small bearings at the forward end of each turbine, to be described presently. The principle is the same as in the main bearings, the gun-metal bush resting on a cast-steel saddle, which again rests on a wedge, admitting of the necessary adjustment for wear. The movement of the wedge, in this case, however, is effected by a screwed nut, driven by bevel-wheels, mounted on a rod, extending below the bearing, the gear being actuated by a spanner. A larger detail of this is shown in Figs. 22 and 23.

The lubrication of the thrust-block has also received special attention. On each ring, both ahead and astern, there are three radial holes, meeting others running at right angles from the working face. Oil grooves are cut between the latter to ensure a distribution of oil across the whole working face. This is clearly shown in Fig. 24, which illustrates one bottom half of a ring. Fig. 25 shows a large-scale detail of the radial holes. The supply of oil to the radial holes is from an annular space provided in the thrust-block and cover, and into this the oil is pumped, Figs. 8 and 10. Communication is established from this annular space to the radial holes in the rings by a series of holes bored through the steel liner. Oil leakage from this space (if any) is inappreciable, on account of the close fit between the liner and the block and between the liner and the cover, so that the oil must pass through the holes (Fig. 8). It may be noted (see Fig. 25) that the phosphor-bronze is kept only $\frac{15}{1000}$ in. clear of the working face of the white metal. This minimising of the clearance was adopted as a safeguard, in order to ensure that, in the event of the white metal running, the rotor would not move forward sufficiently to injure the dummy strips, as the collars would come into contact with the phosphor-bronze face before there was any rubbing at the dummy strips. Moreover, the thrust-collars can be run on the phosphor-bronze without injury.

THE TURBINE BEARINGS AND BUSHES.

In the bearings of all the turbines provision is made for adjustment of "wear down." The details of this arrangement as applied to the low-pressure turbine are shown on page 47. The system generally consists of a cast-steel saddle, into which is fitted a bush, supported by an adjustable wedge, which, in turn, rests on a specially prepared surface of the bearing-block itself. It will be understood, of course, that very true surfaces had to be aimed at, so that in all cases they were machined and scraped most carefully. The system is applied to all the turbine bearings, and differs only in detail. Fig. 26 is a half section and half elevation of the forward bearing-block of the low-pressure turbine, and here also will be seen the provision made for the stool to allow for the longitudinal expansion of the turbine, as already described. Fig. 27 is a longitudinal section, Fig. 28 an outside elevation, Fig. 29 a half elevation looking aft, and Fig. 30 a plan. Fig. 31 is a plan and elevation of the wedge, Figs. 32 and 33 details of the cast-steel saddle, and Figs. 34 and 35 details of the adjusting-screw.

The upper surface of the bearing-block at A is parallel to the centre line of the turbine over its whole plane, and the wedge B is accurately machined to fit this surface, the top surface of the wedge having a taper of 1 in 50. The saddle C has its bottom surface machined to a corresponding taper. The top surface of the saddle is made to suit the curvature of the bush. On the surface of the wedge which is in contact with the saddle a transverse key is forged, as shown at D, and fits into a recess on the saddle provided for it, and forward and aft movement in relation to the saddle is thereby prevented. The saddle, in its turn, cannot move in the fore and aft direction because of the flanges of the bush, shown at E. These flanges also bear against strips provided in the block for them. By these means the bush and saddle are constrained to move only in a vertical direction, and the wedge only in a transverse direction. The movement of the wedge in a transverse direction, to compensate for "wear down," is effected by means of screws, as shown in the details, Figs. 34 and 35. Hardened steel-plates F

THE CUNARD LINER "AQUITANIA;" LOW-PRESSURE TURBINE BEARING-BUSH.

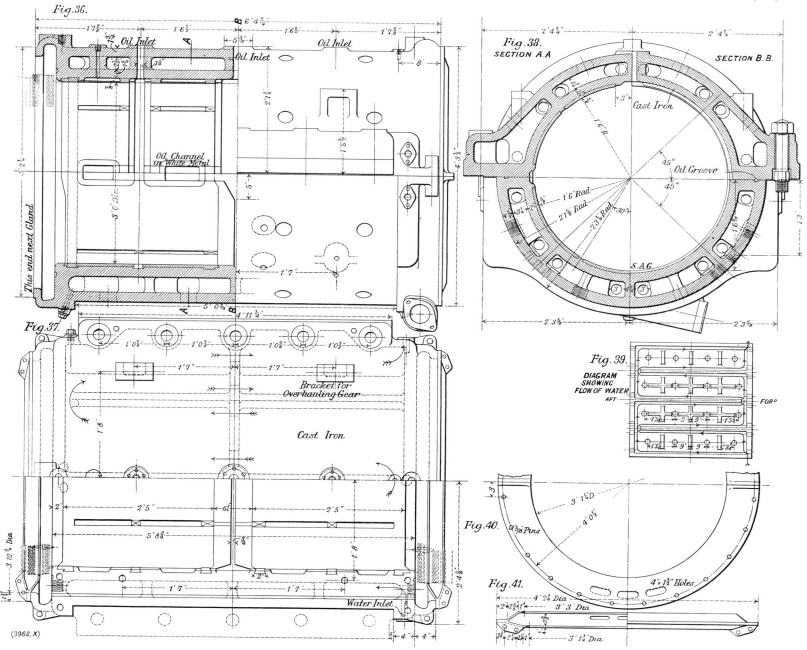

(3962.X)

are fastened to the sides of the wedges, four being fitted along the thick end of the wedge and two at the thin end. Against these plates about the points of square-threaded screw steel pins with hardened points. These pins work in gun-metal bushes, as shown. A square head is provided to take a special spanner. Index-plates are also provided, and one turn of the screws lifts (or lowers) the rotor to the extent of $\frac{5}{1000}$ in. Special attention has been given to the lubrication of different parts of this gear, as will be seen from Figs. 31 to 33.

The low-pressure bearing-bush is illustrated above; Fig. 36 is a half elevation and half section; Fig. 37 a half plan at top and half plan at bottom; Fig. 38 represents separate half cross-sections; Fig. 39 shows the flow of water through the bush, and Figs. 40 and 41 the gun-metal oil-baffles. These drawings are largely self-explanatory. They also show the arrangement provided for lubrication and the design of the keep, combined with the top half, which has already been described. The oil-baffles at the ends of the bush are shown on Fig. 37. By means of sub-division of the annular space around the bush there is ensured as perfect a water circulation as is possible (Fig. 39).

STEAM DISTRIBUTION, MANŒUVRING, AND ALTERNATIVE SYSTEMS OF WORKING.

We come now to the general arrangement of the turbines and their controlling gear. Longitudinal

sections through the low-pressure and high-pressure turbine-rooms and condenser compartments, and a plan of all three turbine-rooms and condenser compartments are given on Plate VII. (Figs. 42 to 44). while sections at various points are shown in Figs. 45 to 52, on pages 50, 51 and 52. The steam-piping arrangement to the turbines is such as to provide for all possible contingencies, and to this we propose now to direct special attention, leaving for future consideration a detailed description of the auxiliaries, already briefly referred to.

It may be noted here that, as shown on the plan, Fig. 43, on Plate VII., while the high-pressure turbines in the wing compartments are placed well forward, the low-pressure turbines are placed aft, partly in order to reduce the length of the eduction-pipe to the main condensers. The space at the after end of the wing compartments is utilised for the evaporating plant, while in the wings there are certain small auxiliary pumps, the auxiliary condenser, and the circulating and air-pumps in connection therewith. The forward end of the central turbine-room, on the other hand, is utilised for the accommodation of the main feed-pumps, as shown in the longitudinal section, Fig. 42, and the plan, Fig. 43. There are here also sanitary and wash-pumps, as well as forced-lubrication pumps. The arrangement further confers the advantage that all these pumps are immediately under the observation of the officer on the starting-platform. Fig. 46, on page 50, shows the arrangement of the machinery as seen from the starting-platform,

excepting, of course, that it is impossible, owing to the longitudinal bulkheads, to see the wing compartments with the high-pressure and intermediate-pressure turbines, the auxiliary condenser, &c. The longitudinal section through the starboard-wing compartment, given in Fig. 47, on page 51, shows the main independent steam lead from the boilers to the intermediate-pressure turbine, with its connection to the ahead and astern turbines, while the lifting-gear is also shown; but this will be described in a later article. In Fig. 48, on the same page, there is a cross-section through the engine-room at frame 98, and here all four turbines are seen and their relation one to the other, while the position of the gravitating oil-tanks and of the ventilating fans is shown. Fig 49, on page 52, is a half-section looking on to the bulkhead separating the turbine-rooms from the condenser compartments, and there are seen in the wings the evaporators and distillers, and in the centre the hot-well pumps and the Harris filters. Fig. 50, on the same page, is a half-section in the same position, but looking forward, and thus the two turbines on the two starboard shafts are shown, the lifting-gear forming a notable feature in the section along with the feed-heaters and filters. Fig. 51 is a half section of the port condenser-room, showing the sea-water outlet, the connection to circulating pumps, and other auxiliaries. It will be noted that there is a cross-connection between the circulating pumps, so that they may be used for service in connection with either or

H

THE CUNARD LINER "AQUITANIA;" GENERAL ARRANGEMENT OF TURBINE MACHINERY.

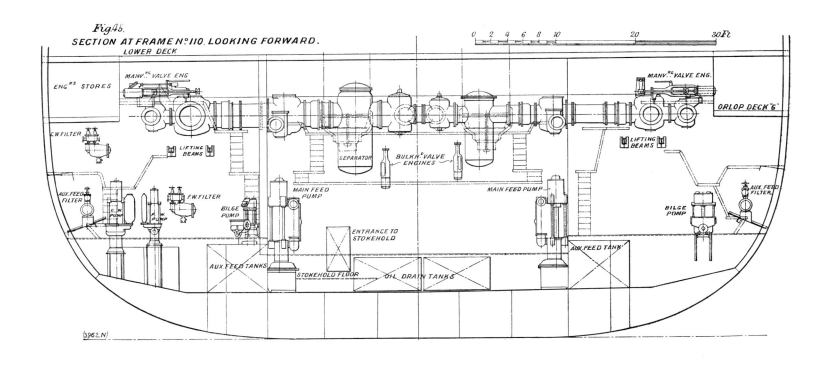

Fig. 45.
SECTION AT FRAME Nº 110, LOOKING FORWARD.

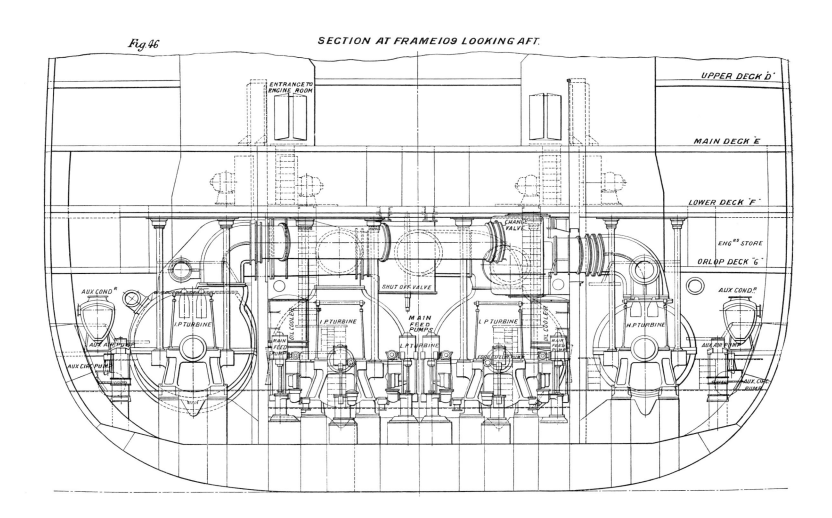

Fig. 46. SECTION AT FRAME 109 LOOKING AFT.

THE CUNARD LINER "AQUITANIA;" GENERAL ARRANGEMENT OF TURBINE MACHINERY.

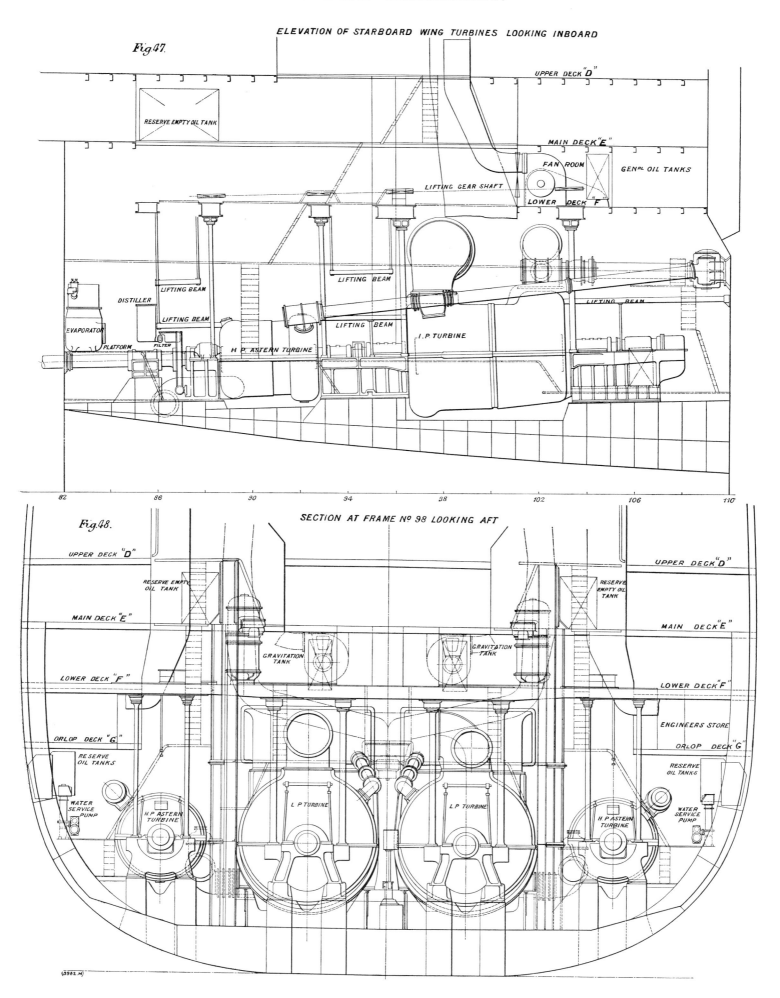

Fig 47.

ELEVATION OF STARBOARD WING TURBINES LOOKING INBOARD

UPPER DECK "D"

RESERVE EMPTY OIL TANK

MAIN DECK "E"

FAN ROOM   GEN⁰ᴸ OIL TANKS

LIFTING GEAR SHAFT

LOWER DECK "F"

LIFTING BEAM

LIFTING BEAM   LIFTING BEAM

DISTILLER

LIFTING BEAM

EVAPORATOR

PLATFORM   FILTER   H P ASTERN TURBINE   I.P. TURBINE   LIFTING BEAM

82   86   90   94   98   102   106   110

Fig.48.

SECTION AT FRAME N⁰ 98 LOOKING AFT

UPPER DECK "D"   UPPER DECK "D"

RESERVE EMPTY OIL TANK   RESERVE EMPTY OIL TANK

MAIN DECK "E"   MAIN DECK "E"

GRAVITATION TANK   GRAVITATION TANK

LOWER DECK "F"   LOWER DECK "F"

ENGINEERS STORE

ORLOP DECK "G"   ORLOP DECK "G"

RESERVE OIL TANKS   RESERVE OIL TANKS

WATER SERVICE PUMP   H P ASTERN TURBINE   L P TURBINE   L P TURBINE   H P ASTERN TURBINE   WATER SERVICE PUMP

(3982.M)

THE CUNARD LINER "AQUITANIA;" GENERAL ARRANGEMENT OF TURBINE MACHINERY.

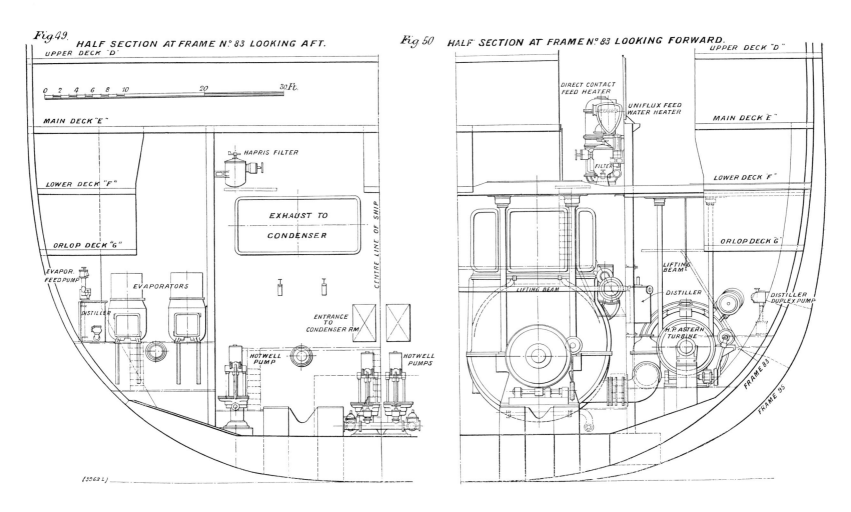

Fig. 49. HALF SECTION AT FRAME N.º 83 LOOKING AFT.

Fig. 50 HALF SECTION AT FRAME N.º 83 LOOKING FORWARD.

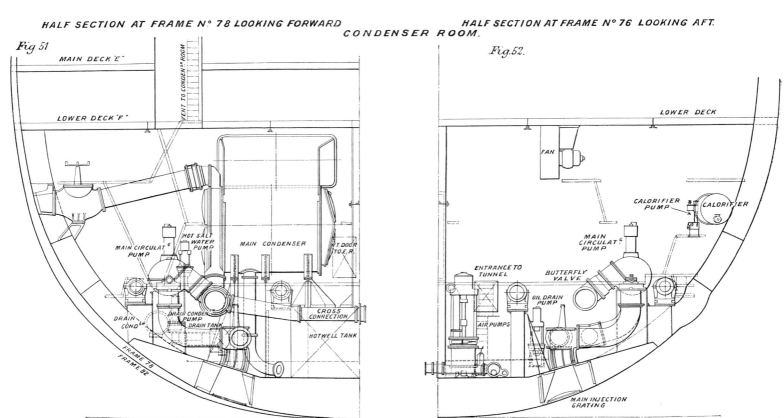

HALF SECTION AT FRAME Nº 78 LOOKING FORWARD
CONDENSER ROOM.

Fig. 51

HALF SECTION AT FRAME Nº 76 LOOKING AFT.

Fig. 52.

THE QUADRUPLE-SCREW TURBINE-DRIVEN CUNARD LINER "AQUITANIA."

FIG. 53. A LOW-PRESSURE TURBINE MAIN BEARING AND THRUST-BLOCK, WITH COVER IN PLACE.

FIG. 54. HIGH-PRESSURE TURBINE MAIN BEARING AND THRUST-BLOCK WITH COVER REMOVED.

THE QUADRUPLE-SCREW TURBINE-DRIVEN CUNARD LINER "AQUITANIA."

Fig. 55. High-Pressure Ahead and High-Pressure Astern Turbines.

Fig. 56. Boring Part of a Low-Pressure Turbine-Casing.

THE QUADRUPLE-SCREW TURBINE-DRIVEN CUNARD LINER "AQUITANIA."

FIG. 57.   A LOW-PRESSURE TURBINE ROTOR IN POSITION IN CASING.

FIG. 58.   A LOW-PRESSURE TURBINE COMPLETE; VIEW FROM FORWARD END.

THE QUADRUPLE-SCREW TURBINE-DRIVEN CUNARD LINER "AQUITANIA."

Fig. 59. View of Turbine Units in the Clydebank Works.

Fig. 60. A Low-Pressure Turbine Complete ; View from Aft End.

THE QUADRUPLE-SCREW TURBINE-DRIVEN CUNARD LINER "AQUITANIA."

Fig. 61. Rotor of a Low-Pressure Ahead and Astern Turbine.

Fig. 62. A Low-Pressure Ahead and Astern Turbine, with Upper Part of Casing Raised.

I

THE QUADRUPLE-SCREW TURBINE-DRIVEN CUNARD LINER "AQUITANIA."

Fig. 63. General View of Turbines in the Erecting-Shop at Clydebank Works.

THE QUADRUPLE-SCREW TURBINE-DRIVEN CUNARD LINER "AQUITANIA."

FIG. 65. A LOW-PRESSURE TURBINE ROTOR BEING LIFTED ON BOARD.

FIG. 64. UPPER HALF OF A LOW-PRESSURE TURBINE CASING BEING LIFTED ON BOARD.

THE QUADRUPLE-SCREW TURBINE-DRIVEN CUNARD LINER "AQUITANIA."

Fig. 66. A Low-Pressure Ahead and Astern Turbine Rotor alongside Ship.

THE CUNARD LINER "AQUITANIA;" THE TURBINE-LIFTING GEAR.

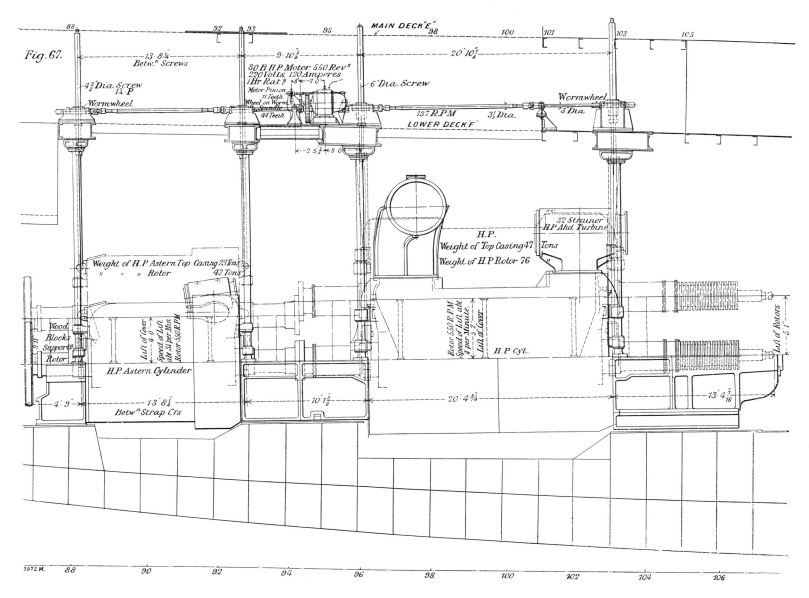

both condensers. Fig. 52 is a half section looking towards the after bulkhead of the condenser-room on the port side, and here are seen the air-pumps, the oil-drain pumps, the circulating-pumps, and the fan for ventilating this compartment.

To return to the steam-distribution leads, two main steam-pipes, 25 in. and 21 in. in diameter, from the boilers, pierce the forward engine-room bulkhead near the centre line of the ship, and terminate in two bulkhead valves on the engine-room side of the bulkhead (Fig. 45). These are operated by Brown's engines and control the supply to the turbines. To port and starboard, and with connection to both bulkhead valves, is an athwartship line of piping, in which are two large separators, distributing the steam through various valves to the respective turbines, all of which receive steam on the top. Master-valves are provided on the athwartship pipes where these pass through the longitudinal water-tight bulkheads. By means of these valves the supply to either wing turbine can be cut off. The ahead and astern manœuvring-valves for the wing turbines are also placed on the bulkhead, and are operated by Brown's engines. The direct low-pressure ahead and astern manœuvring-valves, also operated by Brown's engines, are arranged on the forward end of the low-pressure turbine-casings. These various valves are shown in the cross-section, Fig. 45, on page 50.

It will be gathered from the foregoing that each line of shafting, with its respective turbines, has a direct live-steam ahead and astern connection. The arrangement, however, does not permit of either wing shaft being run independently of the inner shafts; that is accomplished by change-valves and shut-off valves, to be described in detail on a later page. The port outer shaft, for instance, when manœuvring carries with it the port inner shaft, the outer-shaft turbines exhausting into the inner-shaft turbines. The same applies to the starboard shafts. The port shafts can, of course, be run independently of the starboard shafts. On the other hand, the two inner shafts may be worked independently of the outer shafts and of each other.

It will be seen that considerable latitude is afforded the engineer in charge when manœuvring. To obtain such exceptional manœuvring powers, especially with turbines arranged on the triple system, is no simple matter, as a study of the steam-runs will show. As has already been stated, the high-pressure ahead turbine, under normal conditions, receives direct boiler steam; the connection is 32 in. in diameter. A 53-in. diameter pipe leads the high-pressure exhaust to the intermediate-pressure turbine. The intermediate-pressure turbine exhausts through a 90-in. pipe to both low-pressure ahead turbines, each with a 66-in. branch. The main eduction branch-pipe on the low-pressure turbines to the condenser is 15 ft. by 6 ft. This, the normal condition of working, is illustrated in the plan on Plate VII. (Fig. 43).

To cut out the high-pressure turbine all that is necessary is to shut off boiler steam from it and close the exhaust connection from it, opening the steam-run from the boiler to the intermediate-pressure turbine, this steam connection being 25 in. in diameter.

To isolate the high-pressure from the intermediate or low-pressure turbine, a change-valve is introduced at the port side on the 53-in. line of piping across the centre engine-room, as shown in Fig. 43. This valve, of the piston type, is operated by a Brown's engine, and is arranged to shut off the high-pressure ahead turbine exhaust from the intermediate-pressure turbine, while opening it to the low-pressure ahead turbines, or vice versâ, this operation occupying two to three seconds. The ship would then be driven by three propellers —the port outer and inner and the starboard inner propeller—as an ordinary compound turbine installation with one high-pressure and two low-pressure turbines.

Again, the two low-pressure ahead turbines must be separated when manœuvring. As they both receive ahead steam from the intermediate-pressure turbine under normal conditions, a shut-off valve between these turbines becomes necessary. This valve, which is suspended from the deck, is of the cock type, is worked by twin reciprocating engines placed beneath the valve, and can be operated in either direction in from 3 to 5 seconds. By the use of this valve the port inner shaft may be thrown out of gear, while by corresponding means the whole of the steam from the intermediate-pressure turbine passes to this turbine, so that the starboard inner shaft is thrown out of gear.

The stowing of the large branch-pieces to permit of lifting the turbine-casings involved a considerable amount of careful scheming on the part of the builders; but this has been successfully accomplished, as will be seen by reference to Fig. 43, on Plate VII.

THE CONSTRUCTION OF THE TURBINES.

We publish on pages 53 to 60 a series of illustrations of the turbines in course of their construction at the Clydebank Works, and it may be useful here briefly to describe these views. The two illustrations on page 53 are specially interesting, in view of the detail drawings and description already given of the thrust-block and main bearings of the low-pressure turbine. Fig. 53 shows the main bearing and thrust-block (covered in) of one of the low-pressure turbines, while Fig. 54 shows the bearing and thrust-block (uncovered) of the high-pressure turbine. These engravings, when examined in conjunction with the detail drawings of the thrust-bearings published on Plate VI. and page 47 may assist towards a fuller understanding of the description of the method of adjustment. In both views there will be seen the nut by means of which the wedge is brought into play for adjusting the block.

Fig. 55, on page 54, illustrates the high-pressure ahead and high-pressure astern turbines partly lagged. These two turbines, when coupled together, as shown in Fig. 5, make up a total length of 63 ft. 1 in. Fig. 56, on the same page, shows the astern part of the low-pressure casing in the lathe for turning the interior grooves to take the blading. The size of the eduction-pipe for the exhaust of the condenser will be realised from the engraving. This portion of the casing alone weighs 33 tons 17¼ cwt.

Fig. 57, on page 55, shows the low-pressure turbine-rotor in its position in the casing, and with it there is seen the change-valve, which passes the exhaust steam from the high-pressure turbine alternately to the intermediate-pressure turbine, or to the low-pressure turbine in connection with the manœuvring of the ship. In Fig. 58, on the same page, there is given a view showing the forward end of the low-pressure turbine completed. There is seen mounted on the turbine the valve for shutting off steam between the two low-pressure turbines, in order that the two shafts on the port and the two shafts on the starboard side may be operated independently in manœuvring.

On page 56 there is a further view of the low-pressure turbine complete, the view (Fig. 60) in this case being from the after end. Again the change-valve is seen in the distance, while the nature of the ribbing of the turbine casing is specially well shown, and the stools on which the turbine rests. The other view on this page (Fig. 59) shows various parts of the turbines of the Aquitania in the course of construction, and gives some suggestion of the immense extent of the turbine department of the Clydebank Works. Perhaps a more significant indication of the volume of work carried on by the firm is the fact that the shaft horse-power of turbine-propelling machinery simultaneously in progress during the building of the Aquitania was between 300,000 and 400,000 horse-power.

Fig. 61, on page 57, shows the rotor of one of the low-pressure ahead and astern turbines preparatory to being lifted into the casing, and Fig. 62, on the same page, shows a rotor in its position and the upper parts of the casing raised. This view shows the method adopted for supporting the upper part of the casing when it has been raised for the inspection of the rotor.

On page 58 there is another general view of the turbines in the erecting-shops at the Clydebank Works, a view which carries conviction as to the immense size of the units forming the propelling machinery of the Aquitania. In this view there is seen in the foreground the thrust-block, with some of the details of the adjusting gear.

On page 59 there are two very striking views, one, Fig. 64, showing the lifting of the upper half of the low-pressure casing into the ship while in the Clydebank dock, and the other, Fig. 65, the rotor of the same turbine being put on board. The load in this case is 140 tons, excluding the lifting tackle, clearly shown in the view.

The last of this series of illustrations (that on page 60) is an impressive view of the rotor for the ahead and astern low-pressure turbine, lying on the wharf alongside the ship and ready to be lifted into place. This rotor has a total weight of 445 tons, the total length of the part shown in the engraving being nearly 50 ft., while the maximum diameter is 15 ft. 5½ in. The blades in both the ahead and the astern turbine are especially well shown. In the former case there are nine expansions, and in the latter, four, the ahead blades ranging in length from 7 in. to 20 in., while for astern driving the range is from 5 in. to 7 in. The whole of the work, including the provision of the shaft, discs, and drum, is by Messrs. John Brown and Co., or by firms allied to them, because the shafting for the ship was made at the Atlas Works of the Company, while Messrs. Thomas Firth and

Co., Limited (who are now part of the great organisation) provided the rotors. The machining and blading, and the building up of the turbine was done at the Clydebank Works, and it may be said of all three establishments that no turbine-manufacturing works have greater experience of high-powered turbine construction than is the case, alike with designing staff and workmen, of Messrs. John Brown and Co.

THE LIFTING GEAR FOR THE TURBINES.

The arrangements for lifting the upper part of the casing of the rotors in the ship are illustrated on page 61 and the present page. The views show the system adopted for the high-pressure ahead and astern turbines, and is typical of the method applied in connection with all the turbines. Strong beams

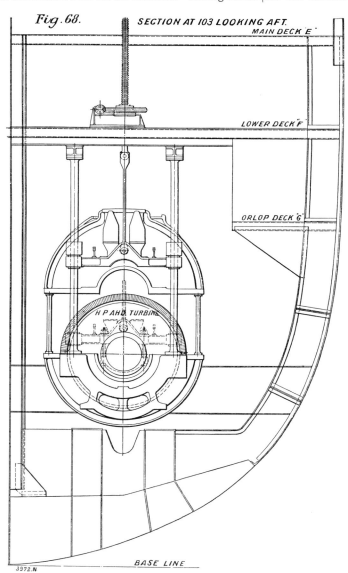

Fig. 68. SECTION AT 103 LOOKING AFT.

MAIN DECK E

LOWER DECK F

ORLOP DECK G

H P AHD TURBINE

BASE LINE

J972.N

FIG. 68. TURBINE-LIFTING GEAR.

are built across the ship at the level of the lower "F" deck, and above the ends of each of the turbines. Upon these beams are fixed large nuts, which form worm-wheels, driven by worms, actuated in each case by a 30-horse-power electric motor. These nuts are threaded to receive vertical screws, each of which is connected at its lower end, by means of links, to a cast-steel beam. This latter is bushed at each end to slide on steel columns, the lower ends of which rest on the top of the turbine bearing-blocks, while the upper ends support the strong beams. When the lifting-gear is in operation, this support is effected by means of distance-pieces, which are inserted only when the gear is in operation, and are removed at other times, so as to prevent any "working" of the ship being communicated to the turbines. The cross-beams, guided on the columns, lift the casing when the nuts are being rotated by the motors. On the casing there are cast horns, seen well in Fig. 60, page 56, which engage with the beams when the latter are lifted. Further,

there are brackets cast on the casing end, through which the guide-columns pass. When the casing is lifted to the desired height, its weight is carried on steel columns, and the beams are then lowered by means of the screws to lift the rotor. For this purpose a strap is passed under the rotor spindle at each end, and fixed to the beam by means of bolts and nuts. When lifted, the rotor is supported on wooden blocks. In the arrangement illustrated the motor that drives the gear for lifting the high-pressure ahead turbine can be disconnected by a clutch, and connected up to the corresponding gear, further aft, for lifting the high-pressure astern turbine. In this case the beams are only used for lifting the rotor, the casing being raised by lifting-plates, which are bolted to the casing ends as shown. The four electric motors for the turbine-lifting gear are of 30 horse-power when running at 500 revolutions per minute. They are of the slat ventilated drip-proof type, and have tramway-type reversing controllers. They were supplied by the Lancashire Dynamo and Motor Company, Limited, Trafford Park, Manchester, who also supplied two similar motors of 40 horse-power at 500 revolutions per minute, and two of 30 horse-power at 600 revolutions per minute, for turning the rotors of the turbines for inspection purposes when in port.

LUBRICATION OF THE TURBINE MAIN BEARINGS.

The efficient lubrication of the main bearings is not the least important system in a turbine installation. The arrangement here is very complete. Each bearing is provided with two supply-pipes from separate mains—one in the wing and one in the centre engine-room, port and starboard —thus ensuring a supply should any one main be rendered inoperative. Six direct-acting pumps, 12½ in. by 10 in. by 24 in. stroke, of Weir's standard type are fitted, four only being required to maintain the oil supply. The main oil-drain tanks from which these pumps draw are situated at the forward end of the centre engine-room. On the oil return from each bearing a sight-glass is introduced, allowing the oil-flow to be easily seen. In the case of the wing-turbine bearings the sight-glasses in connection are brought into the centre engine-room near the starting-platform. On each pump suction an oil-strainer is fitted, and on the discharge side also are fitted four filters for further cleaning the oil. Large and efficient coolers, two on each side of the ship, are provided. From the coolers the oil is pumped into large gravitation tanks, from which the supply to the bearings is taken, or, alternatively, the pumps may discharge direct to the bearings. All the tunnel shaft-bearings have forced-lubrication connections. The return from these bearings drains into tanks placed in the tunnel, from which two auxiliary pumps, 9 in. by 7½ in. by 18 in. stroke, of Weir's type, placed in the condenser-rooms, discharge it into the main drain-tanks. These pumps are automatically controlled by Weir's float-gear placed in the tanks. Two large reserve tanks are provided in the engine-hatch for use when overhauling, or as may be required. These tanks are of sufficient capacity to hold half the oil in the entire system. As the port and starboard systems are separate, one side need only be dealt with at a time. Additional reserve supply-tanks capable of holding sufficient oil to charge the whole system are placed in the wing turbine-rooms on a stringer, being compactly arranged between web-frames.

FROM BOILER TO CONDENSER.

WE may now turn to a consideration of the valves for controlling the main turbines under normal conditions, and the special valves installed for the purpose of effecting the changes briefly described in connection with alternative systems of working in the event of any one of the turbines being put out of gear, intentionally or otherwise.

THE MAIN STEAM AND MANŒUVRING-VALVES.

Apart altogether from the power of the installation, and the consequent large diameter of the steam-pipes and valves, great ingenuity has been exercised in ensuring that these immense valves will be manipulated in the shortest possible period of time. With such a large ship steaming at great speed it is of the first importance that one valve should be closed and another opened very rapidly, in order that manœuvring can be done with exactitude and promptness. To ensure the former of these desirable qualities a most carefully-conceived system of interlocking gear has been arranged, and, as will be shown by the details which we illustrate and the full description which follows, the manœuvring gear has been rendered fool-proof. While, therefore, it is possible to manœuvre with the two inner shafts, using only the combined low-pressure ahead and low-pressure astern turbines on each shaft, it is arranged that manœuvring may also be done with the ahead and astern turbines on the port side working separately from those on the starboard side of the ship. Unless the valves were manipulated in due sequence, there would be liability of steam entering simultaneously at the ahead and the astern ends of the starboard low-pressure turbines. All this has been rendered impossible by the interlocking of the valves, so that one valve cannot be opened until what might be termed the opposing valve is closed. As regards the rapidity with which the change-over can be made, separate engines are fitted for manœuvring the valves through specially-devised levers or gear, so as to decrease greatly the time otherwise necessary to effect the desired closing or opening. The details of this mechanism are therefore of great interest.

In describing in detail the steam-distribution system in the three turbine-rooms, and the successive valves for steam-control and manœuvring, it may be noted first that the steam from the boilers passes through the two bulkhead-valves, one to the port and the other to the starboard of the centre line of the ship, as shown in the elevation and plan, Figs. 126 and 127, on page 66. These bulkhead-valves are of the double-beat type, and are mounted on the after side of the athwartship bulkhead, separating the three turbine-rooms from the after boiler-room. The pipe leading into the valve on the port side is 25 in. in diameter, and on the starboard side the pipe is 21 in. in diameter, the difference being due to the grouping of the boilers.

There are two steam-separators with connection to both bulkhead-valves, one of these separators on the port side passing steam through a 32-in. pipe, and the other on the starboard side through a 25-in. pipe. On the port and starboard sides of these connections again are two master-valves, one for ahead and the other for astern working, on each side. The astern valves control the direct admission of steam at boiler pressure to fore and aft leads, which communicate with additional valves for the admission of steam alternatively to the low-pressure ahead or the low-pressure astern turbines for manœuvring with the centre shafts only ; while the ahead valves control the admission of steam to the wing compartments. In the wing compartments, but still on the athwartship bulkheads, there are the main manœuvring-valves. On the port side, on which the high-pressure turbine is situated, the pipe for ahead working is 32 in., and for astern working 18 in. in diameter ; while on the starboard side, where the intermediate-pressure turbine is placed, the ahead pipe is 25 in., and the astern pipe 18 in. in diameter.

All the valves fixed in this athwartship bulkhead are, as will be understood, of massive proportions, and it was necessary to specially stiffen the bulkhead to carry them. Heavy transverse beams were therefore introduced on the forward side of the bulkhead. Where the longitudinal bulk-

heads separating the turbine installation into three compartments join this transverse bulkhead, heavy brackets were introduced, so that very great stiffness was ensured for the support of the various valves.

The bulkhead-valves, of the double-beat type, are controlled by small direct-acting steam-engines of the Brown type, which may be controlled by hand or through emergency governors mounted on the forward end of each of the four lines of shafts ; these governors are of the Proell type, and when the speed of any turbine exceeds a predetermined rate of revolution, a weight located on the bulkhead is released, and in its fall acts through rods and levers upon the hand-levers controlling the valves of the Brown engines, releases the triggers of the hand-levers from the quadrant, and moves the levers into the shut position ; this arrangement will be described later when we come to deal with the interlocking system applied. In addition to the steam-gear there is a rack and pinion fitted to each of the valves to enable them to be operated manually.

THE STEAM-SEPARATORS.

The steam-separators are of an improved design suggested by Sir Charles Parsons. The aim in design was not only to ensure the separation of any water which might come over from the boiler with the steam, due to priming, but to obviate corrosion in the turbines. The drawings which we reproduce on page 64, Figs. 69 to 75, show how this has been achieved. The principle underlying the design is due to the acceptance of the theory that any corrosive element in the steam might be absorbed in the separator by the use of certain metals similar to those in use in the turbines—viz., cast iron, brass, and steel—and thus cast-iron grids were introduced with brass and steel perforated plates forming alternate layers. The construction is shown in the drawings reproduced. Fig. 69 is a sectional elevation, the arrows showing the direction of flow of the steam through the cells of the separator. Fig. 70 is a sectional plan. Figs. 71 and 72 are respectively a section and plan on a larger scale of the top cell. Figs. 73 to 75 give details of the remaining four cells. It will be seen that there are five cast-iron cells placed at different levels, and arranged so that the steam flows in parallel through them. Each cell is composed of a cast-iron case containing the cast-iron grids, which are separated from one another by alternate layers of brass and steel perforated plates. The support for each cell is of gun-metal, which was used on this occasion merely for constructional reasons; steel would have been equally satisfactory had it been possible within the time to obtain a satisfactory casting. Special care is taken to eliminate as much moisture as possible from the steam. As shown in Figs. 73 to 75, any water that might flow along the sloping division is induced to run in a small channel to the region near division A, Figs. 70 and 74. The arrows again show the course of the water. The bottom of the separator is fitted with a splash-plate in the usual way.

THE MASTER-VALVES.

The 32-in. master-valve, into which the steam passes from the port separator, is fixed to the longitudinal bulkhead, separating the centre engine-room from the port or high-pressure turbine-room, and alongside it there is the smaller valve, 16-in. in diameter, for controlling the direct steam to the port low-pressure turbines, ahead and astern. The 32-in. valve is illustrated in Figs. 76 and 77, on Plate VIII. The arrangement of gear for the 16-in. valve is generally similar to that for this valve, both valves being operated by the hand-wheels (Fig. 126, on page 66). It will be understood that on the starboard side of the ship there is a similar arrangement of 25-in. and 16-in. valves. Each pair of valves is controlled solely by hand from the starting-platform. They are all of the double-beat type, and the interesting feature is the arrangement made for ease in opening and for rapid handling. Each valve is, as shown in Figs. 76 and 77, operated by means of a worm working on a quadrant, which is fixed to a shaft to which a couple of levers are connected. These levers are coupled up to the valve spindle by two rods. The valve-spindle is fitted with a

crosshead, guided as shown, and the arrangement is such that there is a relatively small travel of the valve for an appreciable movement of the lever at the initial stage of opening, during which time there has to be overcome the load due to the difference in area of the two beats and tending to keep the valve shut. When this load has been overcome the arrangement accelerates the rate of travel of the valve, owing to the change of angle of the levers. The effect is to enable the valve to be opened or closed with a very small effort at the hand-wheel on the starting - platform. This reduction of effort is very advantageous on account of the distance between the starting-platform and the valve and the indispensable multiplicity of bevel gears in the line of transmission. The 32-in. valve can either be used for shutting off the port-wing turbines or for regulating purposes. Similarly, the 25-in. valve on the starboard side of the ship can be used for shutting off the starboard-wing turbines or for regulating purposes. The control-wheels for the two master-valves on each side are superposed at the starting-platform to economise space, the rods for each of the 16-in. valves passing through tubes which form the shafts for actuating the 32-in. and 25-in. valves respectively.

MAIN MANŒUVRING VALVES.

The next in series of the valves on the bulkhead are the main manœuvring-valves, ahead and astern, and these are illustrated in Figs. 78 to 86, on Plate VIII. On the port side they consist of a 32-in. ahead and an 18-in. astern valve, and on the starboard side of a 25-in. ahead and an 18-in. astern valve. They also are of the double-beat type, and are operated by Brown direct-acting steam-engines controlled from hand-levers on the port and starboard quadrants at the starting-platform, the lines of transmission having the necessary bevel sectors, as shown in Fig. 126. The port manœuvring-valves themselves are illustrated in Figs. 78 to 86. Figs. 78 and 79 are respectively a vertical section and sectional plan, and Fig. 80 an outside elevation of the two valves ; Fig. 81 a plan of the operating gear ; Fig. 82 is a section through the 32-in. valve-chest, the valve itself being removed ; Fig. 83 a similar section through the 18-in. valve-chest ; Fig. 84 a large-scale detail of the 32-in. valve ; Fig. 85 a similar detail of the 18-in. valve ; while Fig. 86 gives details of the 32-in. valve-spindle and its crosshead. The spindle for the 18-in. valve is generally similar, but of smaller dimensions. These valves are, it may be said, typical of the manœuvring-valves used throughout the installation.

Figs. 80 to 82 show clearly the method of operating the way-shafts A and B respectively for the 32-in. and the 18-in. valves. To these shafts are fixed levers, through which the action of the steam-engine is transmitted to the valve-spindles as desired. The engine acts through two connecting-rods on to the lever C, which is attached to the horizontal shaft D, supported in bearings as shown. To the inner end of this shaft are attached two levers E, and to these again are secured three rods, two of which, marked F, are for the astern valves, and one, marked G, for the ahead valve. The duplication of the rods F, in the case of the astern valve, was necessitated in the interests of stiffness, because of their length and of their being in compression when the valve has to be raised. The rod G, on the other hand, is, in similar circumstances, under tension, and thus a single one sufficed. For ahead working, the way-shaft A carries two levers, which, in turn, are attached to a pin passing through the crosshead of the valve-spindle. This pin is shown at J in Fig. 86, and to it are attached links K, which are connected to a pair of rocking-levers L, in Figs. 80 and 81, at the centre of which a rod M is fixed, carrying an arrangement of springs to assist the return of the valves to their seats. A similar arrangement of levers N is attached to the way-shaft B and to the pin through the crosshead of the 18-in. valve, and similarly coupled by means of links to the rocking-lever L.

Upon an order being given for ahead working, the piston of the Brown engine moves the levers C and E to the right when looking at Fig. 80. The rods F and G are also moved by means of the levers, but the ends of rods F, being slotted, as shown, are free to move without affecting the levers N. The rod G, although slotted, is so arranged that its movement is at once communi-

THE CUNARD LINER "AQUITANIA;" THE STEAM-SEPARATORS.

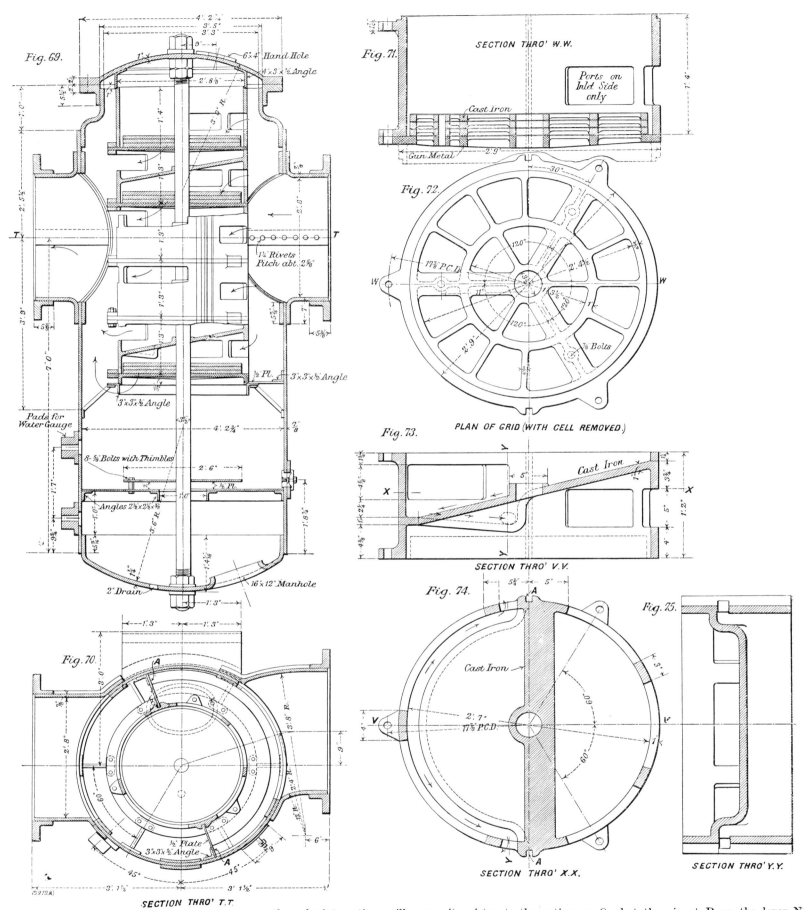

Fig. 69.

Fig. 71. SECTION THRO' W.W.
Ports on Inlet Side only
Cast Iron
Gun Metal

Fig. 72. PLAN OF GRID (WITH CELL REMOVED.)

Fig. 73.
Cast Iron
SECTION THRO' V.V.

Fig. 70. SECTION THRO' T.T.

Fig. 74.
Cast Iron
SECTION THRO' X.X.

Fig. 75.
SECTION THRO' Y.Y.

cated to the levers H through the pin O, and thereby the valve is lifted, the springs on the rod M being compressed by the links K to an extent corresponding to one-half the distance through which the valve is raised.

Assuming that an order is then given for the ship to be driven astern, the Brown engine, when brought into action, will move its piston to the left, as shown looking at Fig. 80, and the rods F and G will be traversed in the same direction. Owing to the action of the rod G, the valve, through its own weight, augmented by the load on the springs transmitted through the rocking-lever L and the links K, will be brought to its seat. The continuation of the movement allows the slot on the rod G to be effective, and thus to obviate any action on O; but the pin at P on the lever N will transmit motion to the rods F and to the lever N, so that the astern valve is lifted. In order to obtain the maximum strength of spring-load in the minimum of space available, two springs are fitted, one inside the other, and this gives a strong yet compact arrangement.

On the starboard side of the ship there is an exactly similar arrangement for giving steam direct.

to the starboard outer and inner shafts, the steam passing from the boilers direct to the intermediate-pressure turbine, so that with the use of these main manœuvring-valves the two lines of shaft respectively on the port and starboard side may be independently manœuvred. In other words, instead of the triple arrangement of turbines there are introduced two entirely separate systems of high-pressure and low-pressure turbines, the intermediate-pressure turbine on the starboard side corresponding in the starboard set to the high-pressure turbine in the port set. But for manœuvring on the inner shafts with the low-pressure ahead and astern turbines only, there are two 16-in. valves at the forward end of each of the low-pressure ahead and astern turbines, each pair being actuated by an engine which is controlled from the starting-platform. The arrangements for working the engines are similar to those for controlling the main manœuvring-valves already described.

The usual strainers are fitted on all the steam connections for all turbines where steam passes direct from the boilers to the turbines. In all cases these strainers are as close to the turbines as possible, so that there is no remaining length of pipe from which any foreign matter may pass direct into the turbine at any time.

THE CHANGE-VALVE.

In order to ensure rapidity of action in passing from the normal condition of steaming ahead with the turbines working in triple series, and to arrange for the port and starboard sets to work independently as compound turbines, much attention was devoted to the details of the change-valves and their operation to ensure the minimum time in changing over. In addition to the master-valves and the manœuvring-valves, which have already been described, it was necessary to cut off the connections between the high-pressure turbine and the intermediate-pressure turbine, and between the intermediate-pressure turbine and the two low-pressure turbines, so that steam from the high-pressure turbine could pass direct into the port low-pressure turbine, and the steam from the intermediate-pressure turbine into the starboard low-pressure turbine. To effect the first of these operations a change-valve is introduced in the line of piping joining up the high-pressure turbine with the intermediate-pressure turbine. From a branch on this valve a pipe makes connection with the two low-pressure ahead turbines.

This change-valve is illustrated in Figs. 87 and 88, on Plate IX. Fig. 87 is a section through the valve, and Fig. 88 a sectional plan. The exhaust from the high-pressure turbine enters at A, and with the pistons in the position shown in the illustration — namely, at the bottom of the stroke — the steam from the high-pressure turbine is in direct communication with the two low-pressure turbines. When the pistons are at the top of the stroke the steam would be able to pass to the intermediate-pressure turbine, which is the normal condition for working at full power in triple series. The valve-pistons are operated by a direct-acting Brown engine controlled from the starting-platform. The weight of the valve-spindle and pistons is about $3\frac{1}{2}$ tons, and owing to the great travel necessary, the lever connecting the direct-acting engine was divided in a ratio of 2 : 1, in order to have a reasonable stroke in the steam-engine actuating the piston. The result is that the load on the engine is about 7 tons, due to the weight of the pistons. This load, under ordinary circumstances, would have been supported entirely by the cataract cylinder attached to the Brown engine. To avoid any possibility of derangement or mishap to the pipes connecting this cataract cylinder, it was thought desirable to balance the load by means of a small steam-piston acting within a cylinder, which is in direct communication with the boiler steam. The diameter of this balancing-cylinder is so fixed that with boiler steam the load is exactly balanced. Two grooves are cut in the side of the balancing-cylinder to drain away any water that may gather owing to condensation, and the underside of the piston is connected to the inlet-belt of the port low-pressure ahead turbine. The piston is packed with ordinary Ramsbottom rings. A special feature of the design of the cylinder is the fitting of an inner liner of gun-metal, which is encased in an outer shell of cast iron. This was introduced in order to obviate any stress on the main bracket, due to the high temperature of the steam continuously inside the balancing-cylinder and the comparatively low temperature of the body of the bracket. The circle shown above the cylinder in the illustration indicates the 16-in. direct steam-pipe to the low-pressure ahead and astern turbine for manœuvring those turbines, and has nothing to do with the balancing-cylinder. The weight of the change-valve complete approximates to about 23 tons, and is supported on a cast-steel branch-piece, shown dotted on the illustrations, and attached to the longitudinal bulkhead dividing the centre from the port-wing turbine-room. This is further supported by a steel chock carried under the flange, but not shown in the illustration. On the other side, that to the left of the section, a 3-in. steel stay is attached to a bracket and fixed to the deck under the ship's casing, which forms a passageway along the centre of the ship above the turbines. In this way the valve is very effectively supported on the structure of the ship.

The outlet from the change-valve to each low-pressure turbine, as well as the outlet to the intermediate-pressure turbine, are each of 53-in. bore, and where the pipes to the intermediate-pressure turbine pass through the bulkhead, a cast-steel branch-piece is fitted with a cast-iron section on the other side of the bulkhead joining up to the inlet branch on the intermediate-pressure turbine.

The 25-in. pipe leading steam direct from the boilers to the intermediate-pressure turbine is connected through its strainer to this cast-iron section, so that, through the same connection on the intermediate-pressure turbine, there is admitted steam from the high-pressure turbine (through the change-valve), as well as from the boilers direct. The exhaust from the intermediate-pressure turbine is a specially-constructed branch-piece of riveted steel plates. This joins up with a short length of cast-iron pipe of 90-in. bore, where it passes through the bulkhead, and this, in turn, is connected to a large cast-iron tee-piece having two branches, 66-in. bore, for coupling up to the two low-pressure turbines.

SHUT-OFF VALVE ON LOW-PRESSURE TURBINES.

The first proposal for cutting off the connection between the intermediate turbine and the two low-pressure turbines was to fit a sluice-valve in the pipe leading to the port low-pressure turbine, but as this pipe was 66 in. in diameter, such a valve, even when operated by a powerful steam-engine, would occupy such a period of time in closing that the idea was abandoned. The next alternative considered was the fitting of a change-valve similar to that adopted for passing the steam from the high-pressure turbine alternately to the intermediate-pressure turbine or to the port low-pressure turbine. But although the speed of operation would have been satisfactory, the space available between the two low-pressure turbines and the structure of the ship generally rendered the fitting of such a change-valve undesirable. There was therefore designed a special system of shut-off valve, which is nothing more nor less than a shut-off cock of immense proportions, actuated by a twin-cylinder steam-engine through a worm and quadrant, to facilitate rapid movement in opening and closing the valve. Tests have proved that this valve, notwithstanding the size of the port, can be closed in from three to four seconds.

This shut-off valve is illustrated on Plate IX. Fig. 89 is a sectional elevation, Fig. 90 a plan through the centre of the branch-pipes, Figs. 91 and 92 are details of the stuffing-box at the top and bottom respectively, Fig. 93 is a longitudinal section, Fig. 94 a detail of the white-metal strips in the valve-bottom, Fig. 95 an elevation of the plug, Fig. 96 a plan, Fig. 97 a plan looking down on the top of the valve, Fig. 98 details of the gun-metal strips in the plug, Fig. 99 a plan of the bottom cover of the chest, and Fig. 100 a view of the same showing the actuating engine and gear.

This special valve acts in principle as an ordinary cock with a parallel plug. The shell of the cock, Figs. 89, 90, and 93, is of cast iron, and the plug shown in Figs. 95 and 96 is of cast steel. The plug is operated by means of a shaft, as shown in Fig. 95, the top and bottom ends having square washers, which are fixed in the recesses in the ends of the cast-steel plug. These washers in turn are driven by means of keys sunk into the shaft, as shown at A in Fig. 90. The washers are allowed a certain amount of freedom of movement in the recess, the reason for which will be indicated later. In the shell four vertical strips of special hard white metal are fitted at B in Fig. 90, and circumferential strips at top and bottom at C in Fig. 93. These strips are shown in detail in Fig. 94. They are checked, as shown at D, Figs. 93 and 94, in order to allow for expansion and contraction. The surfaces of the plug that bear against these strips are sheathed with gun-metal circumferentially, as shown at E in Figs. 89, 95, and 96, and vertically at F, as shown in Fig. 95, and in detail in Fig. 98. Provision is also made in these strips for expansion and contraction by means of slots, shown at G in Fig. 96, and at H in Fig. 95, and in detail again at H in Fig. 98. Fig. 100 shows the arrangement of the small engine actuating the worm which drives the quadrant for moving the plug. The steam inlet to and exhaust from the engine are controlled by the valve marked J, which is operated from the starting-platform through the rod K and the links and bell-crank, as shown in Fig. 100.

Turning now to a description of the working of this valve, it may be said that when the quadrant is in the position shown, by pulling the rod K to the left, looking at Fig. 100 as engraved, the bell-crank O would raise the piston of the control-valve J, admitting steam to the engine, which, in revolving in the required direction, would swing the quadrant round until the pin S engaged with the lever M. The continued movement of the quadrant would push this up by means of the link N working on the rocking lever L, and the valve would then be brought back to its middle position, cutting off both steam and exhaust. By this time the quadrant would have travelled sufficiently far to open or to close the valve as the case might be, the movement of the rod K to the left corresponding to the movement of the handle on its quadrant at the starting position sufficiently to enable it to engage in a notch on the quadrant. This engagement results in the link P being rigidly held, constituting a fulcrum on which the various levers come into operation so as to bring the valve back to its middle position.

An exactly similar series of movements takes place in the reverse operation, the handle being moved to the right into a corresponding notch on the quadrant to give a fulcrum for the action of the levers in the corresponding direction. In regard to admitting a certain amount of freedom to the square washers in the recess, this was provided to give steam-tightness on the side of the valve remote from that on which the steam pressure was acting when the valve was shut. This clearance enables the valve to move under the influence of the pressure, so that it may bear against the strips already referred to. Thus the pressure on one side of the valve is utilised to ensure steam-tightness. During the operation of moving the valve the clearance mentioned reduces the friction by enabling the valve to clear itself from the rubbing surfaces. The form of the valve shown in Figs. 90, 95, and 96, was adopted in order to facilitate the casting of it. The attachment of the shut-off valve to the structure of the vessel was made as strong as possible, in view of its enormous weight, approximating to 28 tons. The deck was reinforced by a solid-steel pillar, 8 in. in diameter, just forward of the valve, in order to take up the load.

THE OPERATING OF THE MANŒUVRING-VALVES.

We come now to the operating of the various valves described and to the system of interlocking the levers by means of which the valves are brought into action. The controlling mechanism of all the machinery is concentrated, along with pressure and other indicators, telephones, &c., on the starting-platform, which is placed at the forward end of the central turbine-room—that containing the two low-pressure ahead and astern turbines—adjoining the bulkhead on which are the main steam, master, and manœuvring-valves.

On page 66 there is given a general arrangement of the levers on the starting-platform, with their connections to the actuating gear on the bulkhead-valves, master-valves, and manœuvring-valves, already described in detail. Figs. 126 and 127 are respectively an elevation looking towards the bulkhead and a plan of all the levers; Figs. 128 and 129 are cross-sections at two of the valves.

The starting-platform is illustrated on Plate X., Fig. 101 being an elevation looking aft, and showing many of the gauges; Fig. 102 is a plan, and it will be seen that the frame with gauges is curved; Fig. 103 shows the gauges on the port-

THE CUNARD LINER "AQUITANIA," GENERAL ARRANGEMENT OF VALVE-CONTROL INTERLOCKING LEVERS.

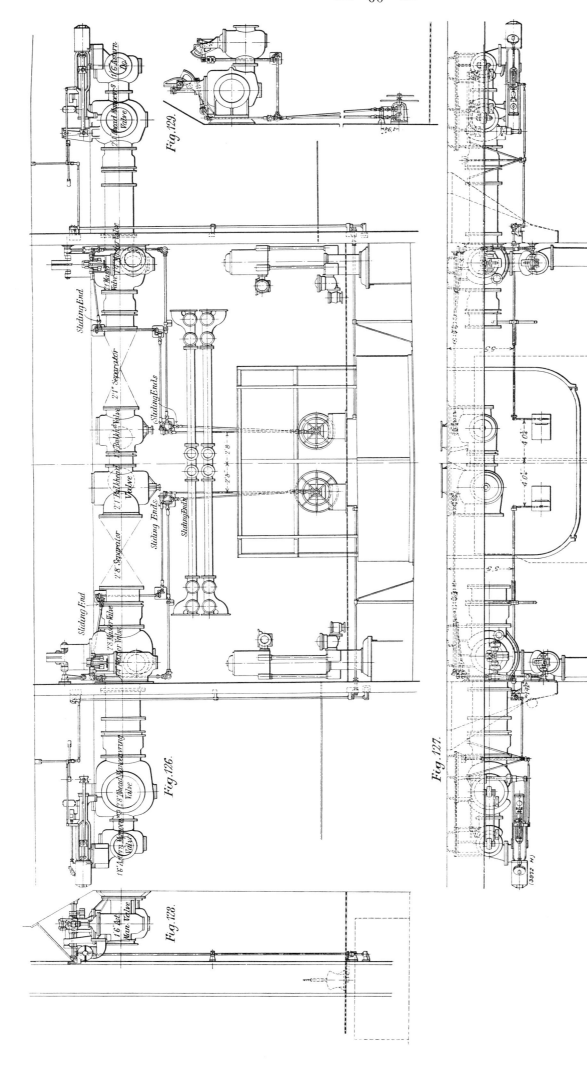

side curve, and Fig. 104 those on the starboard-side curve. Fig. 105 is a view looking towards the bulkhead, with the main steam handles and levers, and Fig. 106 is a side elevation looking towards the port side, showing the handles, levers, and gauges. On the next page is given an index to all the gauges, &c.

This platform, which forms quite a notable feature in the engine-room, is 16 ft. wide by 10 ft. long. Enclosing this space at the aft end, and partly at the sides, is erected a curved frame, on which, as already mentioned, are arranged the engine telegraphs, tell-tales, counters, gauges, telephones, clocks, &c., all of the latest and most efficient type. The chances of error in the transmission of orders from the bridge to the engine-room are reduced to a minimum by the system of reply telegraphs and tell-tales adopted.

On the bulkhead which forms the forward end of this platform, the stokehold telegraphs, stoking indicators, Stone Lloyd's door index-board, &c., are all arranged in positions most convenient to the eye and within the arms-reach of the engineer in charge. The hand-gear for operating the main steam bulk-head-valves is also conveniently disposed on this bulkhead, together with that for the master-valves on the main steam athwartship pipes (Fig. 105, Plate X). Facing the engine telegraphs, and in the centre of the starting-platform space, are placed two quadrant boxes, each with four hand-levers for controlling the bulkhead-valves, manœuvring-valves, 53-in. change-valve, and 66-in. shut-off valve (see Figs. 102 and 106). The operation of the various valves and levers when manœuvring must follow a certain sequence. The possibility of error in the working of the levers to perform these operations is entirely eliminated by the use of an ingenious locking device arranged inside the quadrant boxes, to be described in detail presently. This locking arrangement ensures the various operations following in their proper sequence.

All the turbine drain-valves are geared to the starting-platform, as also are the steam heating and gland steam main control-valves, and those controlling the auxiliary exhaust and turbo-generator exhaust to auxiliary condensers and low-pressure turbines. The hydraulic hand-gears in connection with the various Brown's engines throughout the engine-rooms are also arranged here, so that the engineer in charge has complete control of the various connections.

THE INTERLOCKING OF VALVE-OPERATING LEVERS.

The operations of the 53-in. change-valve and the 66-in. shut-off valve are dependent on one another, and on these also depends the operation of the manœuvring-valve admitting steam direct to the intermediate-pressure turbine or to the starboard astern turbine. When the engineer desires to manœuvre with the two starboard shafts working independently of the two port shafts, the change-valve must be open to the port low-pressure turbine, and closed to the intermediate-pressure turbine, before steam can be admitted direct from the boiler to the latter. Further, there must be no connection between the port and the starboard low-pressure turbines, so that the shut-off valve must be closed before steam is admitted from the boilers to the intermediate-pressure ahead turbine, or to the starboard high-pressure astern turbine. Interlocking gear has been introduced to ensure that the intermediate - pressure turbine manœuvring-valve cannot be opened until the change-over valve passing steam from the high-pressure to the intermediate-pressure turbine has been closed to the intermediate-pressure turbine, and until the shut-off valve passing steam from the intermediate-pressure turbine to the port low-pressure turbine has also been closed. This interlocking gear, along with the starting-platform, is illustrated on Plate X. and on page 66.

In order to bring into one set of quadrants all the valves which have to be interlocked one with the other, the quadrants on the starboard side of the starting-platform actuate the intermediate-pressure manœuvring-valve, the 66-in. shut-off valve, the 53-in. change-valve, and the starboard low-pressure ahead and astern direct manœuvring-valve. This quadrant is illustrated in Figs. 107 to 112. On the port side of the starting-platform there are concentrated the levers for the remaining valves, which do not require to be interlocked, since their action is independent of any other valve—namely, the high-pressure man-

œuvring-valve, the 21-in. and the 25-in. bulkhead-valves, and the port low-pressure ahead and astern direct manœuvring-valves. This quadrant is shown in Figs. 113 to 115. There is on both quadrants supplementary gear, as shown in Figs. 116 to 118, but this will be described later. Referring to Fig. 109, which shows a plan of the starboard quadrant with the top plate removed, the lever operating the change-valve is shown at A in the position when the change-valve is open for the passage of exhaust steam from the high-pressure turbine direct to the intermediate-pressure turbine. The lever operating the shut-off valve is shown at B in the position when the shut-off valve is open. The lever for operating the manœuvring-valve of the intermediate-pressure turbine is shown at C in the position when the manœuvring-valve is shut off. This lever C cannot be worked in the position shown on account of the locking-plate D. In order to release lever C lever A must be moved until its trigger engages in the notch F in Fig. 108. Before this happens the edge G of the lever A has come into contact with the edge H of the relieving-plate J, and the latter has been moved in the direction of the arrow. In so doing the recess K fits round the lever A. This operation being performed, plate E receives a motion of translation to the right sufficient to relieve the plate L, which is carried by the lever B. The latter is now free to move. The movement of A until the trigger engages with the notch F has made the necessary alteration in the direction of the flow of steam through the change-valve. The lever B being now moved, a similar operation is effected on plate M as was effected by lever A on plate J, the movement again being in the direction of the arrow. This gives plate D a motion of translation similar to plate E, and thereby releases a plate N fixed to the lever C, which is now free to move in either direction as necessary for manœuvring.

The locking-gear thus described may be thrown out of action for the adjustment of the valves or other reason. This disengagement is effected in the following manner :—The plates L and N, which are attached to the levers B and C, are carried on an eccentric keyed to the shaft on which the various levers rotate, as shown in Fig. 111. By rotating this shaft the plates L and M receive a vertical motion along the sides of the levers, so as to bring them clear of the plates D and E. This throws the locking-gear out of action. The end of the shaft is shaped in such a way that it necessitates a special key for rotating it, and when out of action the key cannot be removed until the locking-gear is again put into action ; the presence of the key indicates to the engineer that his locking-gear is out of operation.

In order to ensure that steam cannot be passed through the low-pressure astern turbine at the same time as steam is free to pass in ordinary sequence through the ahead turbines on each side of the ship, the supplementary interlocking gear mentioned above has been fitted, as illustrated in Figs. 116 to 118. In referring to the starboard quadrant-box (Fig. 108 or Fig. 118), any movement of the lever giving steam to the intermediate-pressure manœuvring-valve ahead at once locks the low-pressure manœuvring-valve lever in such a way as to prevent any movement of it except in a direction corresponding to the intermediate turbine lever, so that the steam supply through the low-pressure manœuvring-valve would simply be supplementary to the steam supply coming from the intermediate-pressure turbine. The port quadrants are arranged in an exactly corresponding manner.

This system of interlocking is effected in the following manner :—On the intermediate-pressure turbine manœuvring-lever, for instance, a link O (Fig. 118) is connected to a lever P (Fig. 116), which is keyed to a shaft Q resting on brackets on the after side of the quadrant. At the end next to the low-pressure manœuvring-lever another lever R (Fig. 117) is keyed, which is connected by means of the link S to a specially shaped plate T, which is pivoted at U. Any movement of the intermediate-pressure lever from its mid or usual position in either direction, ahead or astern, causes a movement of the special piece T in such a way as to prevent the low-pressure turbine lever from being moved in a direction opposite to the movement of the intermediate - pressure lever. A similar action by the low-pressure lever, by means of links, &c., acts on the intermediate - pressure lever. Instead of having two shafts, the low-pressure lever motion is transmitted to its interlocking

plate by means of a tube through which the shaft for the intermediate-pressure lever works. This is shown in Figs. 116 to 118.

The governing-gear and its action upon the bulkhead-valves is illustrated in Figs. 119 to 125. An interesting feature here is the fact that instead of working on to a throttle-valve, the governor-gear works directly on to the bulkhead-valves. Fig. 119 is an elevation, looking at the transverse bulkhead, showing the connections from the four turbines. Fig. 120 is a plan, Fig. 121 is an elevation of the high-pressure turbine ; and this also is typical of the intermediate-pressure turbine. Fig. 122 is an elevation of the low-pressure turbine, showing the connections to the governor-gear. Excepting for descriptive purposes, the arrangement of the high-pressure turbine is typical of all four turbines. A, Fig. 119, is a weight which is pivoted at B, and is supported in its position by the lever C, which, in turn, is actuated through necessary gearing by means of the rod D in Figs. 120 and 121, and the governor E on the forward end of the turbine. This governor is driven by spiral gearing from the turbine-spindle. When the governor acts, due to the attainment of a speed exceeding a predetermined rate of revolution, the lever C is released and allows the weight A to fall. The dropping of this weight, acting through the successive rods F and successive rods G and the shaft H, operates the two handles on the quadrant, which control the 21-in. and 25-in. bulkhead-valves. The action is shown on a larger scale in Figs. 123 to 125. The rod G is connected to a bell-crank lever J, to one end of which a shaft K is fixed. The ends of the shaft carry the rollers L, which bear against the pawls M. The latter are supported by the hand-levers P, which act on the two bulkhead-valves. The effect of the weight A falling is to cause the bell-crank J to move forward. Through the medium of the rollers acting on the pawls the triggers N are raised clear of their respective slots on the quadrant. The further movement of the bell-crank J brings the special plates O, which are bolted to the bell-crank, into contact with the backs of the handles P, and these are now carried forward on the quadrant, and through the rods Q, acting on the shaft R, on to the rods S and levers T to the valves of the valve-operating engines, which then act and close the bulkhead-valves. The rack and pinion for the hand operation of these valves is shown respectively at U and V. A small winch is shown at W, and is used for raising the weight, in order to reset the governor. The operation which we are describing is typical of that effected by the governor-gear of all the turbines.

The exhaust from the high-pressure astern turbines, port and starboard, can be cut off from the low-pressure astern turbines by means of a sluice-valve, seen in the general arrangement, Fig. 43, on Plate VII. Gear is fitted for operating this sluice-valve from the centre engine-room as well as from the wing engine-rooms.

Throughout the engine-room the steam leads are of lap-welded pipes with riveted flanges. The valves and all high-pressure connections are generally of cast steel ; the exhaust connections between the turbines are mostly of cast iron, but the straight lengths are all steel pipes. Expansion in the high-pressure line of piping is provided for by the usual stuffing-boxes, and in the connections between the turbines copper bellows are extensively used, as shown on the general arrangement plan on the same plate. Special care has been taken to provide adequate support for the various parts of the steam-distribution units, so as to minimise any undue strain. In some cases stay-rods are used, in others brackets are secured to the adjacent structure of the ship.

ENGINEERS' STORES AND WORKSHOPS.

A workshop containing two lathes, one drilling-machine, planing-machine, and grindstone, is fitted up in the port-wing turbine-room, with a large issuing store attached. There are also two large store-rooms in the tunnel compartments, and one between Nos. 3 and 4 boiler-rooms ; also a sufficient number of vice-benches, with lockers, &c., are distributed over the various rooms, &c., for overhauling purposes.

THE QUADRUPLE-SCREW TURBINE-DRIVEN CUNARD LINER "AQUITANIA"

FIG. 151. WEIR'S "UNIFLUX" CONDENSER.

FROM CONDENSER TO BOILER.

Having described the main turbines to drive the ship, and the steam distribution to the turbines, with the several valves for various alternative systems of working, we may now turn to the mechanical appliances connected with the condensation of the steam and the return of the condensed water to the boilers, as well as the supply of "make-up" feed-water. As has already been explained, each of the low-pressure turbines exhausts through an eduction-pipe into a separate condenser, which is placed, along with the requisite pumps, in a separate compartment abaft the turbine-room. The two condenser-rooms are separated by a longitudinal bulkhead in the centre line of the ship, these rooms together occupying 36 ft. 6 in. of the length of the ship and the full width ; but at the point where the turbine-room transverse bulkhead joins the hull of the ship there is a splayed joint forming a **V**, to

There is in each condenser 23,000 sq. ft. of cooling surface, making collectively 46,000 sq. ft. There are two circulating pipes to each condenser 30 in. in diameter, and for inspection purposes large double doors are fitted to each end, each door again having a large number of man-hole doors for easy access to all tubes, without the removal of the main doors. This is well shown in the perspective view of the condenser on page 68.

There are four main circulating-pumps supplied by Messrs. W. H. Allen, Son and Co., Limited, of Bedford. They have suction and discharge-branches 30 in. in diameter, and each is fitted with a turbine type of disc. Each pump is driven by a double-acting enclosed engine, having a steam-cylinder 14 in. in diameter by $10\frac{1}{2}$ in. stroke. The pumps and engines are arranged in two pairs, as shown in Fig. 152, annexed. The engine crank-shafts are extended on the side remote from the pumps, and

and Kinghorn valves on gun-metal seats. The rationale of the "Dual" air-pump, it may be said, is as follows :—The duty of an air-pump is to take from the condenser a mixture of air, water, and vapour, and to obtain economical working ; this should be done at the highest possible temperature. If a single pump be used to deal with this mixture, the hotwell temperature for a given vacuum is dependent on the amount of air leakage and the air-pump capacity. Consequently, with a single air-pump the temperature of the mixture must be considerably colder than the theoretical temperature, due to the vacuum. By the use of separate pumps handling the air and water, the dry pump has a cold injection non-returnable to the feed, and the above conditions are changed, higher thermal efficiency being thus rendered possible. The wet (or water) pump is enabled to handle water at approximately the steam temperature,

FIG. 152. MAIN CIRCULATING PUMPS, BY MESSRS. W. H. ALLEN, SON AND CO., LIMITED.

obviate both the turbine and the condenser-rooms on the port or starboard side respectively from being put in connection with the sea as a result of collision at a point of junction between the transverse bulkhead and the skin of the ship. The arrangement of the machinery in the condenser-rooms is illustrated on Plates VII. and XI.

THE CONDENSING PLANT.

The condensers, of Weir's "Uniflux" design, and constructed by Messrs. John Brown and Co., Limited, are illustrated in detail on Plate XI. and page 68. The drawings reproduced are largely self-explanatory and dimensions accompany them. Each condenser is built up of $\frac{3}{4}$-in. steel plates, riveted with double lap-joints. The water ends are of cast iron, $1\frac{1}{8}$ in. thick. The tube-plates are of yellow metal, the distance between these being 12 ft. $6\frac{1}{2}$ in. The tube-plates are stayed by steel rods having capped nuts. There are altogether 18,706 tubes in the two condensers, these tubes being $\frac{3}{4}$ in. external diameter, while the pitch varies from $1\frac{3}{8}$ in. at the top to $1\frac{1}{8}$ in. at the bottom. The circulation is on the double-flow principle, and in the design of the condensers and pumps a vacuum of $28\frac{1}{2}$ in., with a barometer at 29 in., is aimed at.

couplings are provided so that the pair can be coupled together or run separately, as desired. The engines are fitted with a system of forced lubrication throughout the working parts. The pump-casings are of cast iron, and are fitted with brass rings where the outer rim of the pump disc approaches the casing. The discs are of gun-metal and the spindles of bronze. Each pumping-engine is capable of delivering 18,500 gallons of water per minute under circulating conditions against a total suction and delivery head of 31 ft. 6 in., which includes condenser, pipe, valve, and bend friction, the speed being 350 revolutions. The circulating water enters the condenser at the bottom, this arrangement following the usual practice, which has been found to give the best results.

Two sets of air-pumps of Weir's "Dual" type work in connection with each condenser. One set is illustrated by Fig. 153, on page 70. The air-cylinders are of 38 in. diameter by 21 in. stroke, and each is driven by one steam-cylinder, 20 in. in diameter by 21 in. stroke ; each pump is suitable for 14,000 shaft horse-power. The pumps are of Weir's standard merchant-service type, having gun-metal barrels, with cast-iron bases and tops, fitted with gun-metal buckets, manganese-bronze pump-rods, steel piston-rods,

while at the same time the dry pump deals with the air and vapour at the volume and temperature conditions imposed by the temperature of the injection water. This aim, sought in many different ways, has been achieved in a comparatively simple manner by the use of the "Dual" air-pump, together with an increased efficiency of the dry pump, due to its contents being densified or decreased in volume through cooling by the injection water, which circulates continuously, never leaves the system, and is never subjected to atmospheric pressure, with consequent aeration. The dry air-pump further works only at less than half the pressure range, as it discharges below the head-valves of the wet pump.

The port and starboard air and circulating-pumps, it may be added, are cross-connected, enabling both condensers to be served by the pumps in either compartment.

For dealing with the exhaust from the auxiliaries and turbo-electric plant a Weir's "Uniflux" auxiliary condenser, constructed by Messrs. John Brown and Co., Limited, with circulating and air-pumps, is placed at the forward end of each of the wing turbine-rooms. These condensers are 7 ft. between tube-plates with 2000 sq. ft. cooling surface each. The auxiliary pumps, like the main circulating-

THE QUADRUPLE-SCREW TURBINE-DRIVEN CUNARD LINER "AQUITANIA."

FIG. 155. WEIR'S HOT-WELL PUMP.

FIG. 154. WEIR'S MONOTYPE PUMP FOR AUXILIARY CONDENSER.

FIG. 153. WEIR'S "DUAL"-TYPE AIR-PUMPS FOR MAIN CONDENSERS.

THE QUADRUPLE-SCREW TURBINE-DRIVEN CUNARD LINER "AQUITANIA."

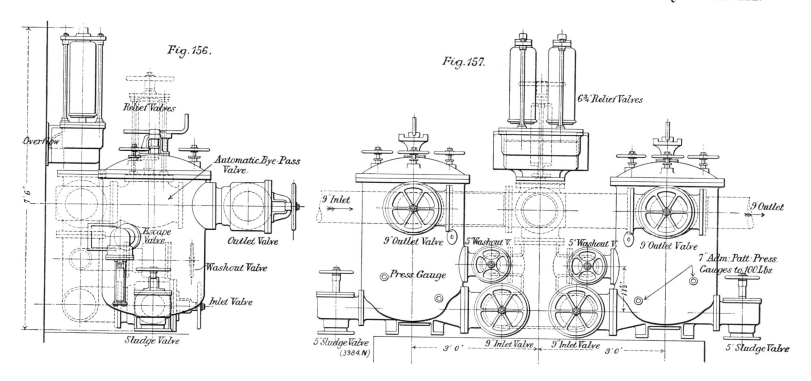

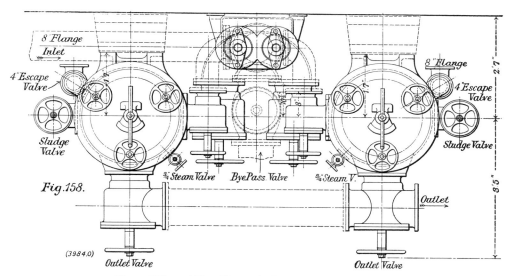

FIGS. 156 TO 158. HARRIS'S FEED-WATER FILTERS.

pumps, have been supplied by Messrs. Allen. Each pump has suction and discharge branches 10 in. in diameter, and is driven direct by a single-cylinder enclosed engine, the cylinder having a diameter of 7 in. by 6 in. stroke. Each of these pumps delivers 2500 gallons of water per minute against 20 ft. head, when running at a speed of 330 revolutions. The air-pumps of Weir's monotype design, illustrated by Fig. 154, on page 70, have an air-cylinder 24 in. in diameter, and a steam-cylinder 12 in. in diameter, both with a 15 in. stroke. The materials used are the same as those adopted in the "Dual" pumps. The mountings, as shown, include steam and exhaust stop-valves. The air-pump discharges through an auxiliary filter to the hot-well tanks or to the auxiliary feed-tanks situated at the forward end of the wing turbine-rooms.

FEED-PUMPS, HEATERS, &c.

From the main air-pumps in the condenser-rooms the feed-water is discharged into two hot-well tanks, one in each compartment. There are four of Messrs. Weir's hot-well pumps, of the light-duty type, shown by Fig. 155, on page 70. Each pump-cylinder is 14 in. in diameter, and the steam-cylinder 12 in., with a 26-in. stroke. Each pump is capable of dealing with the feed-water for 14,000 shaft horse-power. The pump ends are of gun-metal, and the pumps are fitted with gun-metal liners, gun-metal buckets, manganese-bronze pump-rods, steel piston-rods and gun-metal valves on gun-metal seats. The pumps are automatically controlled by Weir's control-gear, fitted in the hot-well tanks, so that the speed of the pumps corresponds to the flow of water into the tanks. These pumps are also regulated by the direct-contact heater control-gear, giving a control on the suction and discharge side of the pumps.

Between its passage from the hot-well tank and the heaters the feed-water goes through filters, of which there are four, of the well-known Harris type. These filters are illustrated by Figs. 156 to 163, on the present and the next pages. They are arranged in pairs (Figs. 156 to 158), one pair being on each side of the centre turbine-room, so that one may be overhauled while the other is in use. The principal feature of their internal construction is the central sludge-outlet—an ingenious arrangement by which the filtering area is divided into eight separate sections, each of which can be sludged out independently of the others (Fig. 161), the whole force of the reversed current of water when cleaning being concentrated on only one-eighth of the surface. In this way the cleaning is most

efficient, and can be effected in a few minutes without the necessity of opening up. Each filter is fitted with a nest of gun-metal grids (Fig. 159) having a central opening, the upper and lower faces and centre of each grid being machined ; shallow recesses are formed in each face of the grids, into which discs of tinned-copper gauze are fitted, and between each grid and the next is placed a disc of filtering material having a centre hole, the inner and outer edges of the material being gripped by the grids, thus forming a water-tight joint. The internal chamber formed by the grids (Fig. 162) is fitted with the central sludge-valve, which is a special patented appliance in the form of a lantern cock with a number of rows of ports (Fig. 163), the external shell of the cock being provided between the rows of ports with collars fitting closely into the interior of the grids and practically making a joint, thus dividing the whole pile into independent sections, each of which, by reversing the flow of water, can be sludged out independently of the rest by moving a handle working over a marked quadrant on the filter-cover (Fig. 160). By this arrangement the filters can be effectively sludged without opening out or removing the filtering medium.

The feed-water, after being filtered, is discharged by the hot-well pumps through Weir's "Uniflux" surface feed-heaters, of which there are two. In

these the exhaust steam from all the auxiliaries, with the exception of the turbo-generators and ash-expeller pumps, is utilised to heat the feed-water. As this steam is impregnated with oil, it flows, after condensation, by gravity to the hot-well tanks, the outlet being regulated by a float-control gear. Each of the two "Uniflux" surface feed-water heaters, which are of the horizontal type, contains 1000 sq. ft. of heating surface, and is capable of dealing with the feed-water for 28,000 shaft horse-power and of raising the temperature of this quantity of water from 90 deg. to 155 deg. Fahr. when supplied with exhaust steam from the auxiliaries, with the exception of the electric-light engines. The shells of the heaters, one of which is illustrated by Fig. 164, on page 73, are of mild steel, with cast-iron end-pieces and covers, rolled-brass tube-plates, solid-drawn copper tubes, fixed into tube-plates by screwed ferrules and packing, neatly covered with planished sheet steel. In addition to the "Uniflux" feed-heaters there are also fitted two of Weir's direct-contact heaters, into which the exhaust from the turbo-generators and ash-expeller pumps is led. The heaters, illustrated by Fig. 165, on page 74, are 48 in. in diameter, and contain automatic-control gear for regulating the speed of the main feed-pumps, and each capable of dealing with feed-water for 28,000 shaft horse-power and of raising the temperature

THE QUADRUPLE-SCREW TURBINE-DRIVEN CUNARD LINER "AQUITANIA."

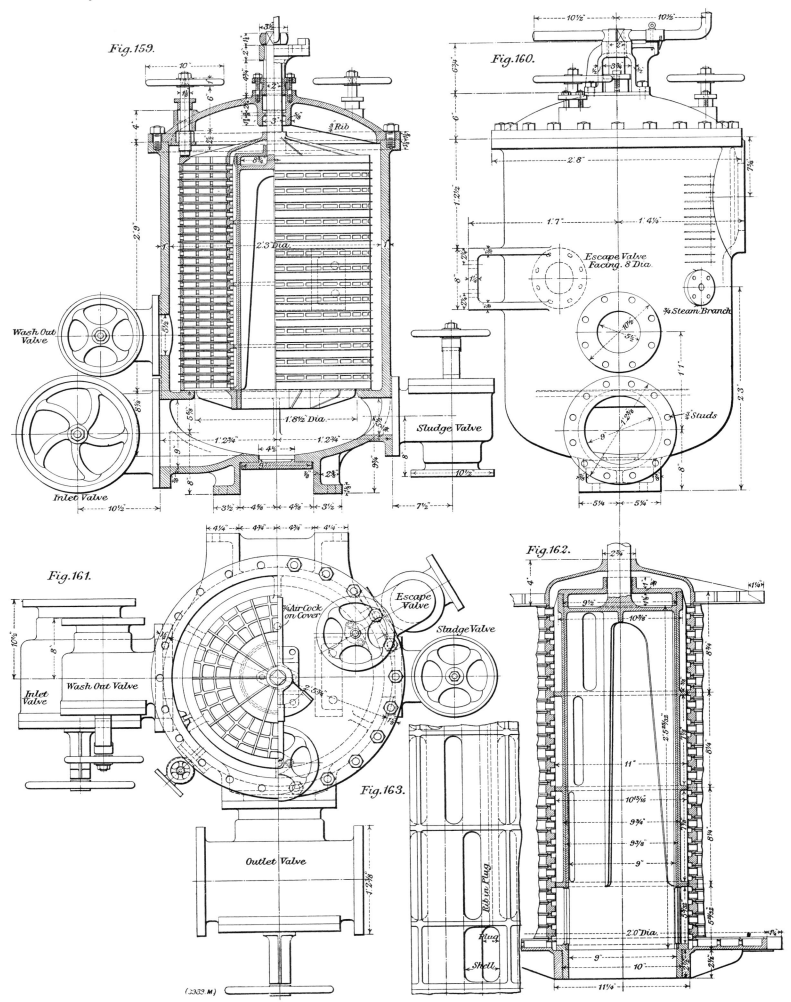

FIGS. 159 TO 163. HARRIS'S FEED-WATER FILTER.

from 155 deg. to 220 deg. Fahr., when supplied with exhaust steam from the electric-light engines. The shells of the heaters are of mild steel, with cast-iron end-pieces and covers. The heaters are fitted with steam-inlet valves, water-inlet valves, relief-valves, pressure-gauges, and all requisite mountings.

There are three pairs of Weir's standard feed-pumps, supplemented by a duplicate installation of auxiliary feed-pumps of the same size and number, all located at the forward end of the centre turbine-room. These pumps are all connected on the suction side to the direct-contact heaters and the hot-well tanks. All of these pumps, one of which is illustrated by Fig. 166, on page 74, have water-cylinders, 13 in. in diameter, and steam-cylinders, 18½ in. in diameter by 27 in. stroke. Each pair is capable of supplying the necessary feed-water for one-third of the boiler power when working at full power—i.e., each pair is suitable for over 18,000 shaft horse-power. It will be noted that on this basis the feed-pumps have a margin of 100 per cent. over their normal duty. The water ends of these pumps are of gun-metal, fitted with gun-metal liners, gun-metal buckets, manganese-bronze pump-rods, steel piston-rods, and bronze valves in gun-metal seats. Each pump is fitted with four suction and four discharge stop-valves, quadruple steam-valve, single exhaust-valves and relief-valves.

EVAPORATING AND DISTILLING PLANT.

The fresh-water distilling machinery consists of two separate plants, placed at the after end of the wing turbine-rooms. These, illustrated in Fig. 167, on page 75, are of Quiggin's well-known design. Each set includes two evaporators of equal capacity, two distilling condensers, one evaporator feed-pump, and one circulating pump for the two condensers. The evaporators, which are of cast iron, have a normal capacity of 75 tons each per twenty-four hours, but are capable of producing considerably over this quantity if required. They are of the "single effect" type, and have all the necessary mountings, including dead shut-off type of automatic feed-water regulator, and specially designed separator for enabling the attendant visually to regulate the condenser boiler-steam drain from the heating surface. The evaporators are lagged with hair-felt and planished steel. Either or both evaporators can be used for feed make-up purposes or for the production of distilled water. An automatic feed-water regulator is fitted on each evaporator, and this maintains the water-level in the evaporators at a constant height.

There are two distilling condensers, of equal size, each having an output of 50 tons (or 11,200 gallons) of distilled water per twenty-four hours when supplied with vapour from the evaporators. Each condenser has its own independent and separate fresh-water filter, specially designed to facilitate cleaning and inspection, with an aerating apparatus fitted between the condenser and filter. The condensers are designed to produce the drinking-water at a temperature within a few degrees of that of the sea-water.

Each set is provided with a Lamont's vertical duplex pump 11 in. by 10 in. by 10 in., for circulating water through the distillers, and each capable of discharging 200 tons of water per hour, and a pump, also of the vertical duplex type, 5 in. by 5 in. by 6 in., by Thom, Lamont and Co., for maintaining the feed supply to the evaporators. The firm also supplied two pumps, 5 in. by 5 in. by 6 in., each capable of delivering 35 tons of water per hour.

PUMPS FOR SUNDRY PURPOSES.

In addition to the auxiliary machinery in connection with the condensers and feed-water, as already described, there are a number of pumps throughout the machinery space for sundry duties. In the centre turbine-room there is a vertical duplex pump, 11 in. by 10 in. by 10 in., in connection with the sanitary system throughout the ship; a similar pump is fitted for wash-deck and fire purposes, and has a capacity of 200 tons per hour. These pumps, of the Carruthers type, are cross-connected, and the view on Fig. 168, page 75, illustrates the type. Of pumps of this or kindred design the firm supplied twelve. The three pumps in connection with the Stone-Lloyd water-tight door system are also situated in the centre engine-room. Together these pumps are capable of delivering without

THE CUNARD LINER "AQUITANIA."

FIG. 164. WEIR'S "UNIFLUX" FEED-HEATER.

shock or noise 150 gallons of water or oil per minute against a pressure of 700 lb. per sq. in. when supplied with steam at 150 lb. per sq. in., and exhausting against a back pressure of 25 lb. per sq. in. above atmosphere. Each pump is fitted with a relief-valve (with internal spring) having a return to suction. On the outboard side of the port-wing turbines two vertical duplex pumps, 12 in. by 10 in. by 12 in., by Carruthers, are placed, with a similar pair on the starboard side for water service to the bearings, oil-coolers, &c. A motor-driven sanitary pump is also situated in the port turbine-room. This motor-driven Allen pump has one 6-in. pump driven by a semi-enclosed motor, and it delivers 170 tons per hour against a maximum head of 75 ft. when running at 1500 revolutions per minute. The motor develops 27 brake horse-power, and the set is furnished with a starter and regulating switch fitted with automatic no-load release and speed-regulator.

The fresh and condensed-water pumps, of Weir's type, are arranged at the forward end of the port-wing engine-room. Each of these pumps has filters. The pump-cylinders are 8 in. in diameter, and the steam-cylinders 6½ in. by 15 in. stroke. Each pump is capable of delivering 9100 gallons of water per hour when running at thirty double strokes per minute. The condensed-water pump is 12½ in. in diameter, with a steam-cylinder 10 in. by 24 in. stroke, and is capable of delivering 80 tons of water per hour when running at fifteen double strokes per minute against a head of 95 ft. when supplied with steam at a pressure of 150 lb. per sq. in. In each wing compartment at the forward end there is a vertical duplex bilge-pump 9 in. by 8 in. by 8 in. A small horizontal duplex pump in connection with the ship's steam-heating system is placed in the starboard wing compartment. There are also two Royle calorifiers, and these will be described later.

In the condenser-rooms, in addition to the pumps already mentioned, there is a bilge-pump similar to those in the wing engine-rooms. A hot-salt-water pump, 6½ in. by 8 in. by 15 in. stroke, to deliver 9100 gallons per hour, for ship's purposes, is situated in the port condenser-room. This pump draws from the main circulating discharge overboard. A small condenser is arranged in the port condenser-room, into which all drains from steam and exhaust-pipes and from thermo-tanks, galleys, and ship's steam heating are led. From a drain-tank in connection with this condenser a pump situated near by delivers the drain-water to the hotwell tanks after being cooled.

The six forced-lubrication pumps, by Messrs. Weir, have steam cylinders 12½ in. in diameter, with pump cylinders 10 in. by 24-in. stroke. Each is capable of delivering 20,000 gallons of oil per hour

when running at 17½ double strokes per minute. The same firm supplied two vertical oil service pumps, 9 in. in diameter with 7½-in. steam cylinder by 18-in. stroke, each capable of pumping 9000 gallons of oil per hour from one tank to another when running at 20 double strokes per minute.

All the necessary valves, &c., for galley, thermo-tanks, and steam heating are placed in the centre engine-room, with all shut-off and reducing valves and gauges, so that the engineer in charge has this system under his entire control.

THE BOILERS.

On the two-page Plate XII. we reproduce a longitudinal section and plan, Figs. 169 and 170, of two of the four boiler-rooms, the other two being practically the same, while Figs. 171 to 173 are cross-sections. In each of the three forward boiler-rooms, which are 78 ft. long by 60 ft. wide, are six boilers, placed three abreast, while in the aftermost boiler-room, which is 42 ft. long by 60 ft. wide, there are three boilers similarly placed. To each boiler-room there is a large double elliptical funnel, the outer casings of each being 24 ft. on the major axis by 17 ft. on the minor axis. The forward funnel is 154 ft. 9 in. high above the fire-grate, and 64 ft. 6 in. above the casing-top. In addition to the ordinary exit there is an emergency escape from each boiler-room to "E" deck. It will be seen that along the whole length of the boiler compartments—369 ft.—on each side of the ship, are coal-bunkers divided from the boiler rooms by a longitudinal bulkhead, which is 18 ft. from the outer skin of the ship, so that no damage to the outer skin can possibly affect the inner wall. The space between the inner walls constituting the boiler-rooms is about 60 ft. wide. In the coal-bunker space there are fitted transverse bulkheads dividing these bunkers into ten water-tight coal sections on each side, varying from 27 ft. to 33 ft. in length. A notable feature in the subdivision is that the coal-bunkers in each of the main divisions separated by the transverse bulkheads are sufficient in capacity to take coal for the voyage for all the boilers in such compartment, so that the isolation of any boiler compartment becomes an easy matter. Moreover, the circuit for the closing of the doors in the main transverse bulkheads from the bridge, and the maintaining of them in the closed position on the Stone-Lloyd system, is separate from the circuit on which the doors in the longitudinal bulkheads are operated. Thus the former doors may be kept closed on the voyage, except where it may be desired to open them for unavoidable communication, and then they automatically close. The doors on the longitudinal bulkheads may be kept open, but can be

THE QUADRUPLE-SCREW TURBINE-DRIVEN CUNARD LINER "AQUITANIA."

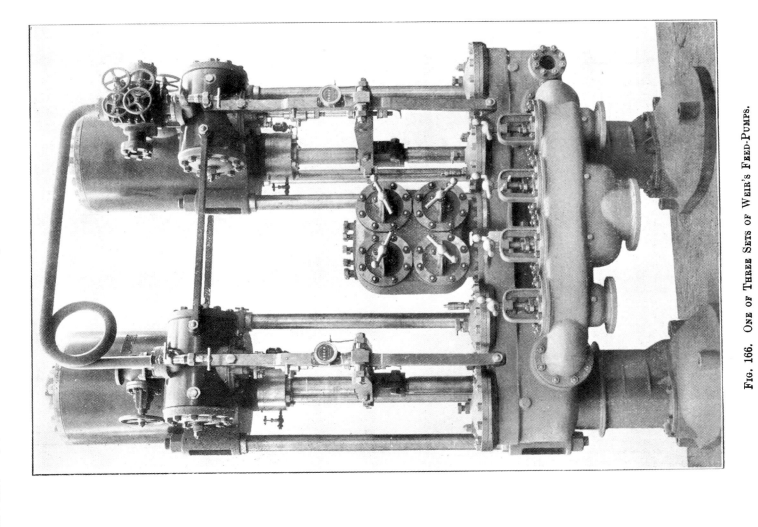

FIG. 166. ONE OF THREE SETS OF WEIR'S FEED-PUMPS.

FIG. 165. ONE OF WEIR'S CONTACT FEED-HEATERS.

THE QUADRUPLE-SCREW TURBINE-DRIVEN CUNARD LINER "AQUITANIA."

FIG. 167. QUIGGIN'S EVAPORATING AND DISTILLING PLANT; THE LIVERPOOL ENGINEERING AND CONDENSER COMPANY, LIMITED.

FIG. 168. ONE OF SEVERAL CARRUTHERS' PUMPS FOR SUNDRY DUTIES.

instantly closed at the will of the captain from the bridge. This is a departure from previous practice, and adds greatly to the security of the ship.

The fore-and-aft bulkheads in all cases are connected to the shell of the ship by strong stays formed of double channels spaced 9 ft. apart. The hatches to the cargo holds are trunked and made water-tight to the weather-deck. The engine and boiler-casings are extra well stiffened by webs and made water-tight to 20 ft. above the load water-line. Thus water entering any of the cargo, engine, or boiler compartments cannot flow into any adjacent compartment, but is confined within the trunk hatches or casings. Moreover, there are transverse coal-bunkers athwart the ship at the forward end of the boiler space and between each pair of boiler-rooms, excepting the space between Nos. 3 and 4 boiler-rooms, where the compartment is given up to the electric generating station on the "H" deck level, and on the hold level on the starboard side to the refrigerating machinery, and on the port side to an assistant feed-pump and ballast-pump, both of the vertical duplex type.

Distributed throughout the boiler-rooms are seven ash-expellers, of Stone's underline type, for the disposal of ashes at sea, as illustrated in Figs. 183 and 184, on Plate XIII. These expellers are arranged in large recesses in the stokeholds, into which all ashes may be stowed for ejection at will, thus facilitating the work of the stokers by leaving a clear firing-platform at all times. The principle on which these expellers work was fully described in ENGINEERING, vol. xcv., page 664.

As the whole of the ashes produced is estimated at 120 tons per day, and as each of the expellers has a capacity for disposing of 15 to 18 tons of ash per hour, they need only be worked intermittently. The ash and stokehold refuse are discharged quickly and noiselessly through the bottom of the ship without ever being brought above the level of the stokehold floor. The advantages of such a system to passengers are obvious. But another important point is that the expellers can be utilised as bilge-pumps, the bilge connection being not made to the pump, but to the discharge flow, so that any sludge or solid matter which can pass through the bilge suction can be discharged without going near the pump. Moreover, in times of emergency, the expeller-pumps can be brought into use; and when it is mentioned that the capacity of the pumps for each expeller—already described—is approximately 4500 tons per hour, it will be seen that the service they are capable of rendering at such times may be of the utmost value. In addition to these expellers there are eight ash-hoists fitted throughout the boiler-rooms for use in port. These ash-hoists are of the Railton Campbell silent type, as shown in Fig. 172, Plate XII.

The arrangement of the main steam-piping—of

THE QUADRUPLE-SCREW TURBINE-DRIVEN CUNARD LINER "AQUITANIA."

FIGS. 185 AND 186. HOWDEN'S FORCED-DRAUGHT FANS AND ALLEN'S ELECTRIC MOTOR AND CONTROLLER.

FIG. 187. HOISTING THE FOURTH FUNNEL INTO THE SHIP IN CLYDEBANK BASIN.

THE QUADRUPLE-SCREW TURBINE-DRIVEN CUNARD LINER "AQUITANIA."

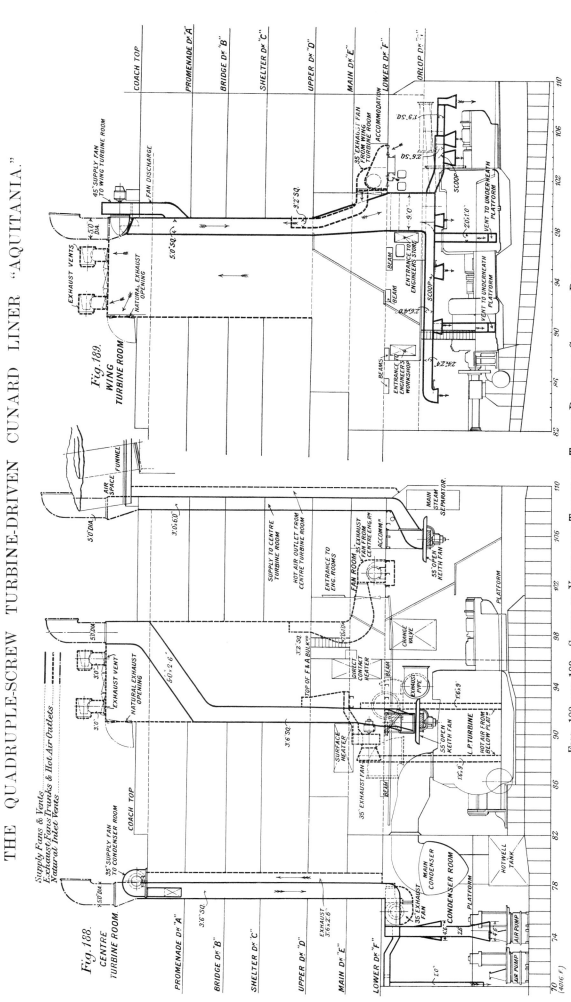

Supply Fans & Vents ——————
Exhaust Fans Trunks & Hot Air Outlets ————
Natural Inlet Vents ....

Fig. 188. CENTRE TURBINE ROOM.

Fig. 188. WING TURBINE ROOM.

FIGS. 188 AND 189. SYSTEM OF VENTILATING TRUNKS FOR TURBINE-ROOMS AND CONDENSER-ROOM.

Stewart and Lloyd's make—and ranging up to $33\frac{1}{4}$ in. in diameter in the turbine-room, is well shown in Figs. 169 and 170. It will be seen that the boilers in Nos. 3 and 4 boiler-rooms are connected to a main on the starboard side of the centre line, and that those in boiler-rooms Nos. 1 and 2—those not shown in the longitudinal section and plan—are joined up to another main on the port side, but there is connection between the valves on the turbine-room side of the after boiler-room bulkhead, as already described. The leads from each boiler to the main are shown in Figs. 170 and 172.

All the boiler blow-down valves are arranged in the auxiliary machinery-rooms, thus obviating any derangement of the stoking-platform for access to valves when blowing down boilers. A very substantial system of flooring has been adopted throughout the boiler-rooms. All the chequered floor-plates are laid on solid-wood floors, carefully fitted on T-bar bearers, so arranged that no dust or ashes can find their way into the bilges, the whole stoking-platform being divided into suitable sections for lifting. Firemen's escapes are provided, as shown in Figs. 169 to 171, Plate XII., and these communicate with central passages to the firemen's quarters in the forecastle.

One of the boilers is illustrated by Figs. 174 to 182, on Plate XIII., and as the details are very complete, little description is necessary. All the boilers are alike, double-ended, with separate combustion-chambers. The mean diameter of each is 17 ft. 8 in., and the mean length 22 ft. There are eight furnaces in each boiler, and these are of the Morison type, 3 ft. 9 in. inside diameter, the fire-grate being 5 ft. 6 in. long. The dimensions of the boilers are given in the next column.

	One Double-Ended Boiler.	21 Double-Ended Boilers.
Grate surface ...	168.66 sq. ft.	3541.8 sq. ft.
Tube-heating surface	5479.6 "	115,071.6 "
Furnace " "	405.6 "	8517 "
Fire-box " "	714.6 "	15,006.6 "
Total " "	6599.8 "	138,595.8 "
Area through tubes	25.12 "	527.5 "
Steam space ...	1231.7 cub. ft.	25,865.7 cub. ft.
Ratio of heating surface to grate area	39.1 to 1	
" grate area to area through tubes ...		6.71 to 1
" steam space to grate area ...		7.3 to 1
" tube surface to grate area ...		32.48 to 1

triple riveted, and the end circumferential joints are double riveted. The front tube-plate is $\frac{25}{32}$ in. thick, and the back tube-plate $1\frac{2}{8}$ in. over the centre fire-box, and $\frac{7}{8}$ in. over the wing fire-boxes. The tubes are of iron, and the plain tubes are $2\frac{1}{4}$ in. in external diameter of 8-wire gauge, while the stay-tubes are from $2\frac{1}{2}$ in. by $\frac{1}{4}$ in. to $2\frac{1}{4}$ in. by $\frac{3}{8}$ in., some of the larger being fitted with nuts as shown. There are altogether 54 miles of Stewart and Lloyd's tubes. Details are given of riveted joints, stays, &c. Figs. 179 and 180 are details of the junction of the furnace with the combustion-chamber.

The boilers are fitted with Howden's latest forced-draught system. The furnace fronts are of the "single-action" safety type, the valves for admitting air to the ashpits being worked by one handle for each furnace, and so arranged

The shell-plate is $1\frac{19}{32}$ in. thick. There are three plates in the length of the boiler, and two in the circumference. The longitudinal joints are double-butt strap, with three rows of rivets on each side of butt; the middle circumferential joints are

THE QUADRUPLE-SCREW TURBINE-DRIVEN CUNARD LINER "AQUITANIA."

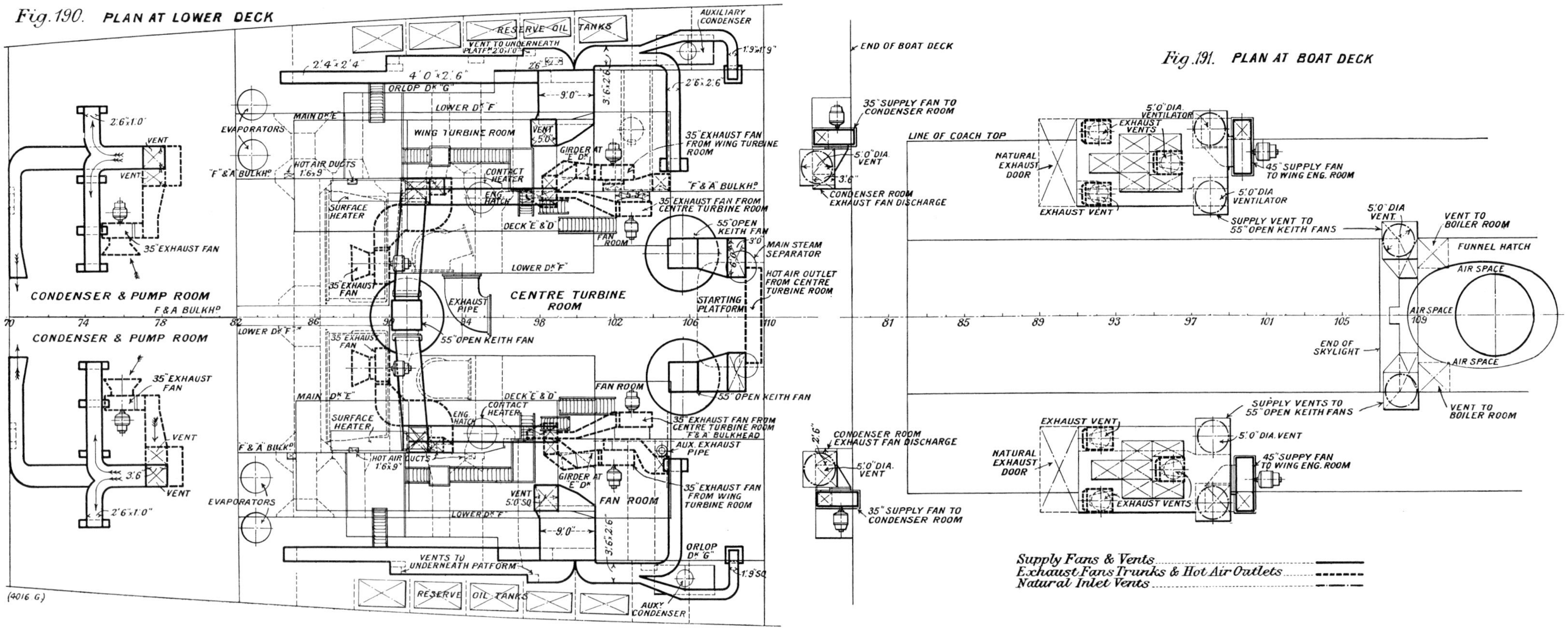

Fig. 190. PLAN AT LOWER DECK

Fig. 191. PLAN AT BOAT DECK

Supply Fans & Vents ——————
Exhaust Fans Trunks & Hot Air Outlets ———————
Natural Inlet Vents — · — · —

FIGS. 190 AND 191. SYSTEM OF VENTILATING TRUNKS FOR TURBINE-ROOMS AND CONDENSER-ROOM.

that the furnace-doors cannot be opened until these air-valves are closed, thereby preventing the possibility of any accident from blow-back through carelessness on the part of the firemen. The electrically-driven fans which supply the air for combustion, also of the Howden type, are illustrated in Fig. 185, on page 76. They are placed in separate fan-rooms on "G" deck level (Figs. 169, 171, and 173). There are twenty-eight such fans, of the single-inlet type, with revolving wheel, 66 in. in diameter, and capable of running at a speed of 450 revolutions per minute against a pressure at the discharge of 3⅜-in. water gauge. The fans are constructed of steel plating, the wheels being built with a cast-steel centre carrying the blades and shrouds, and giving great rigidity. The suction branches of the fans are connected to trunks leading to the stokeholds, and arranged with air inlets, to ensure efficient ventilation. Hinged doors also are fitted on the suction inlet branch of each fan, for the purpose of giving ventilation to the fan-room.

Each pair of fans is driven by one Allen electric motor of 50 horse-power, as shown in Fig. 185. The motors are of the pipe-ventilated pattern, fitted with internal fan, by which circulation of

air through the windings is obtained. Under such conditions the temperature rise is kept within the limits of 70 deg. Fahr. This arrangement of ventilation to all intents and purposes provides a machine having all the advantages of a totally-enclosed motor, but of less size than would be the case were it totally enclosed. The motors are shunt-wound, and by field-control have a speed range of 225 to 450 revolutions per minute at 50 horse-power, with an overload speed of 500 revolutions per minute for 68 horse-power. The motors are provided with auxiliary poles, by which sparkless commutation is obtained at all loads with fixed position of brushes.

The controllers, illustrated by Fig. 186, on page 76, are of somewhat special design, the drum being shifted in a step-by-step action, one position for every fourth turn of a spoke-wheel, which latter is so guarded that too rapid starting is prevented. For operating the controllers in the stokehold a similar gear is provided at the end of the extension equipment. The first movement of the drum closes the main circuit by energising the double-pole clapper switches. Further movement of the drum decreases the resistance in the armature circuit, and afterwards increases the resistance

in the shunt circuit, thereby bringing the motor from rest to full speed. The controllers fully protect the motors against failure of supply and overloads, and press-buttons are provided both in the fan-flat and in the stokehold by which the motors can be instantaneously stopped. Apart from these special features the details of construction are of the type which are found in tramway controllers, accessibility of the resistances and working parts being a feature of design.

With the forced-draught fans and controller, on page 76, is a view, Fig. 187, showing the shipping of one of the funnels into the ship while lying in the Clydebank basin. This view indicates the great range of height of the powerful crane used—one of two at the dock—the other, of the hammer-head type, being on the further side of the basin, and just discernible to the extreme right of the engraving.

VENTILATION OF MACHINERY COMPARTMENTS.

With a vessel having machinery spaces of the huge dimensions of this liner, the problem of efficient ventilation becomes rather difficult, for

the following reasons :—The vessel's propelling engines, consisting as they do of turbines, are the cause of a very hot stratum of air at the lower platform or working level. In the case of a reciprocating-engine arrangement this is in a large measure obviated by the fact that the hottest parts of the machinery are situated at the level of an upper grating, and often conveniently situated for hot-air egress by the main-engine hatch. With reciprocating engines also a larger hatch is a necessity for the shipping of the engines, and hence what may be termed the main outlet for hot air in this particular case is much greater in proportion to the total volume of the machinery space than it is in the case of turbine installations. Again, as turbines occupy much less space in a vertical direction, this has resulted in the utilisation of additional accommodation at each side of the ship on the lower decks. This, of course, tends to the boxing-in of the wing compartments, and it is often difficult under these circumstances to avoid the formation of awkward air-pockets and hot corners. Moreover, with turbine machinery there is a long line of main steam-pipes extending athwart the vessel at the forward bulkhead and over the starting-platform, and unless efficient means are provided for promoting rapid displacement of the air and its frequent renewal, the convected heat effects become very noticeable and make working conditions unbearable.

Preliminary investigations were made with the object of ensuring adequate air changes, and it was first thought advisable to approach this from the point of view of nullifying the effect of the constant output of heat units from the various hot surfaces in the engine-room, lagged or otherwise. This was carefully gone into, and there were obtained the temperature gradients representing the flow of heat through the various thicknesses of lagging, as well as the working inside temperature and the desired outside temperature. On this basis it was possible approximately to estimate the amount of air required to carry off the superfluous heat.

It was decided that the plenum system should, in the main, be adopted—that is to say, the largest air volumes were dealt with by supply-fans, the exhaust being principally utilised for the removal of, and the better circulation of, air in the pockets, corners, and enclosed hot spaces below the level of the floor-plates. It has been usual in cases of machinery space ventilation on ship board to restrict the areas of the downcast trunking. This has, of course, been due to the unwillingness of owners to sacrifice space, but it was here recognised that for the obtaining of efficient working conditions, large

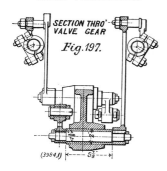

FIG. 192. KEITH BLACKMAN FAN FOR ENGINE-ROOM VENTILATION.

SECTION THRO'
VALVE GEAR
Fig. 197.

(3984J)

an exact replica of the machinery spaces, to a scale of ¼ in. to the foot. The interior of the model was fitted with electric heaters, capable of regulation by the introduction of suitable resistance, and representing the vessel's turbines. It was thus possible to fix the various initial temperature conditions, and then, by experiment, to obtain the number

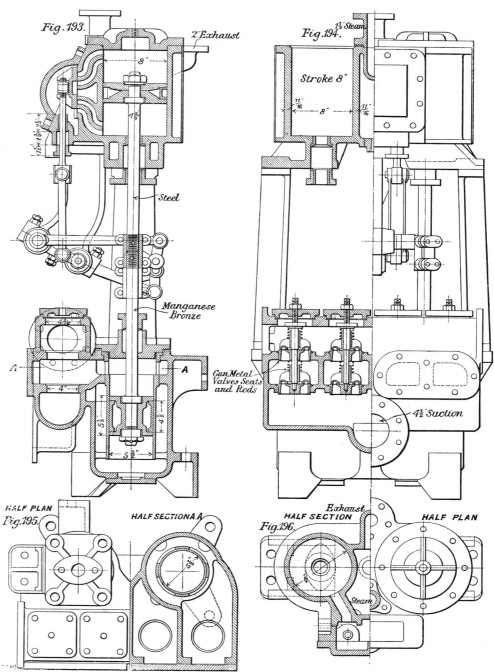

FIGS. 193 TO 197. LAMONT ASSISTANT BOILER FEED-PUMPS.

of air changes necessary to produce the desired temperature drop. A complete trunking installation, to scale, was fitted to the model, together with arrangements for obtaining air supply and exhaust, and their regulation. Time-tests were carried out for comparison of (1) plenum or all supply system; (2) all exhaust; (3) supply and exhaust; and results showed the superiority of the plenum system, which was in the main adopted, as already mentioned.

A further series of experiments was carried out for the purpose of determining the most suitable form of engine-hatch skylight, and here it may be mentioned that propeller-fans were placed so as to obtain a breeze corresponding to the ship's motion at 23 knots, the same being utilised as efficiently as possible both for supply and exhaust purposes. Again, the form of skylight was made dependent on its non-interference with hot-air outlets. It was found that with the ship in motion the current of air passing aft through panels of a cambered top produced a blanketing effect on the hot upcast. A flat top with torpedo exhaust ventilators suitably arranged thereon gave the best results in this

respect, as also in regard to its accelerating effect on the hot upcast. Experiment further suggested the advisability of fitting an adjustable flap opening at the aft-end top, and the utilising of the head wind or breeze above-mentioned for natural supply to one fan in the centre turbine-room.

The skylight being thus arranged for, an induced-draught system has proved very successful in practice. Temperature readings were taken by means of small specially-made thermometers, introduced at various parts of the model most representative of actual working spaces, as also in the hatch. During each experiment, light silk threads, attached to the bulb of each thermometer, indicated the presence and direction of the various air currents, while these currents and eddy formations were further studied by introducing smoke into the compartments of the model under various conditions of both supply and exhaust. The tendency of the air to form hot " stagnant " pockets was very clearly demonstrated, and leads to exhaust trunking were based to a large extent on the results obtained.

On pages 77 and 78 we illustrate the system of trunks adopted. Fig. 188 is a longitudinal section through a low-pressure turbine-room, and Fig. 189 a section through a wing turbine-room, while Figs. 190 and 191 are plans at the lower-deck and boat-deck levels respectively. In the low-pressure turbine-room the three open-type fans fitted required no trunking from the fan to the

cross sectional areas for trunking were an absolute necessity, unless much of the power required to produce the output was to be wasted on frictional water gauge. Again, the Cunard Company's experience with regard to previous ships had shown them the inadvisability of introducing tortuous leads for trunking, and the carrying of numerous branches from a single supply main basis of small dimensions. Trunking areas were thus calculated to ensure that the possible outputs of the fans under free discharge would be most nearly realised, and that the total static and frictional water gauge was kept at a minimum. The outlet air velocity was also, by this means, kept low, in no case exceeding much above 2000 ft. per minute, and the obtaining of large air volumes without unpleasant draught sensations was thus ensured.

With the object of more fully investigating the working conditions, a model of the machinery spaces in wood and glass was constructed at the Cunard Company's works, and experiments were continued by Mr. A. Galbraith, the Superintending Engineer of the Cunard Company. This model was point of discharge, and consequently an enormous amount of trunking of large dimensions was saved. Moreover, as the trunking would have had to be removed when the turbine casing and rotor were raised for overhauling purposes, there was further gain in this arrangement. The fans can be run at different speeds to suit the atmospheric conditions, and, in addition, dampers are fitted to the downcast trunks supplying the fans. The same figures show the method adopted for the condenser-room.

In the case of the wing turbine-rooms, shown in Fig. 189 and in the plan, Fig. 190, owing to the lack of head-room, the open type of fan could not be adopted, and consequently there had to be downcasts as well as upcasts.

Fig. 191 shows the arrangement, at boat-deck level, of the ventilators for the supply of air to the fans in the wing turbine-rooms and in the condenser-rooms. It will also be seen that a part of No. 4 funnel is used as the uptake, the inner funnel from No. 4 boiler-room being smaller than the others, owing to the less number of boilers in this stokehold.

The fan equipment—19 supply and exhaust fans of the Keith-Blackman type — has an aggregate capacity of 660,000 cub. ft. of air per minute. Of these, the greatest interest perhaps attaches to the open-type Keith fans, three of which (having 55 in. diameter inlets and a total output of 150,000 cub. ft. of air per minute) are installed in the centre turbine-room, on the system adopted on board the Lusitania with marked success. The arrangement of these open-type fans is shown in Fig. 192, page 79. The impellers, which are designed for efficient working without any surrounding casing, are keyed direct to the shafts of vertical-spindle Laurence-Scott motors, and the heavy angle-iron framework renders each unit self-contained and ready for bolting to the lower end of the fresh-air ducts brought down to the engine-rooms from the top deck. It was impossible to find room in the machinery spaces for distribution ducts of the sizes necessary to convey an adequate supply of cool air for maintaining a satisfactory temperature, and it was regarded as the characteristic advantage of these open-type fans that exceptionally large volumes of air could be distributed over a wide area without the use of any branch ducts, and at a comparatively low expenditure of power for the effective work done. It has also been found that the cooling effect is obtained with an absence of objectionable draughts.

For the wing turbine-rooms, the condenser rooms, and the turbo-dynamo rooms, the fresh air is supplied by two 45-in. and four 35-in. fans of the cased type, fitted with dust-proof motors by the Electromotor Company. For exhausting the heated air from various points in these machinery spaces, ten Keith fans are employed, with a combined capacity of 270,000 cub. ft. of air per minute, these being of the cased type also, and combined with semi-enclosed motors. For assisting the ventilation of the stokeholds, seven motor-driven Keith fans of smaller size are in use.

During the trials of the ship the writer made careful observation of the temperature in the various boiler and machinery spaces, and the result was thoroughly satisfactory. The coolness experienced was most exceptional, and showed that the Cunard Company had acted wisely in undertaking the experiments, that Mr. Galbraith had made sound deductions, and that Messrs. John Brown and Co., Limited, had carried out his proposals efficiently.

CONCLUSION.

In concluding our account of the Aquitania we desire to acknowledge our indebtedness to the Cunard Company, and especially to the chairman, Mr. A. A. Booth, and to Messrs. John Brown and Co., Limited, Clydebank, and notably to Mr. Thomas Bell, the chief of the Clydebank establishment, for permission to illustrate the important features of the vessel. To the technical officers on their respective staffs, and particularly Mr. W. J. Luke, naval director, and Commander Wood, engineering manager of the builder's firm, and Mr. L. Peskitt, the naval architect, Mr. A. Galbraith, the engineering superintendent, and Mr. John Currie, of the Cunard Line, we wish also to express thanks for the assistance given in conducting the writer over the ship on many occasions during the progress of the construction of the vessel and her machinery.

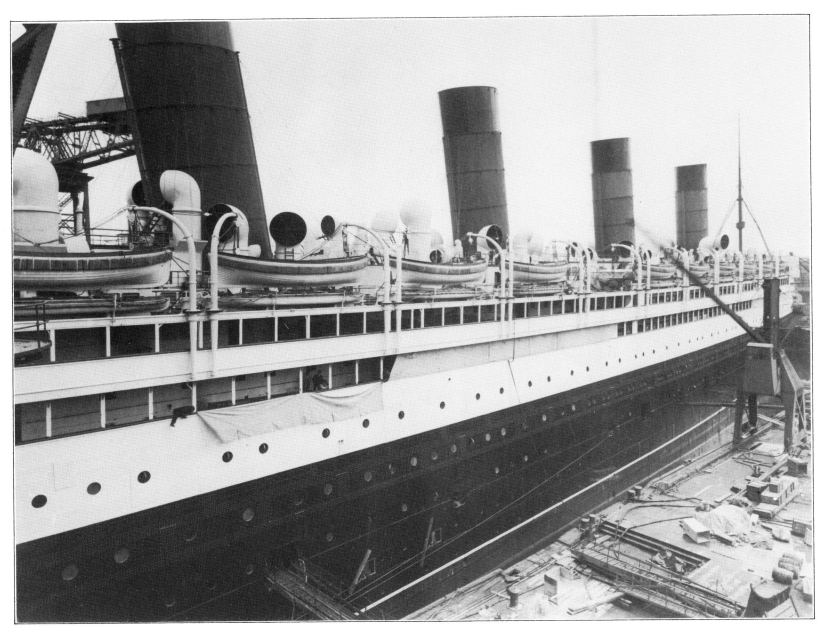

FIG. 198. TOP SIDES STARBOARD.

THE WORKS OF THE BUILDERS.

FROM what we have said in the preceding pages, it will be readily accepted that the shipbuilding works of Messrs. John Brown and Co., Limited, are equipped for the greatest and best of ships, but it may render this book more complete if some brief reference is made to the establishment at Clydebank, and also to the other works of the Company, where a great part of the constructive material for ships and machinery is produced.

The Clydebank Works had their origin in a small factory within the city of Glasgow in 1846, and the present establishment, about seven miles from Glasgow, was first laid out in 1873. In recent years, however, there have been enormous developments, so that the establishment now covers over

realised by the fact that their machinery collectively represents about 250,000 horse-power. Of lighter cruisers a large fleet has been constructed, while the firm have been particularly successful with their torpedo-boat destroyers, having been amongst the first British firms to take up the manufacture of this type.

As regards merchantmen, some reference has already been made on page 1 to the work done at Clydebank, but there consideration was given only to the Atlantic liners completed. In other craft equally pronounced success has been achieved. The firm have taken a high place among the constructors of fast Channel mail steamers. Thus we find that on the Fishguard and Rosslare service of

To achieve this there are at Clydebank shops for all classes of work, and, as can be understood from our description of the Aquitania, the wood-working department, the copper smithy, the sheet-iron department, the plumbing department, and the electrical department are equally prominent with the various steel and iron-workers' shops, turbine and boiler shops, &c. Dominating the whole factory is the spirit of enterprise and of experimental research, associated with a determination to ensure that the results attained by the vessels in service will be thoroughly efficient from every standpoint. Thus, the Company have not only an experimental tank for the testing of models, with a view to arriving at the best form from the point of view of propulsive efficiency, but they have a large experimental turbine station, so that guaranteed results may be realised with as great precision as is possible within the limits of human error.

THE ATLAS WORKS.

Equally important with the shipbuilding and marine engineering works are the Atlas Works at Sheffield, where, as we have said, much of the material of construction for warships and liners is produced; notably, the armour, gun-forgings, and the forgings for turbine machinery for warships, and the forgings, of various kinds, for the propelling machinery of merchantmen. Some remarks regarding the Sheffield Works of the Company are therefore necessary. These works were established in 1857, and now cover an area of over forty acres in the east end of the city of Sheffield. The history of this important establishment also is already well known, and has been frequently published, and it would occupy too much space to recount it in detail; but, in view of the wonderful strides the turbine, as a means for propelling ships, has made, it is interesting to notice the position occupied by Messrs. John Brown and Co., in its exploitation. Realising the importance of this growing industry, they early installed a patent rolling mill for producing hollow cylindrical bodies in steel, such as rotor drums, &c. On this page is an illustration of this hollow rolling mill.

By this process the ingots, as cast, are first punched vertically in a 3000-ton hydraulic press; they are then drawn longitudinally to the desired length by a powerful horizontal hydraulic press. The ends are then machined to remove the waste portions. The next operation consists of rolling the annular piece. For this the works arranged the powerful rolling mill illustrated; it is actuated by a 12,000 horse-power steam engine. This comprises two principal rolls placed horizontally the one above the other and parallel. The lower roll is worked directly by the engine by means of a shaft with a Cardan joint. The upper roll is worked by the principal shaft by means of gears and a coupling which can work freely when the speed of the two rolls ceases to be proportionate, in consequence of the reduction in the thickness of the metal. The axis of the upper roll remains always in the same position, or changes only within the smallest limits. The position of the lower roll, on the contrary, can be changed with regard to that of the upper roll in such a manner as to give the pressure desired to the rolling at all thicknesses; the variations are obtained by means of two identical vertical screws which act on the support of the lower roll, and are themselves actuated by toothed pinions worked by hydraulic pistons. The turbine drum is rolled between the two rolls, and meanwhile is guided by four roller bearings turning freely. The position of these latter can be modified with regard to the

Hollow Rolling Mill for Turbine Rotor Drums at the Atlas Works.

eighty acres and gives employment to 9000 workmen, while the output of tonnage per annum has reached a total of over 80,000 tons, and the horse-power of machinery manufactured an aggregate of 239,000 horse-power; these figures apply to the year 1913.

A long list of battleships have emanated from the Clydebank Works, and to name some of these suffices to prove that the establishment has taken a prominent place in the development of the present day warship. Among the best known of the battleships built are H.M.S. Ramillies, H.M.S. Hindustan, the Japanese battleship Asahi, and H.M.S. Inflexible, the first of the Dreadnought cruisers; while at the present time they have on hand simultaneously the battleship Barham and the battle-cruiser Tiger, both unexcelled in size in their respective classes. As regards cruisers, the list is even more numerous, and includes a number of armoured ships, culminating in the battle-cruisers Inflexible, Australia and Tiger, while the machinery for the Queen Mary was completed by the firm. The importance of these four British ships will be

the Great Western Railway Company, three of the four vessels in service were constructed by Messrs. John Brown and Co., while all of the five vessels on the Harwich and Hook of Holland route were built by them. All of these vessels are propelled by turbines, and are notable, not only for their speed, but for their great regularity on the passage. The Channel Islands service has also many ships representative of Clydebank design and workmanship; indeed, it would be difficult to name a service where the influence of the Clydebank establishment, in design and workmanship, has not been experienced. In practically all the seven seas the Clydebank ships take a prominent place, and the firm have at present in hand an Orient liner (the third built by the firm within recent years) which promises to be of unusual interest, as the vessel will be the first on this service to have geared turbines.

As to the various departments of the works, the only remark which need be made is that, practically in every respect, every type of merchantman and warship can be completed within the establishment.

VIEW OF A TURBINE ROTOR DRUM AFTER BEING ROLLED.

ARMOUR PLATE ROLLING MILL AT THE ATLAS WORKS.

6000-Ton Forging Press at the Atlas Works.

lower roll. The upper roll can be withdrawn horizontally, so as to allow the annular piece to be inserted in position on the lower roll. This machine has rolled in twenty-six minutes perfectly cylindrical drums of a uniform thickness, having a diameter of 12 ft., the ingot originally being of about 24 tons. It can roll drums up to 15 ft. diameter, 10 ft. in length, and weighing 30 tons.

The work so produced has not only an exceedingly beautiful finish, but the fact of the material being punched, then drawn in the direction of its length, and subsequently rolled in a transverse direction, gives unusually good physical results. It will also be observed that since the work put on the material by the action of rolling is in the direction of the circumference of the cylinders, the material obtains special advantages, as the strains it has to carry are in the direction in which most beneficial work has been given to it. On page 82 is a view of a finished drum. The figure of the man alongside will give some idea of the magnitude of the article produced.

Owing to the superiority of the process, it has superseded the previous method of producing these drums by means of hollow forging, except when special design necessitates this process still being adhered to. Messrs. John Brown and Co., Limited, have already been entrusted with most of the turbine-drums, &c., required for the various vessels built and now building in Great Britain. In the past they have supplied drums for the Cunard liners Carmania and Lusitania, so well known to all engineers. They have also supplied turbine-drums, &c., for H.M. ships :—

Barham	Inflexible
Emperor of India	Invincible
King George V	Comus
Thunderer	Calliope
Colossus	Bristol
Temeraire	Yarmouth
Dreadnought	Southampton
Tiger	Nottingham
Queen Mary	Chatham
Australia	&c. &c.

In addition they have produced the drums for over 50 torpedo-boat destroyers for the British Government, and for many Foreign Government vessels of all classes, as well as for a great number of turbine vessels for the mercantile marine.

To meet the ever-increasing demands for turbine forgings, considerable extensions have been made in the machinery plant at the Atlas Works, including large turning and boring lathes, and special machinery for dealing with a new type of turbine wheel. Recently the firm installed a turning lathe of exceptional size, and weighing 270 tons, specially designed to deal with the large forgings already named.

The manufacture of turbine drums is, however, by no means the only industry of the Atlas Works. The reputation which this firm enjoys as manufacturers of armour plate dates long anterior to the manufacture of turbine parts, and its position with the various admiralties of the world is well established.

On page 82 is a view of the new armour-plate mill recently installed at the Atlas Works. It is reputed to be amongst the finest in the world The armour plates are produced by the firm for the British Government, and from time to time for nearly all the navies of the world.

Forgings are also made at this establishment from the smallest to the largest dimensions, and on page 83 is an illustration of the new 6000-ton forging press, with intensifier driving power, which has been erected in a large new forge, the whole shop area being traversed by two 200 ton cranes. This plant has proved a very satisfactory addition to the firm's producing power.

The firm is also largely engaged in the manufacture of railway material, being the first practical makers of steel rails, and they still enjoy an unexcelled reputation in the railway world for axles, tyres, springs, buffers, castings and the like. The collieries of the Company—namely, Aldwarke Main, Rotherham Main and Dalton Main—are among the largest and best equipped in the country, and employ upwards of 15,000 hands.

The above, together with the firm's interests in various allied companies, notably Thomas Firth and Sons, Limited, Harland and Wolff, Limited, the Coventry Ordnance Works, and others, constitute it one of the largest employers of labour in the world. The firm is alike strong in the industries of peace and war.

FIG. 199. PORT SIDE FORWARD.

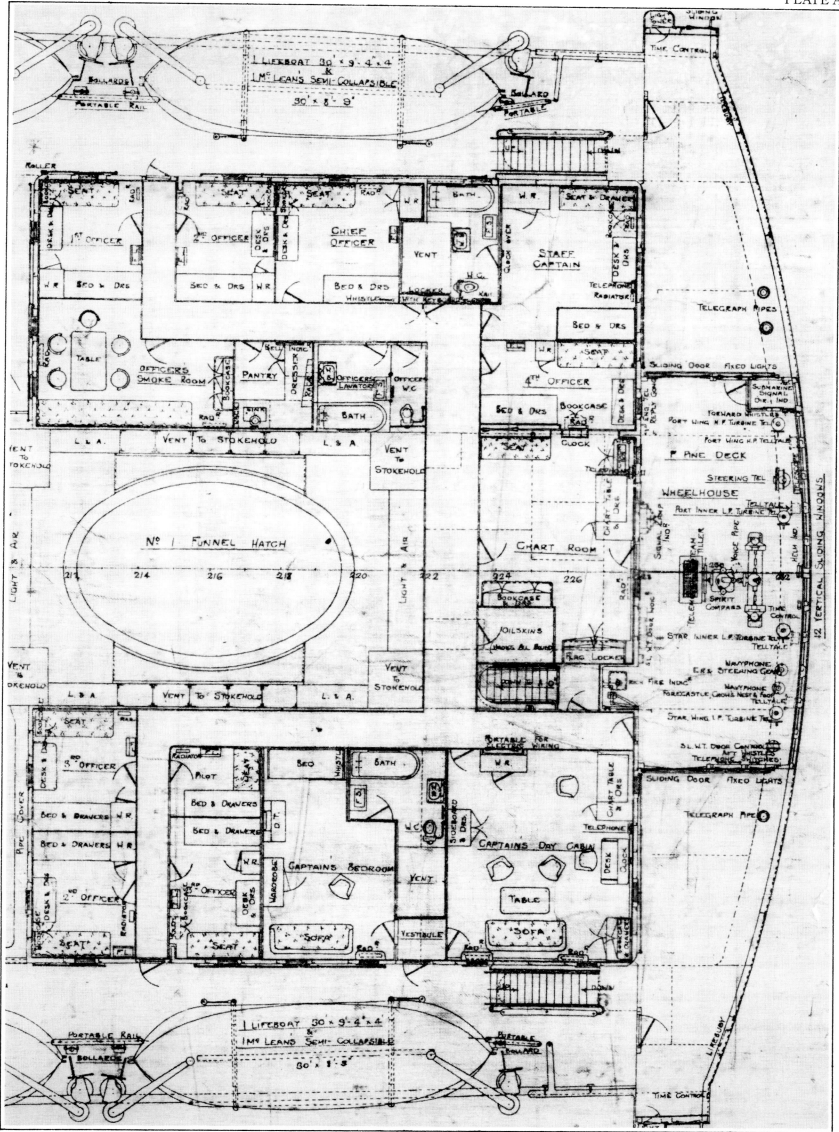

PLAN OF NAVIGATING BRIDGE — WHEELHOUSE AND OFFICERS' QUARTERS
SCALE: ⅛″ = 1 FOOT
CROWN COPYRIGHT.

PLATE I.

D LINER "AQUITANIA" BEFORE THE LAUNCH.

D CO., LIMITED, SHEFFIELD AND CLYDEBANK.

see Page 4.)

Fig.50.

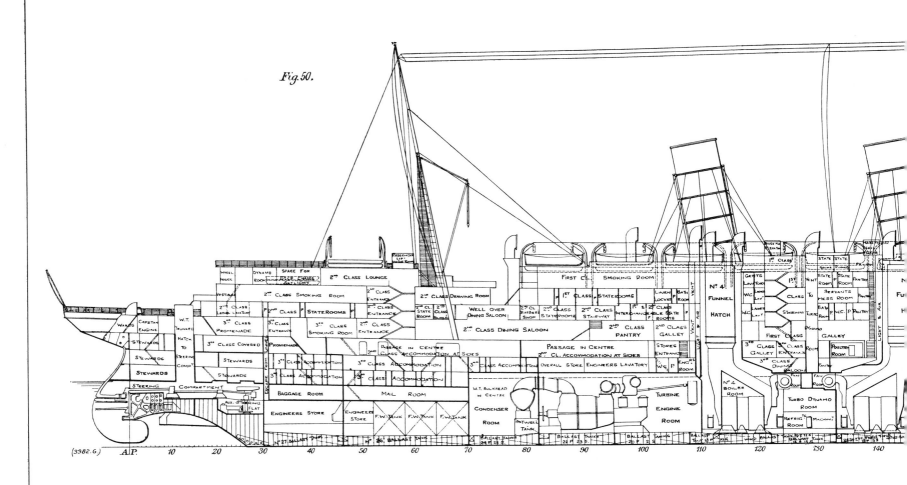

Fig.51. "H" DECK

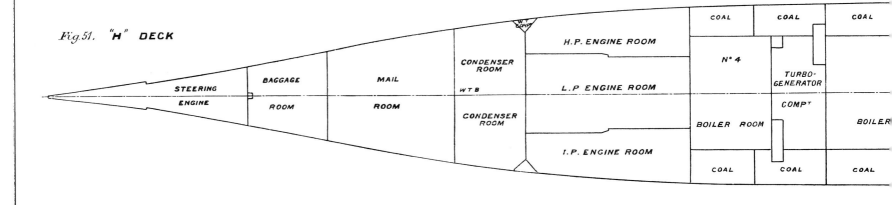

Fig.52. HOLD PLAN.

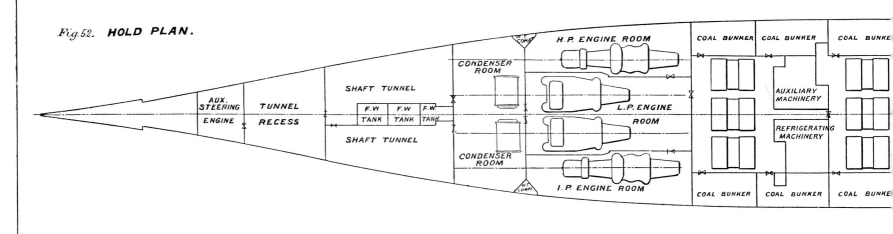

PLATE II.

QUITANIA;" LONGITUDINAL SECTION AND HOLD PLANS.

., LIMITED, SHEFFIELD AND CLYDEBANK.

es 11 *and* 25.)

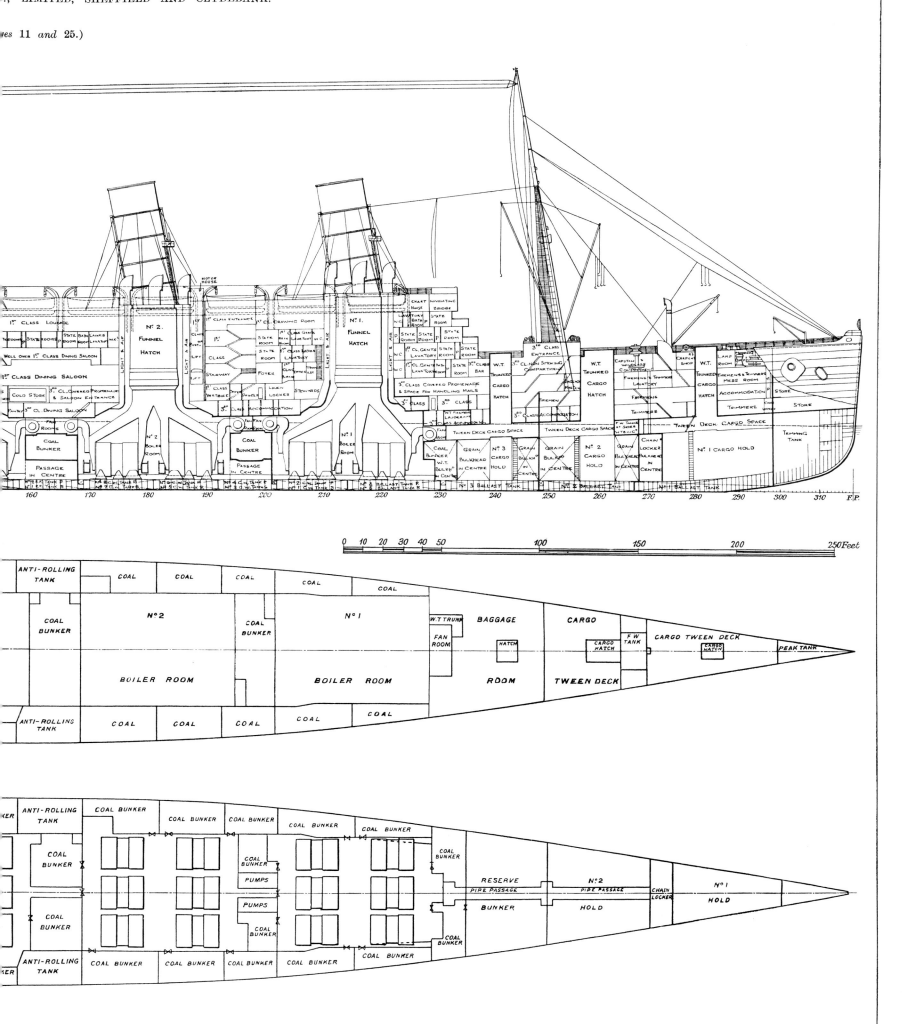

Fig. 53.

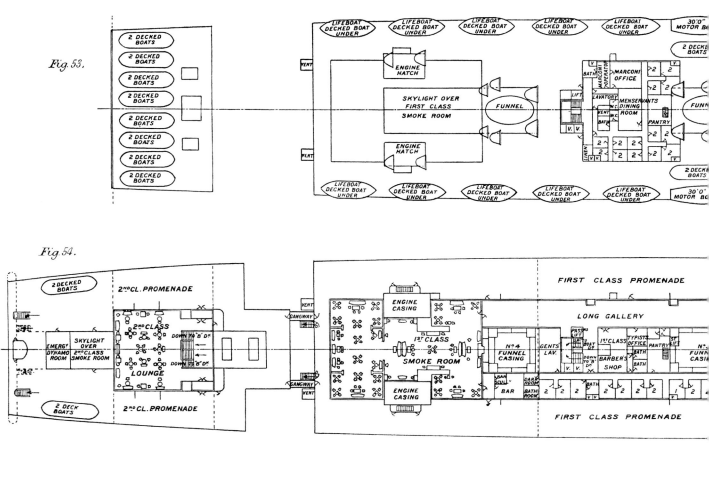

Fig. 54.

Fig. 55.

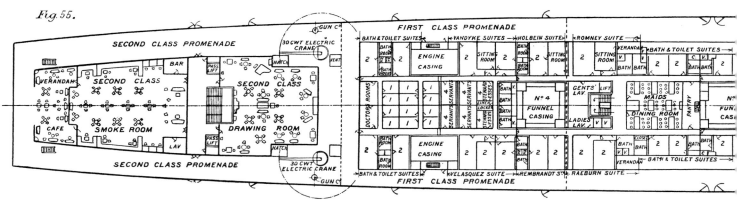

Fig. 56.

SHELTER DECK "C"

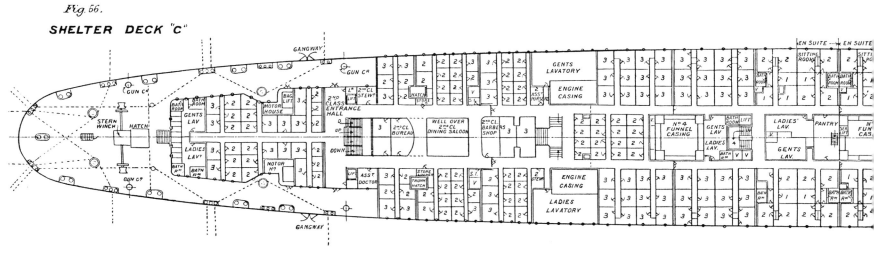

PLATE III

NARD LINER "AQUITANIA;" DECK PLANS.

D., LIMITED, SHEFFIELD AND CLYDEBANK.

Page 25.)

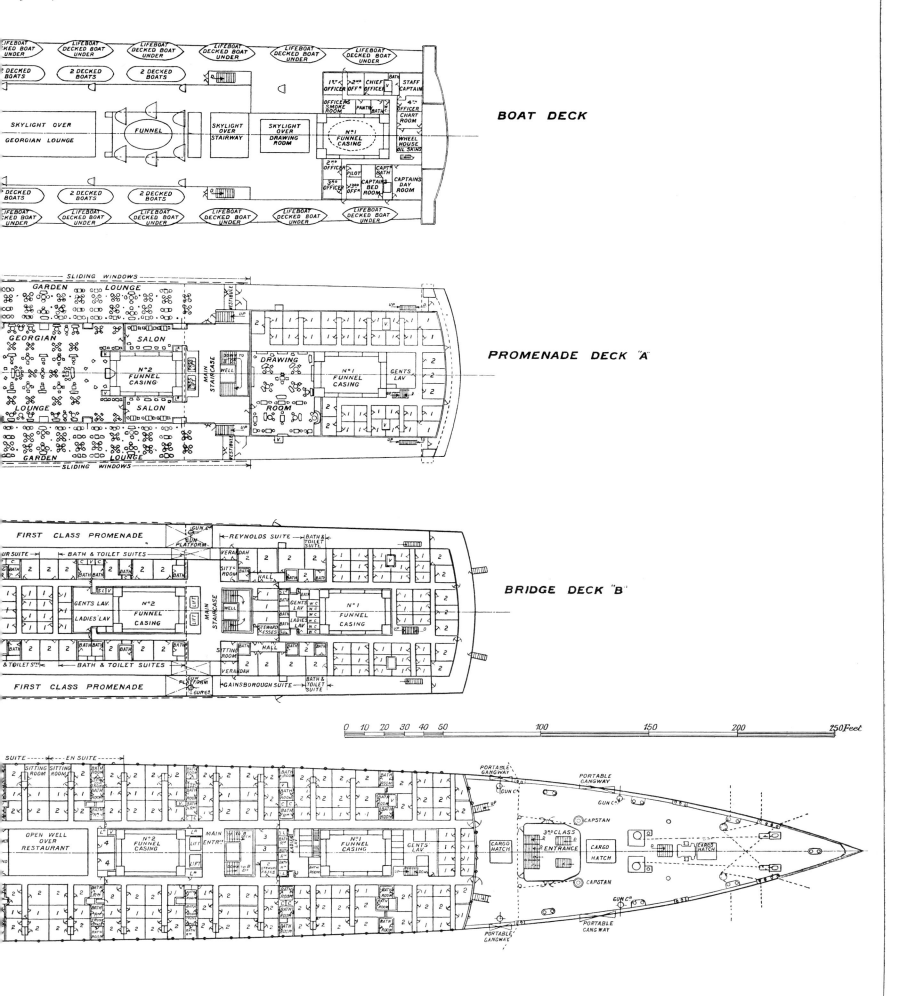

BOAT DECK

PROMENADE DECK "A"

BRIDGE DECK "B"

0 10 20 30 40 50   100   150   200   250 Feet

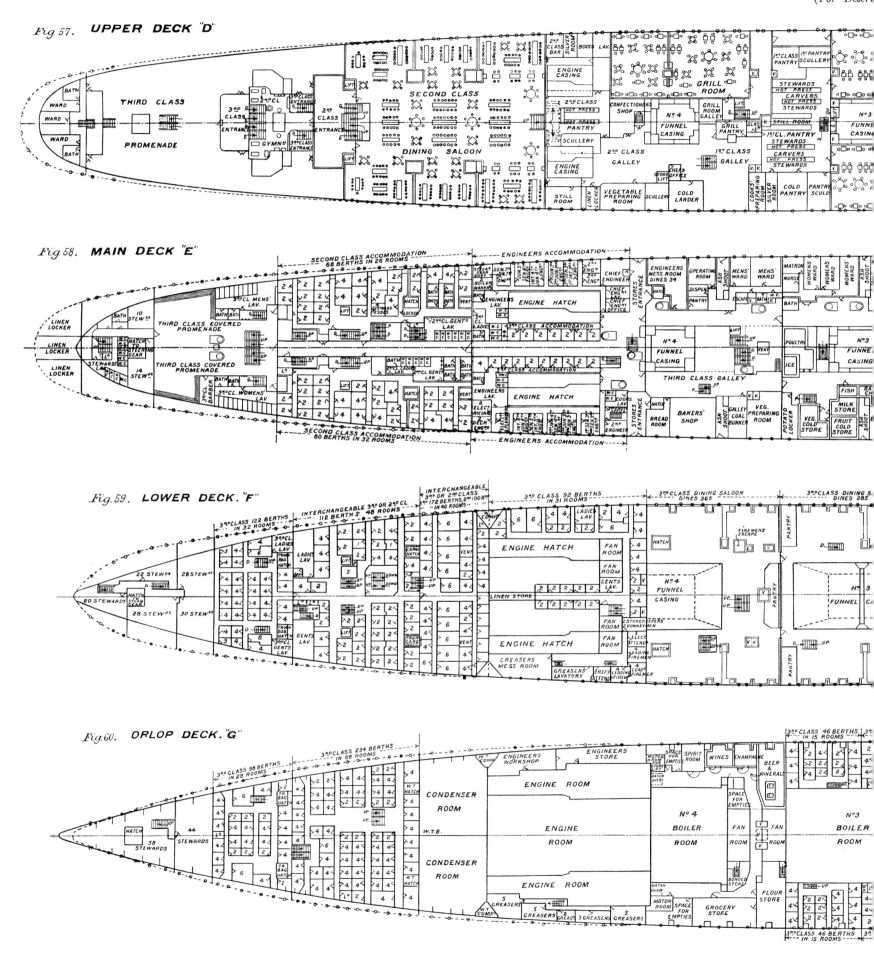

Fig. 57. UPPER DECK "D"

Fig. 58. MAIN DECK "E"

Fig. 59. LOWER DECK "F"

Fig. 60. ORLOP DECK "G"

PLATE IV.

NARD LINER "AQUITANIA;" DECK PLANS.

, LIMITED, SHEFFIELD AND CLYDEBANK.

Page 25.)

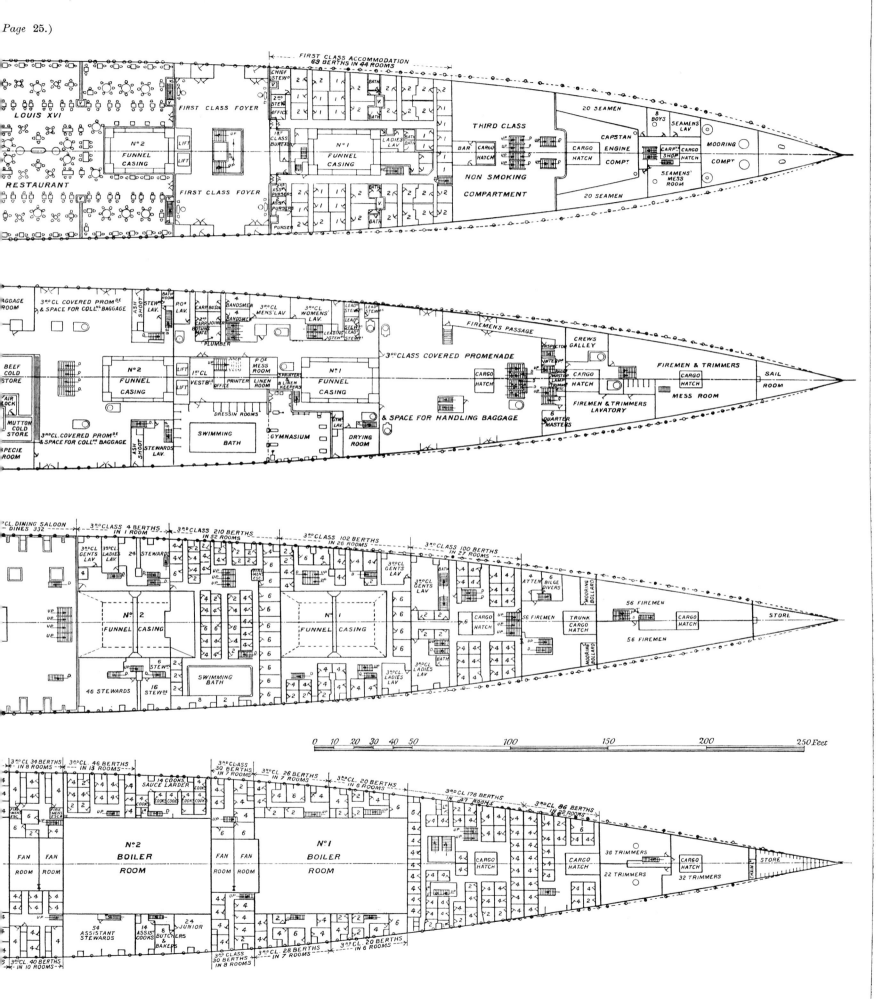

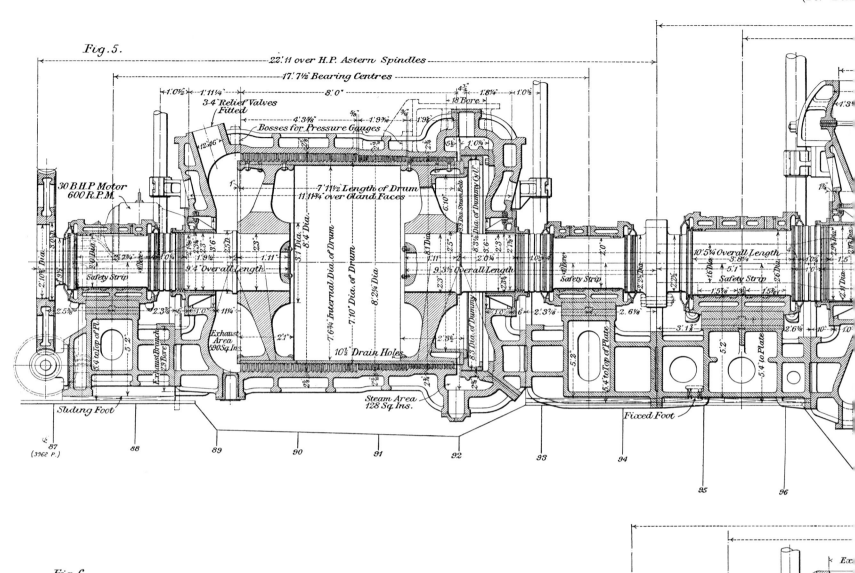

Fig. 5.

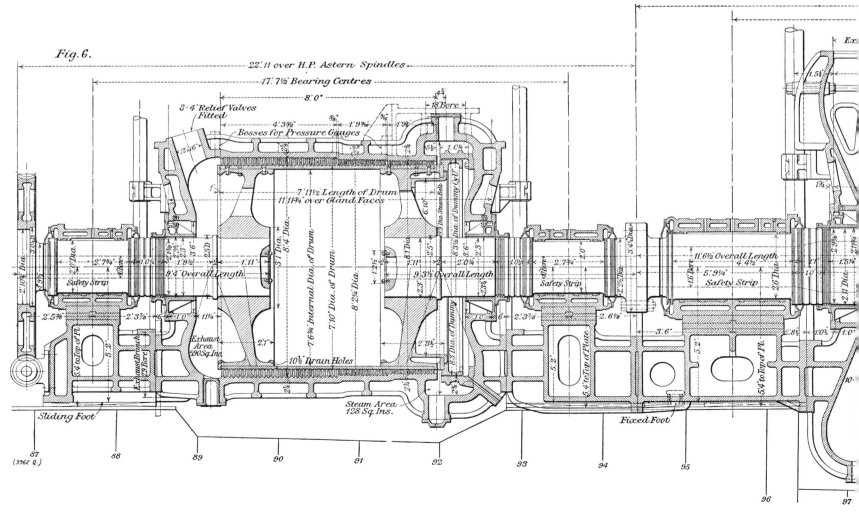

Fig. 6.

PLATE V

PRESSURE AHEAD TURBINES, AND HIGH-PRESSURE ASTERN TURBINES.

LIMITED, SHEFFIELD AND CLYDEBANK.

Page 46.)

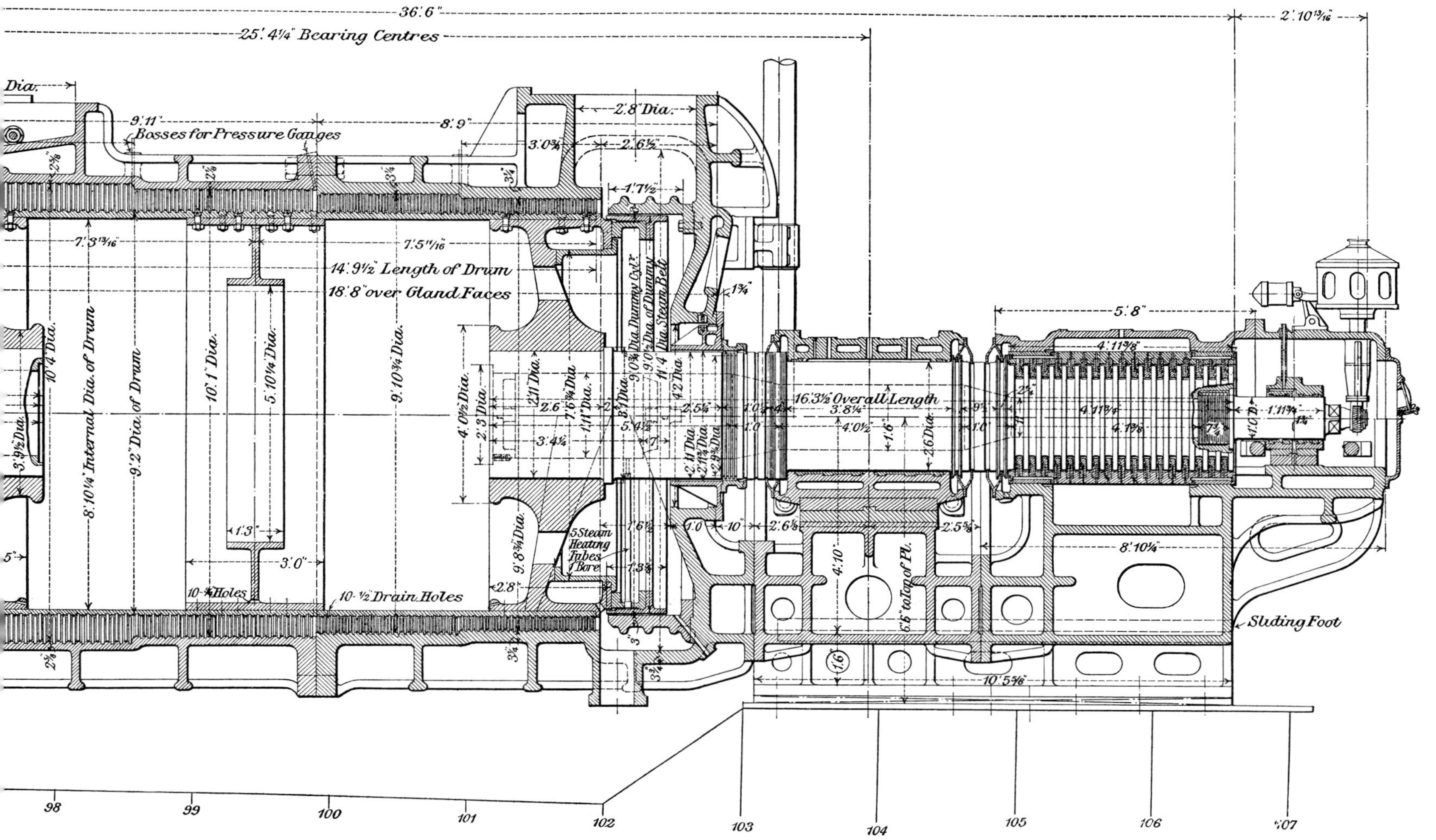

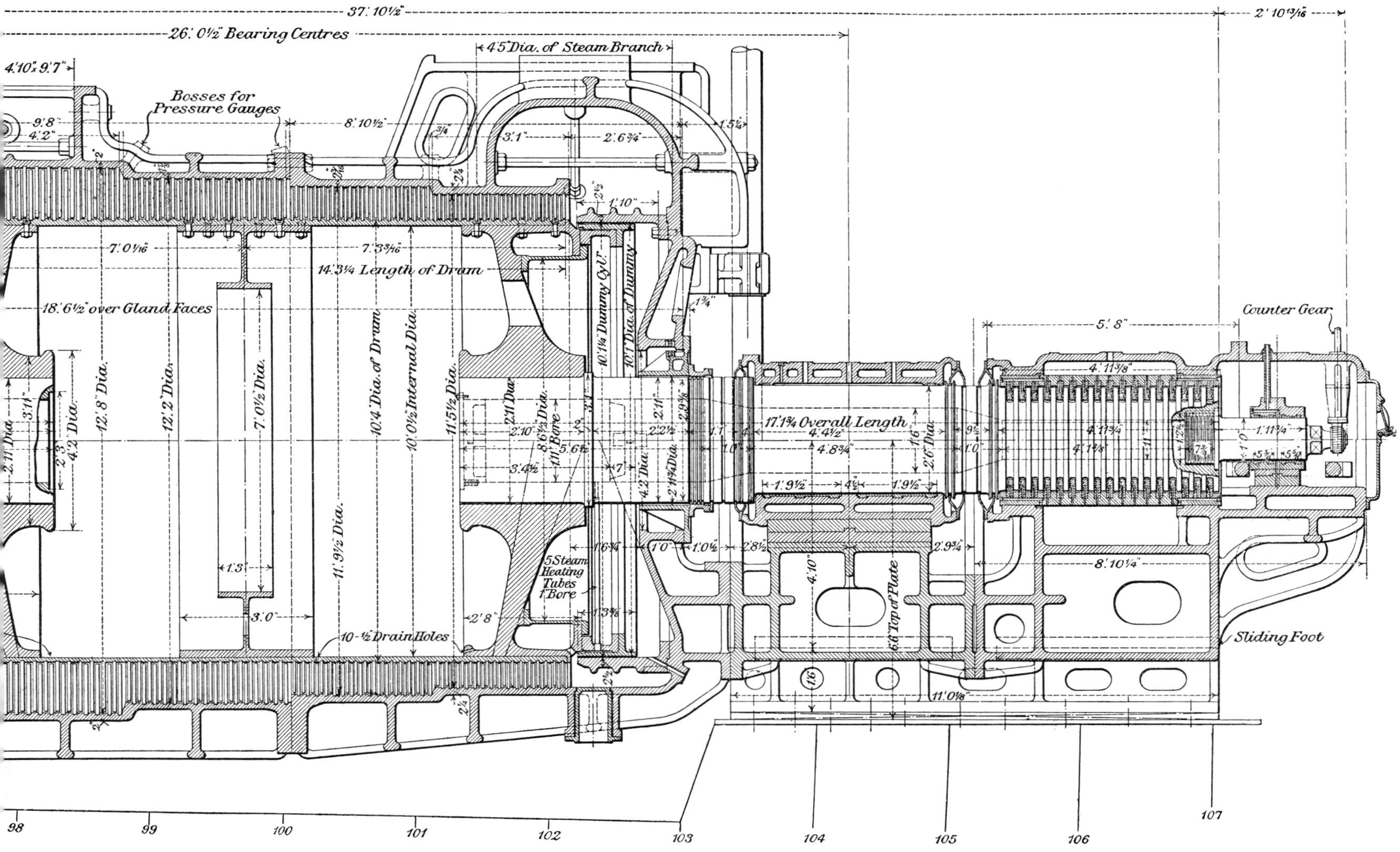

Top figure:

36'.6"

25'.4¼" Bearing Centres

2'.10¾₆"

Dia.

9'.11"
Bosses for Pressure Gauges

8'.9"

2'.8" Dia.

3'.0¾"

2'.6½"

4'.7½"

7'.3¹³⁄₁₆"

7'.5"⁄₁₆"

14'.9½" Length of Drum
18'.8" over Gland Faces

1¾"

5'.8"

10'.4" Dia.

8'.10¼" Internal Dia. of Drum

9'.2" Dia. of Drum

10'.1" Dia.

5'.10¼" Dia.

9'.10¾" Dia.

4'.0½" Dia.

2'.3" Dia.

4'.11⅞"

16'.3½" Overall Length
3'.8¾"
4'.0½"

4'.11¾"
4'.1⅞"

2'.6" Dia.

3'.9¾" Dia.

1'.3"

3'.0"

5 Steam
Heating
Tubes
1 Bore

2'.8"

9'.8¾"Dia.

10-¾ Holes

10'.½" Drain Holes

8'.10¼"

Sliding Foot

6'.6" to Top of Ft.

10'.5¾₆"

98   99   100   101   102   103   104   105   106   107

Bottom figure:

37'.10½"

26'.0½" Bearing Centres

4'.5" Dia. of Steam Branch

2'.10¾₆"

4'.10½" 9'.7"

Bosses for
Pressure Gauges

8'.10½"

3'.1"

2'.6¾"

1'.5½"

9'.8"
4'.2"

1'.10"

1¾"

7'.0¹⁄₁₆"

7'.3³⁄₁₆"

14'.3¼" Length of Drum

18'.6½" over Gland Faces

12'.8" Dia.

12'.2" Dia.

7'.0½" Dia.

10'.4" Dia. of Drum

10'.0½" Internal Dia.

11'.5½" Dia.

4'.11⅞"

5'.8"

Counter Gear

2'.11" Dia.
4'.2" Dia.

8'.6½" Dia.

17'.1¾" Overall Length
4'.4½"
4'.8¾"

4'.11¾"
4'.1¼"

2'.6" Dia.

1'.3"

11'.9½" Dia.

2'.8"

5 Steam
Heating
Tubes
1 Bore

3'.0"

10-½ Drain Holes

8'.10¼"

Sliding Foot

6'.6" Top of Plate

1'.9½"   1'.9½"

2'.9¾"

11'.0¼"

4'.10"

98   99   100   101   102   103   104   105   106   107

Fig. 7.

Fig. 8. SECTION ON CENTRE LINE

Fig. 9.

Fig. 10. AFT END LOOKING FORWARD — SECTION THRO' A.A. LOOKING FORWARD

Fig. 11. SECTION THRO' C.C. LOOKING AFT — FORWARD END LOOKING AFT

Fig. 12.

Fig. 13. SEC. THRO' B.B. LOOK'G FOR

Fig. 14. FORE & AFT SEC. THRO' D.D.

PLATE VI.

AND ASTERN TURBINES, WITH DETAILS OF THRUST-BLOCK.

O., LIMITED, SHEFFIELD AND CLYDEBANK.

Page 46.)

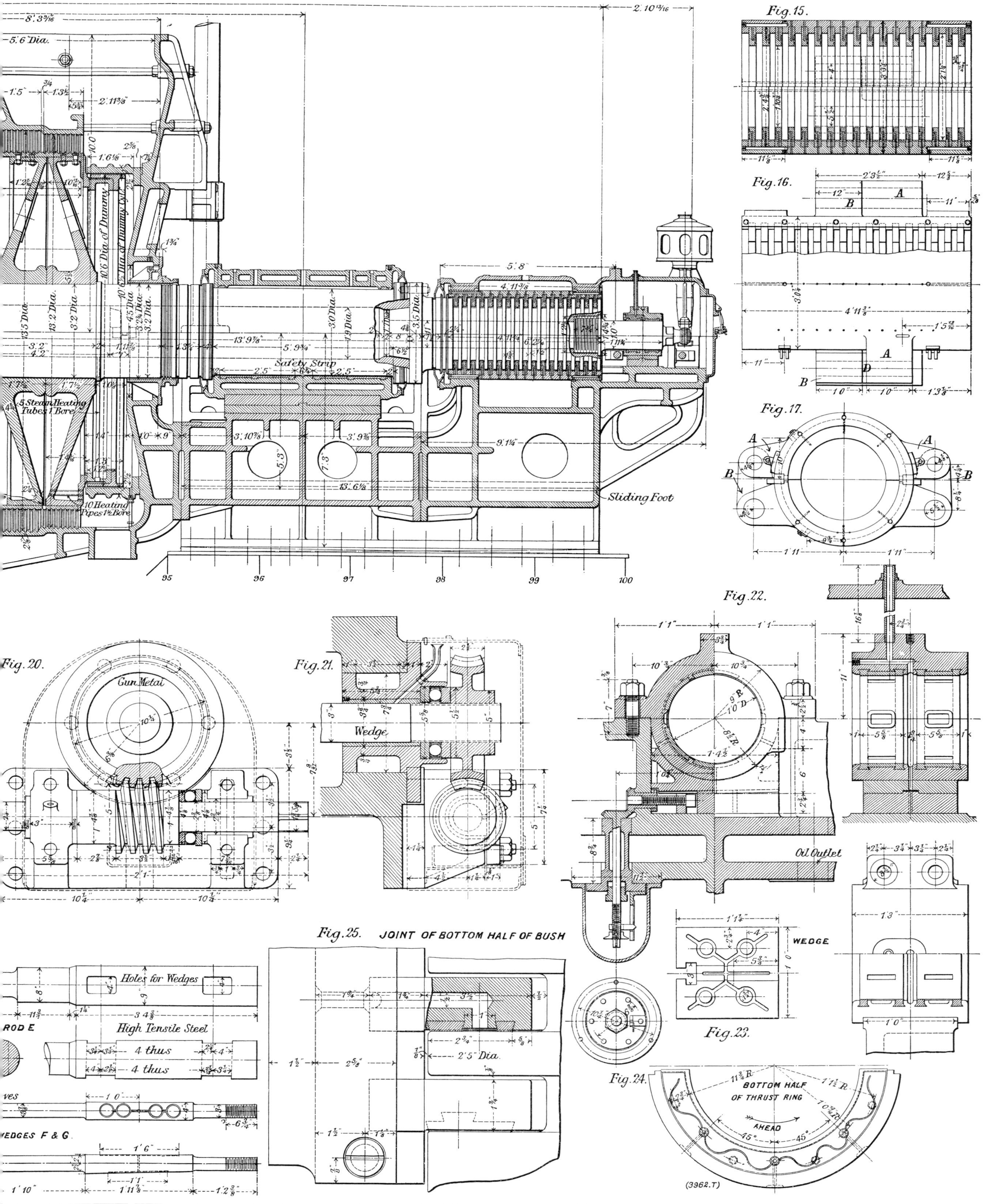

Fig.15.

Fig.16.

Fig.17.

Fig.20.

Gun Metal

Fig.21.

Wedge

Fig.22.

Oil Outlet

WEDGE

Fig.23.

Fig.24.

BOTTOM HALF
OF THRUST RING

AHEAD

Fig.25. JOINT OF BOTTOM HALF OF BUSH

Holes for Wedges

ROD E

High Tensile Steel

4 thus

4 thus

WEDGES F & G.

Safety Strip

Sliding Foot

Steam Heating
Tubes 1 Bore

Heating
Pipes 1½ Bore

(3962.T)

PLATE IX.

THE CUNARD LINER "AQUITANIA;" STEAM-VALVES FOR THE MANŒUVRING OF THE SHIP.

CONSTRUCTED BY MESSRS. JOHN BROWN AND CO., LIMITED, SHEFFIELD AND CLYDEBANK.

(For Description, see Page 65.)

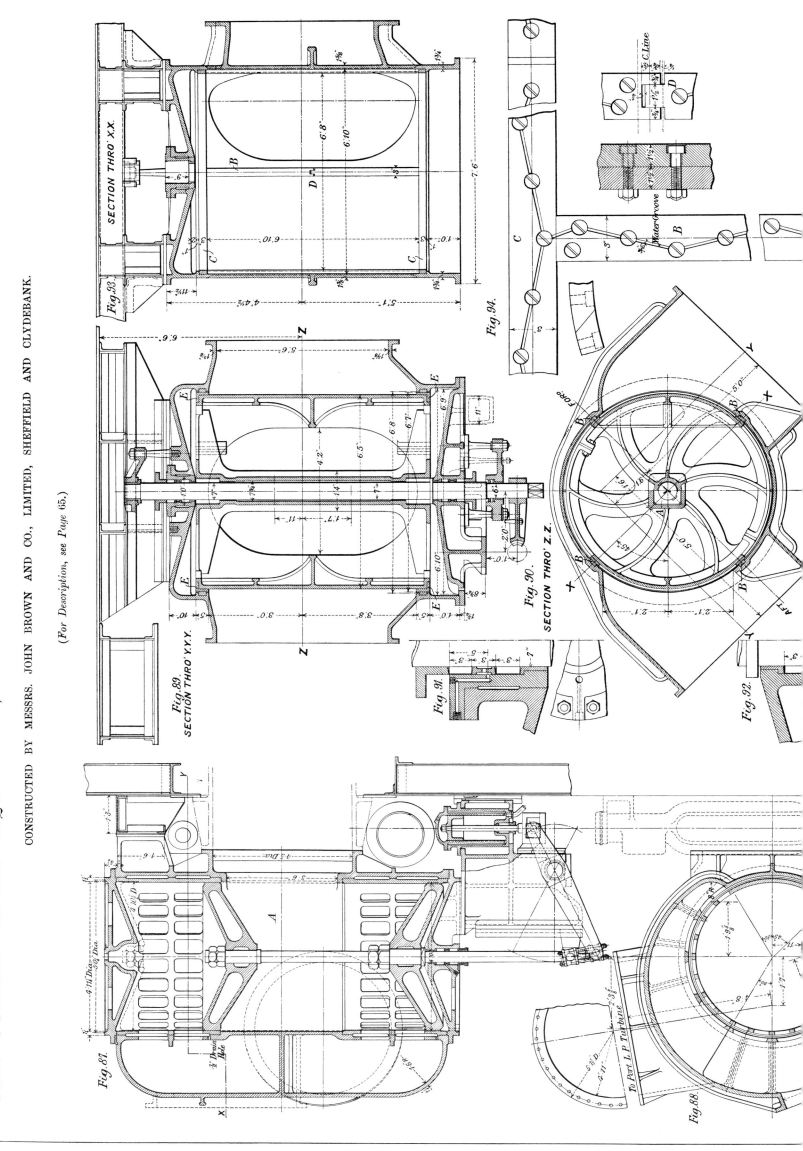

Fig. 87.

Fig. 88.

Fig. 89. SECTION THRO' Y.Y.Y.

Fig. 90. SECTION THRO' Z.Z.

Fig. 91.

Fig. 92.

Fig. 93. SECTION THRO' X.X.

Fig. 94.

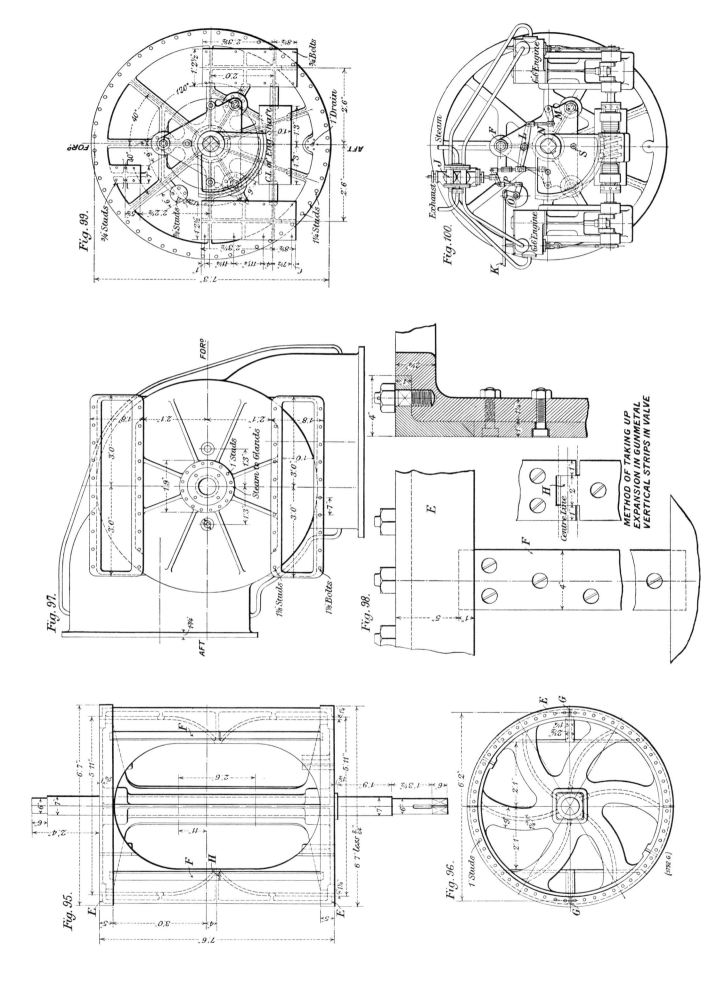

SECTION AT X.Y.

Figs. 87 and 88. The Change-Valve.

Figs. 89 to 94. The Shut-Off Valve between the Intermediate and Low-Pressure Turbines.

Fig. 99.

Fig. 100.

Fig. 97.

Fig. 98.

METHOD OF TAKING UP
EXPANSION IN GUNMETAL
VERTICAL STRIPS IN VALVE

Fig. 95.

Fig. 96.

Figs. 95 to 100. Details of Shut-Off Valve between the Intermediate and Low-Pressure Turbines, and the Actuating Gear.

PLATE X.

THE CUNARD LINER "AQUITANIA;" STARTING-PLATFORM AND VALVE-INTERLOCKING GEAR.

CONSTRUCTED BY MESSRS. JOHN BROWN AND CO., LIMITED, SHEFFIELD AND CLYDEBANK.

(For Description, see Page 65.)

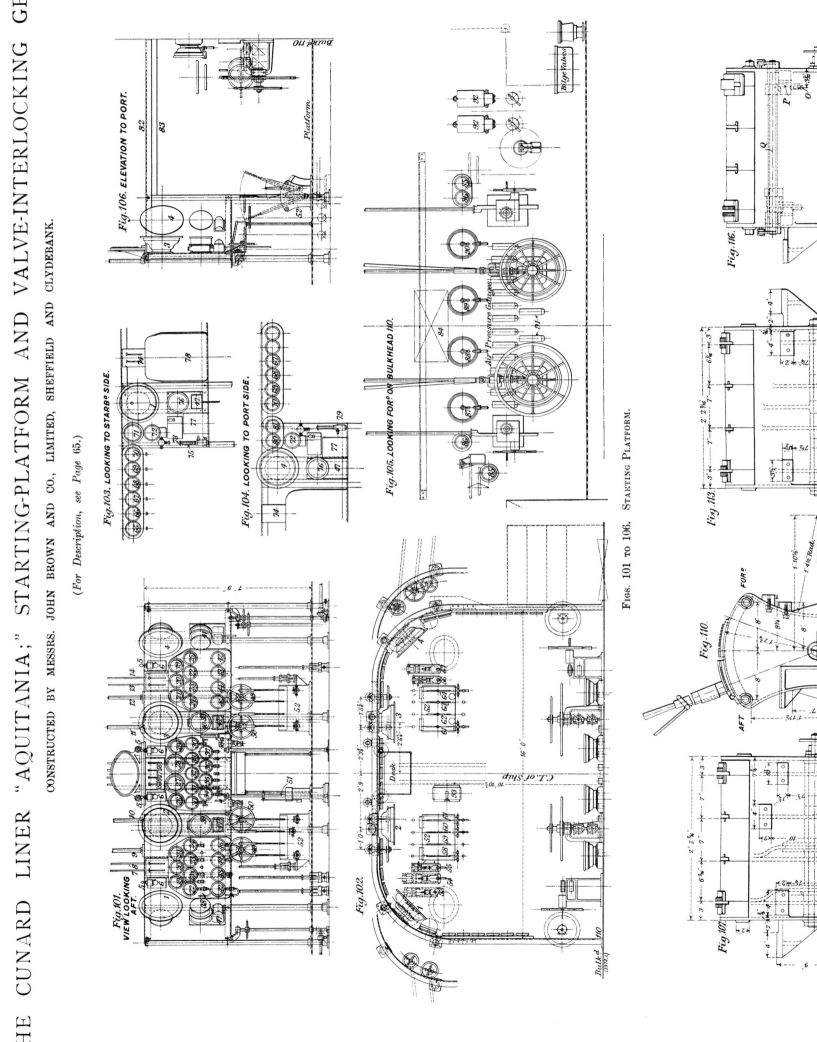

Fig. 106. ELEVATION TO PORT.

Fig. 103. LOOKING TO STARB? SIDE.

Fig. 104. LOOKING TO PORT SIDE.

Fig. 105, LOOKING FOR? ON BULKHEAD 110.

Fig. 101. VIEW LOOKING AFT.

Fig. 102.

Fig. 116.

Fig. 117.

Fig. 113.

Fig. 114.

Fig. 110.

Fig. 111.

Fig. 107.

Fig. 108.

FIGS. 101 TO 106. STARTING PLATFORM.

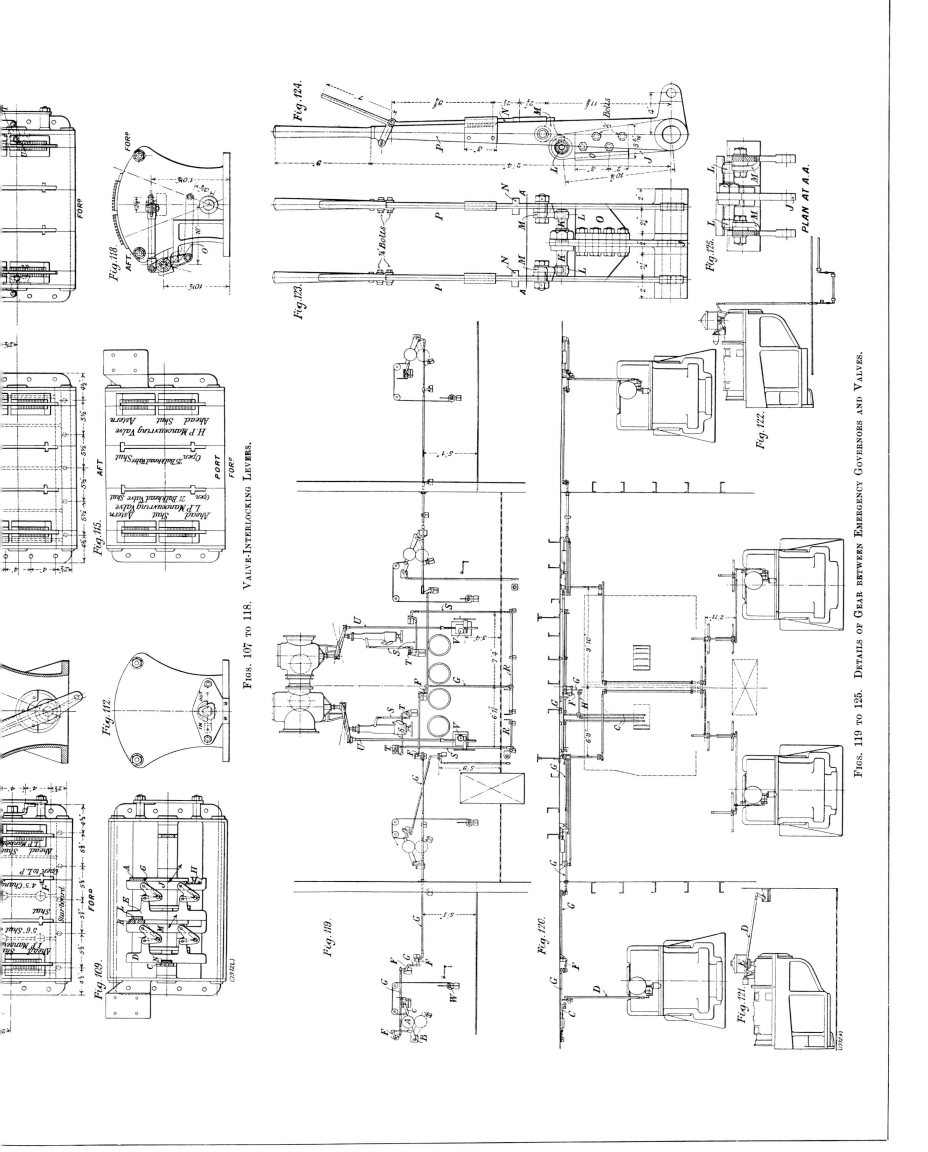

FIGS. 107 TO 118. VALVE-INTERLOCKING LEVERS.

FIGS. 119 TO 125. DETAILS OF GEAR BETWEEN EMERGENCY GOVERNORS AND VALVES.

PLATE XI.

THE CUNARD LINER "AQUITANIA;" WEIR'S "UNIFLUX" CONDENSERS.

CONSTRUCTED BY MESSRS. JOHN BROWN AND CO., LIMITED, SHEFFIELD AND CLYDEBANK.

(For Description, see Page 69.)

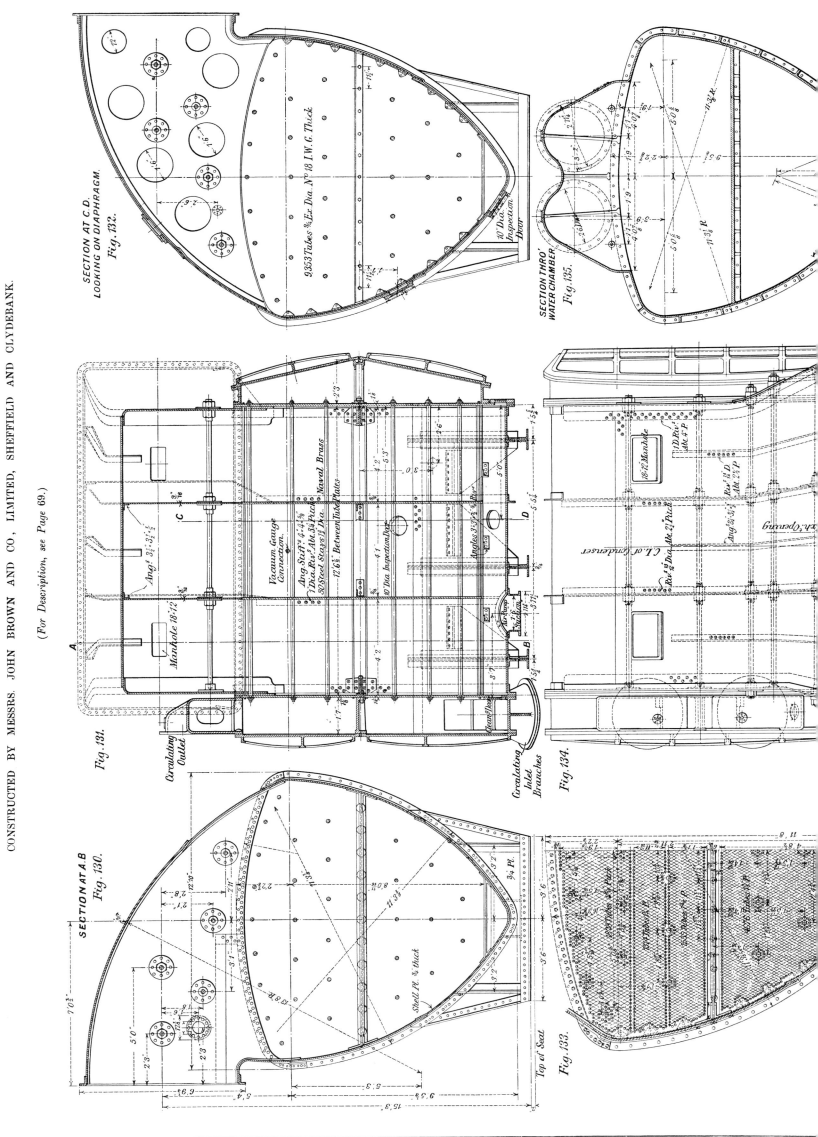

SECTION AT C.D.
LOOKING ON DIAPHRAGM.
Fig. 132.

9353 Tubes ⅞ Ex. Dia. Nº 18 I.W.G. Thick

10' Dia. Inspection Door.

SECTION THRO'
WATER CHAMBER.
Fig. 135.

Fig. 131.

Circulating Outlet

Manhole 18·12

Angs 3½·3½·½

Vacuum Gauge Connection.

Angs Stays 4·4·⅜
1"Dia. Rivs. Abt. 3¾ Pitch.
80 Steel Stays 1½ Dia.
Naval Brass

12·6½ Between Tube Plates

10 Dia. Inspection Door.

Angles 3½·3½ Rivs

Air-pump Suction.

Circulating Inlet Branches

Clean'Door

SECTION AT A.B
Fig. 130.

Shell Pl. ¾ thick

¾ Pl.

Top of Seat

Fig. 134.

18·12 Manhole

1"D.Rivs. Abt. 4" P.

Rivs.⅞ Dia. Abt. 2½"P.

Rivs.⅞ Dia. Abt. 2½"Pitch

Angs.3½·3½ R

CL.of Condenser

Ex.Opening

Fig. 133.

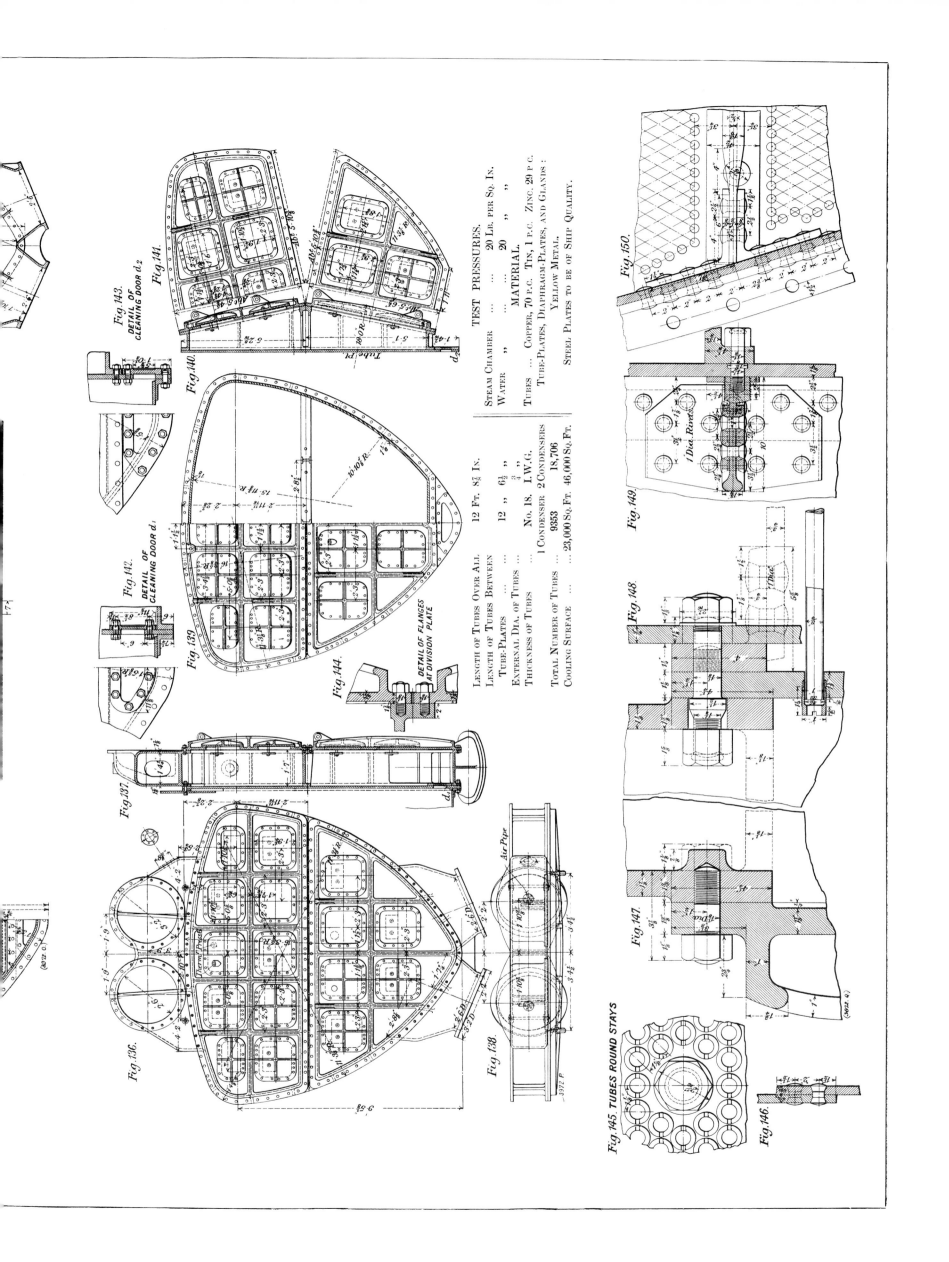

Fig.143.
DETAIL OF CLEANING DOOR d₂

Fig.141.

Fig.140.

Fig.142.
DETAIL OF CLEANING DOOR d₁

Fig.139.

Fig.144.
DETAIL OF FLANGES AT DIVISION PLATE

Fig.137.

Fig.136.

Fig.138.

Fig.145. TUBES ROUND STAYS

TEST PRESSURES.

STEAM CHAMBER	...	20 LB. PER SQ. IN.
WATER ,,	...	20 ,, ,,

MATERIAL.

TUBES ... COPPER, 70 P.C. TIN, 1 P.C. ZINC, 29 P.C.
TUBE-PLATES, DIAPHRAGM-PLATES, AND GLANDS :
Yellow Metal.
STEEL PLATES to be of Ship Quality.

LENGTH OF TUBES OVER ALL		12 FT. 8⅞ IN.
LENGTH OF TUBES BETWEEN TUBE-PLATES	...	12 ,, 6½ ,,
EXTERNAL DIA. OF TUBES	...	¾ ,,
THICKNESS OF TUBES	...	No. 18. I.W.G.
		1 CONDENSER 2 CONDENSERS
TOTAL NUMBER OF TUBES	...	9353 18,706
COOLING SURFACE	...	23,000 SQ. FT. 46,000 SQ. FT.

Fig.150.

Fig.149.

Fig.148.

Fig.147.

Fig.146.

PLATE XII.

CUNARD LINER "AQUITANIA;" GENERAL ARRANGEMENT OF TWO OF THE FOUR BOILER-ROOMS.

CONSTRUCTED BY MESSRS. JOHN BROWN AND CO., LIMITED, SHEFFIELD AND CLYDEBANK.

(For Description, see Page 73.)

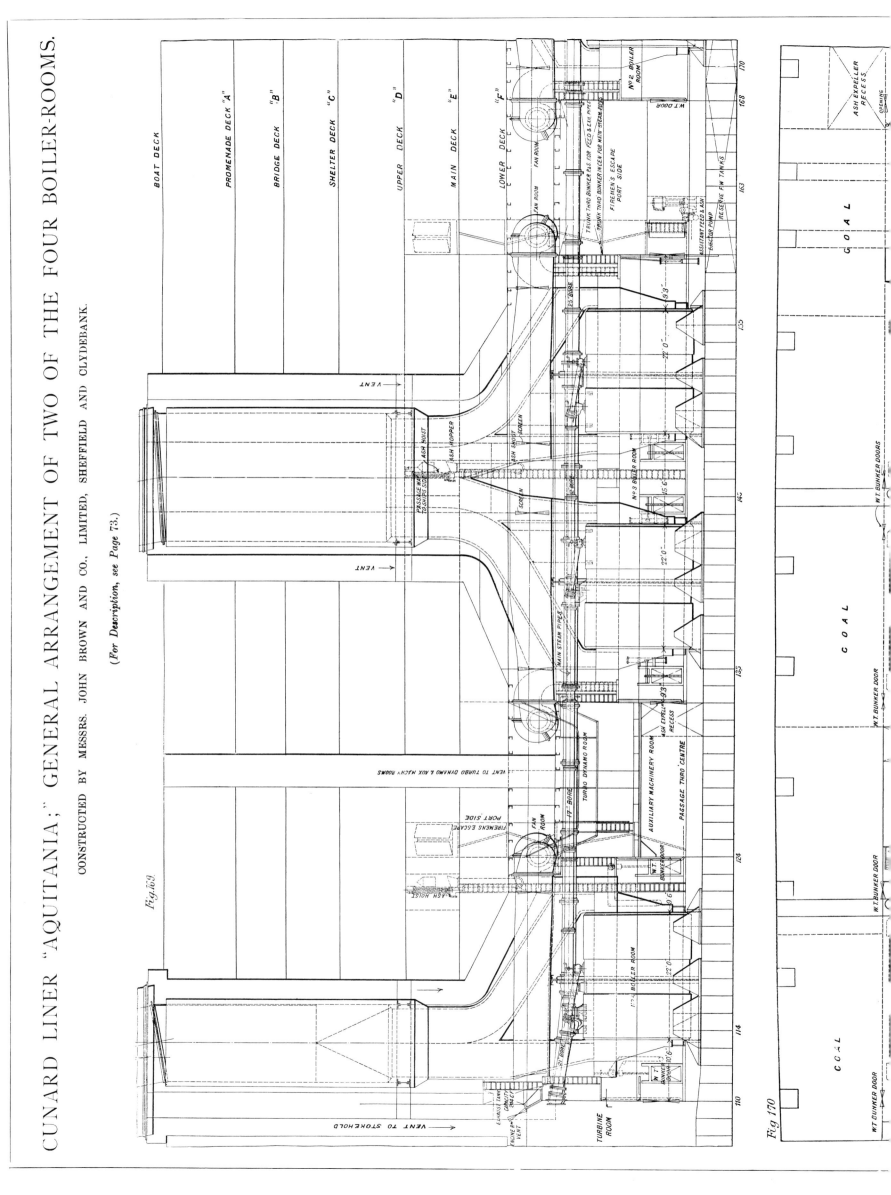

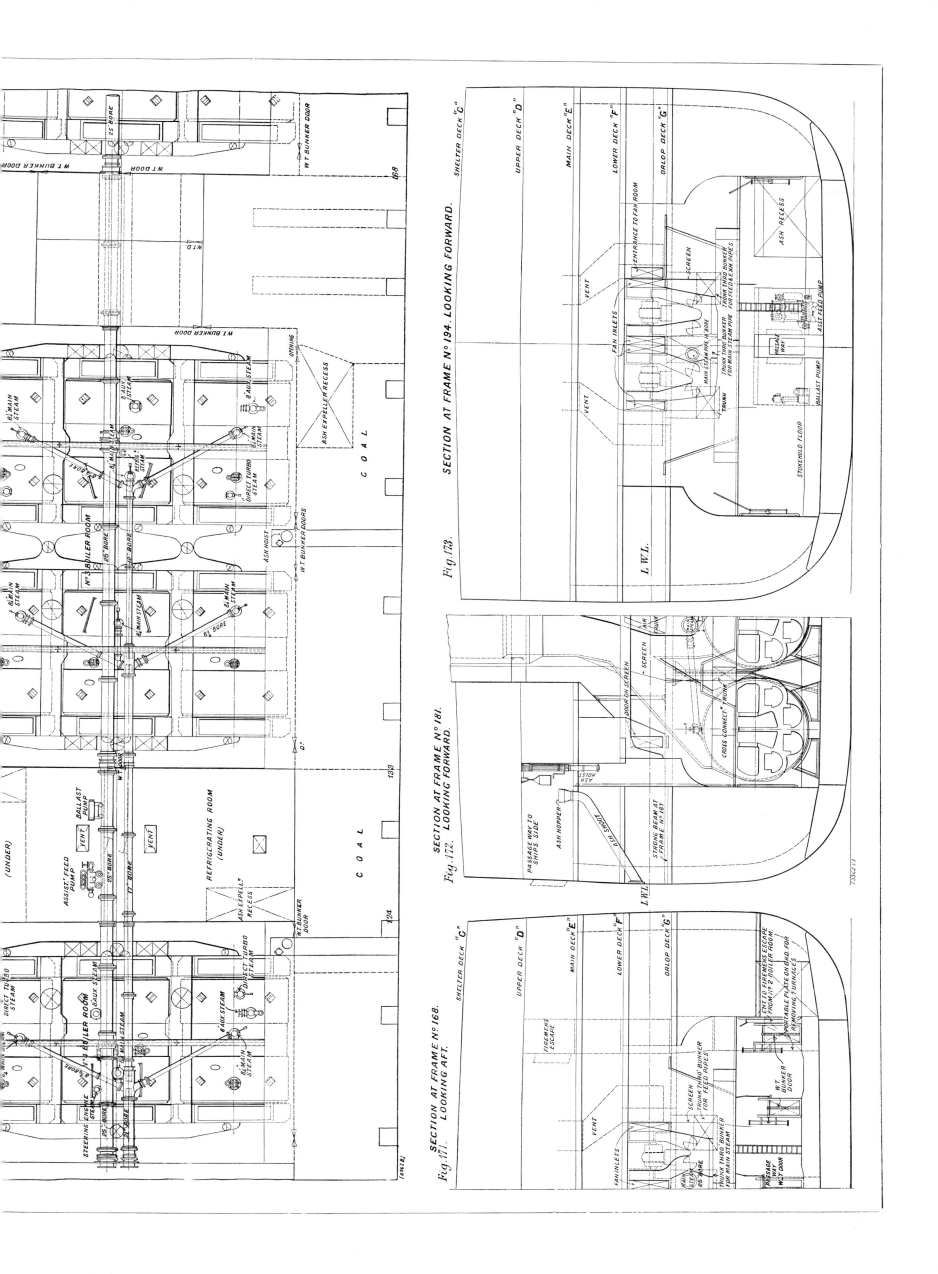

SECTION AT FRAME Nº 194. LOOKING FORWARD.

Fig. 173.

SECTION AT FRAME Nº 181. LOOKING FORWARD.

Fig. 172.

SECTION AT FRAME Nº 168. LOOKING AFT.

Fig. 171.

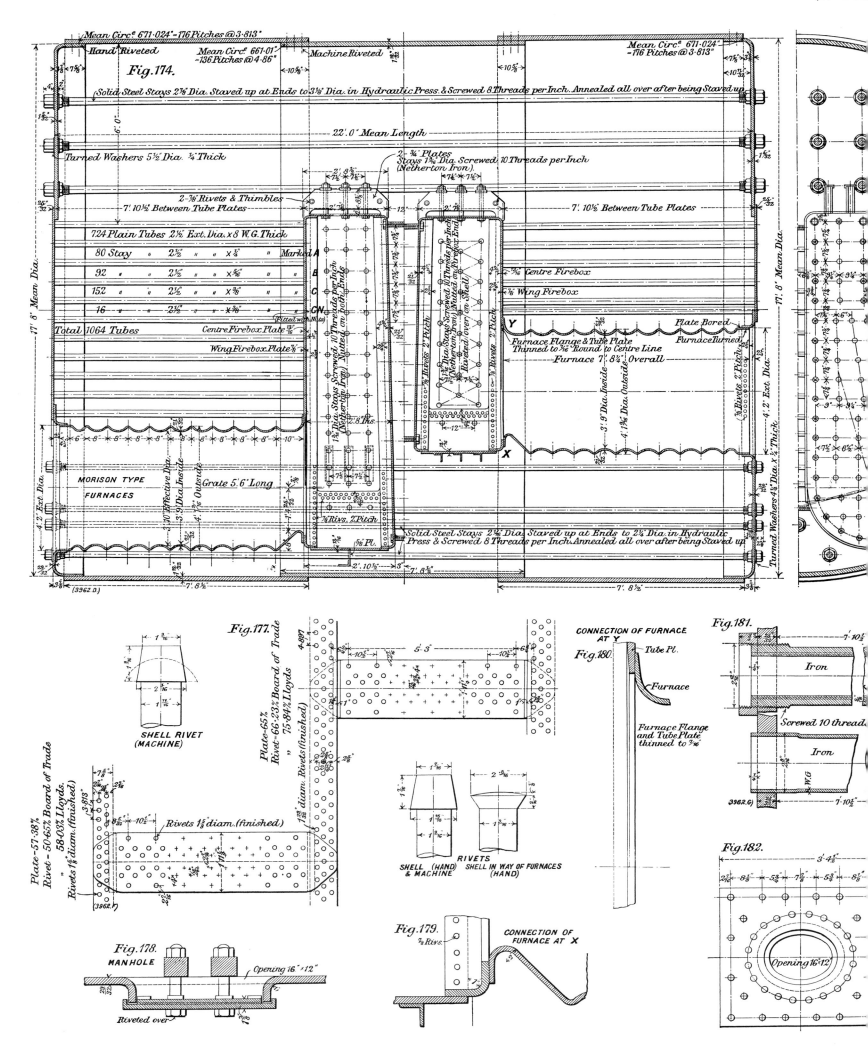

Fig.174.

Fig.177.

Fig.178.
MANHOLE

Fig.179.

Fig.180.
CONNECTION OF FURNACE AT Y

Fig.181.

Fig.182.

SHELL RIVET (MACHINE)

RIVETS
SHELL (HAND) & MACHINE
SHELL IN WAY OF FURNACES (HAND)

CONNECTION OF FURNACE AT X

PLATE XIII.

NER "AQUITANIA;" THE DOUBLE-ENDED BOILERS.

, LIMITED, SHEFFIELD AND CLYDEBANK.

Page 77.)

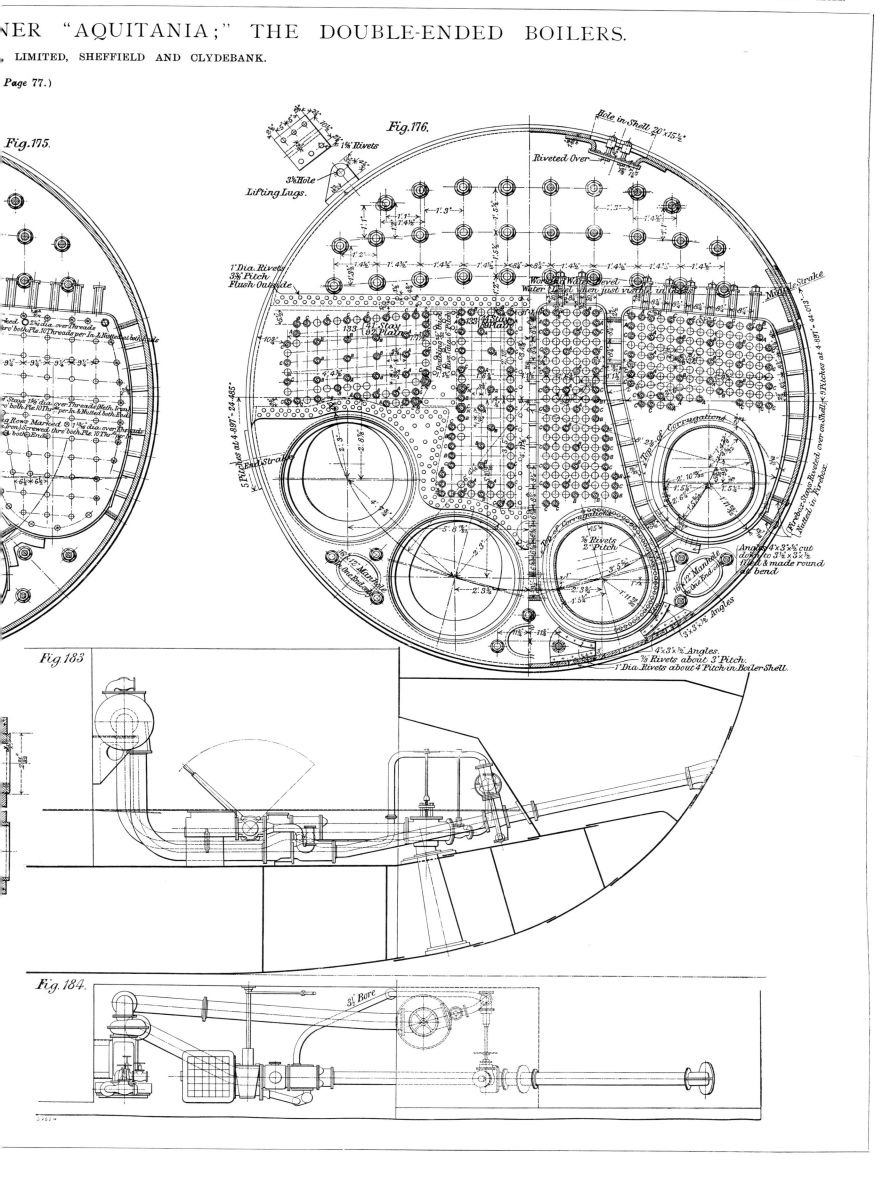

Fig.175.

Fig.176.

Fig.183

Fig.184.

PLATE XIV

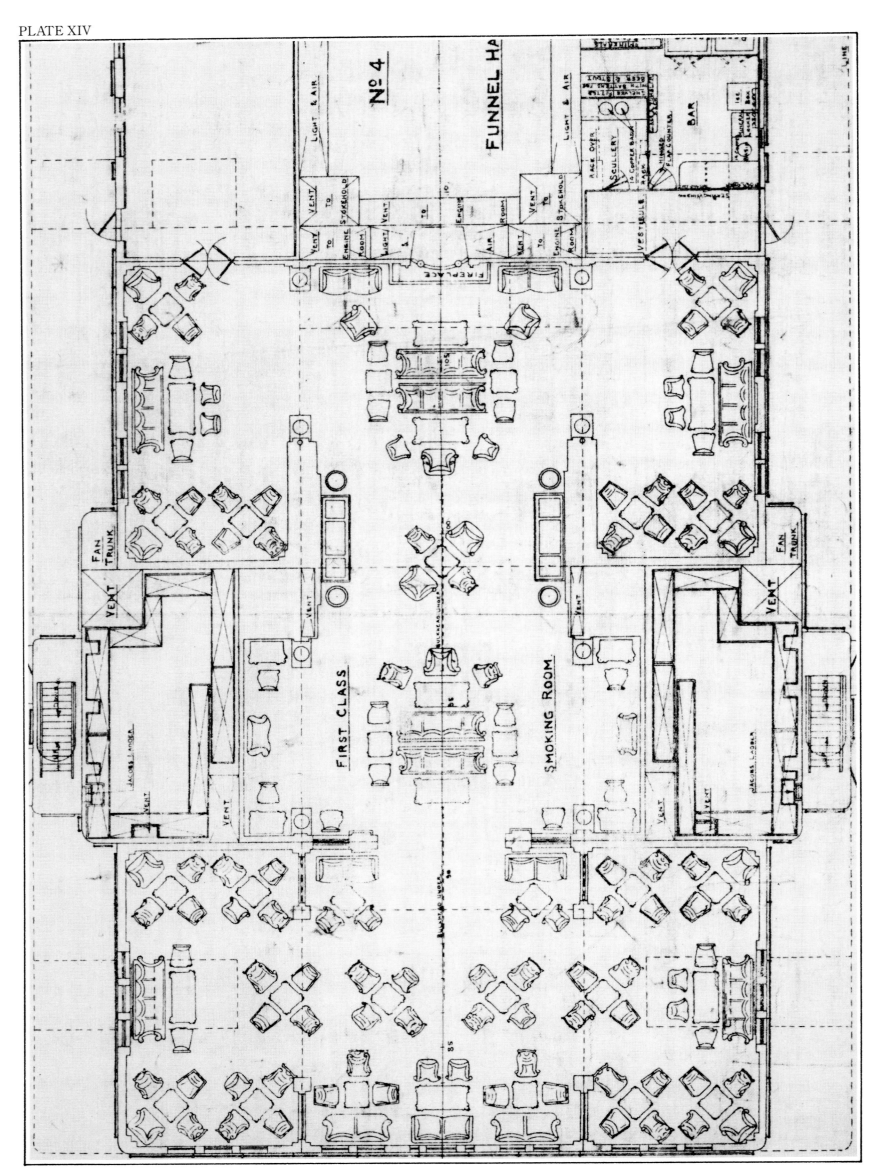

PLAN OF FIRST-CLASS SMOKING ROOM. SCALE: 1/8″ = 1 FOOT.

PLATE XV

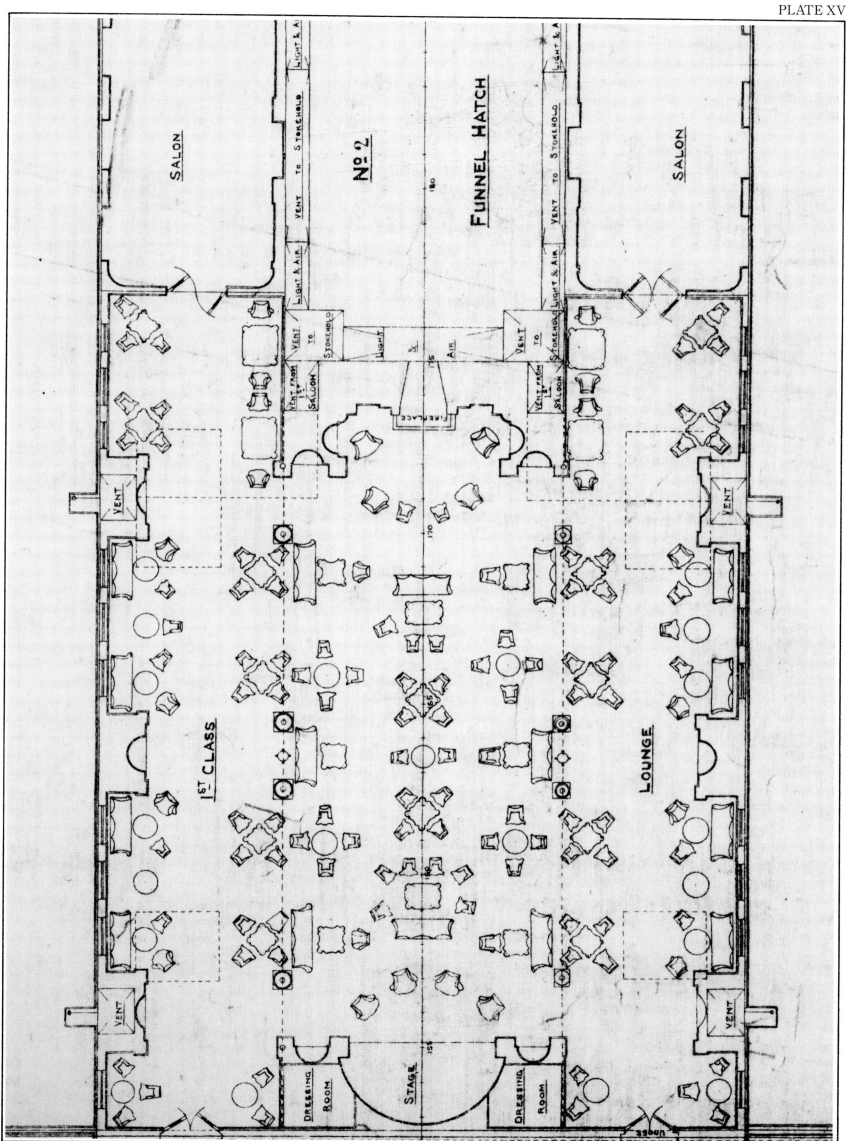

PLAN OF FIRST-CLASS LOUNGE. SCALE: 1/8″ = 1 FOOT.
CROWN COPYRIGHT.

PLATE XVI

THE QUADRUPLE-SCREW TURBINE-DRIVEN CUNARD LINER "AQUITANIA."

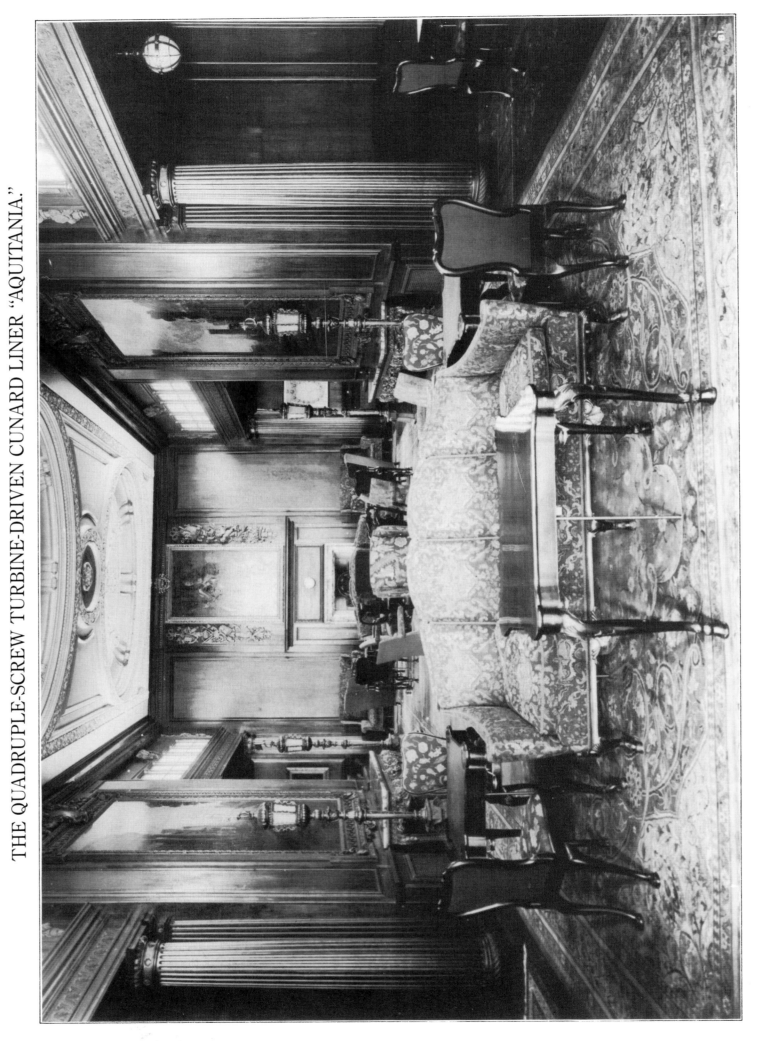

FIG. 200. FIRST-CLASS SMOKING ROOM LOOKING FORWARD.

PLATE XVII

THE QUADRUPLE-SCREW TURBINE-DRIVEN CUNARD LINER "AQUITANIA."

FIG. 202. STARBOARD SIDE FIRST-CLASS SMOKING ROOM PAINTING "EMBARKATION OF ST. URSULA."

FIG. 201. PORT SIDE FIRST-CLASS SMOKING ROOM PAINTING "SEAPORT WITH FIGURES."

PLATE XVIII

THE QUADRUPLE-SCREW TURBINE-DRIVEN CUNARD LINER "AQUITANIA."

Fig. 204. First-Class Lounge, Looking Aft.

Fig. 206. First-Class Lounge Fireplace.

Fig. 203. First-Class Smoking Room, Port Side, Aft.

Fig. 205. First-Class Lounge, Looking Forward.

PLATE XIX

THE QUADRUPLE-SCREW TURBINE-DRIVEN CUNARD LINER "AQUITANIA."

FIG. 207. LONG GALLERY, LOOKING FORWARD.

FIG. 208. LONG GALLERY, LOOKING FORWARD.

FIG. 209. FIRST-CLASS DRAWING ROOM AND LIBRARY READING SECTION.

FIG. 210. FIRST-CLASS DRAWING ROOM AND LIBRARY WRITING SECTION.

PLATE XX

THE QUADRUPLE-SCREW TURBINE-DRIVEN CUNARD LINER "AQUITANIA."

FIG. 211. FIRST-CLASS GRAND STAIRCASE.

FIG. 212. FIRST-CLASS GRAND STAIRCASE AND LIFTS.

FIG. 213. FIRST-CLASS SALON ENTRANCE. PORT SIDE.

FIG. 214. FIRST-CLASS FOYER.

PLATE XXI

THE QUADRUPLE-SCREW TURBINE-DRIVEN CUNARD LINER "AQUITANIA."

FIG. 215. GARDEN LOUNGE ENTRANCE, PORT SIDE, FORWARD.

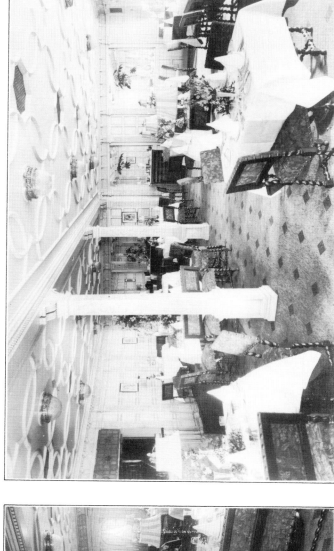

FIG. 216. GARDEN LOUNGE, PORT SIDE, LOOKING AFT.

FIG. 217. FIRST-CLASS GRILL ROOM.

FIG. 218. FIRST-CLASS GRILL ROOM.

PLATE XXII

THE QUADRUPLE-SCREW TURBINE-DRIVEN CUNARD LINER "AQUITANIA."

Fig. 220. Louis XVI Restaurant Ceiling Painting. "The Triumph of Flora".

Fig. 222. Louis XVI Restaurant Wall Painting. "Parc du Grand Trianon.".

Fig. 219. Louis XVI Restaurant. Looking Forward.

Fig. 221. Louis XVI Restaurant. Port Side. Looking Forward.

PLATE XXIII

THE QUADRUPLE-SCREW TURBINE-DRIVEN CUNARD LINER "AQUITANIA."

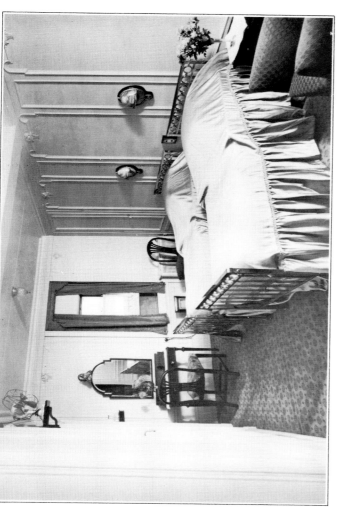

FIG. 223. GAINSBOROUGH SUITE DINING ROOM — B55.

FIG. 224. CABIN-CLASS SUITE BEDROOM - B132.

FIG. 225. REYNOLDS SUITE SITTING ROOM — B56.

FIG. 226. REYNOLDS SUITE SITTING ROOM FIREPLACE — B56.

PLATE XXIV

THE QUADRUPLE-SCREW TURBINE-DRIVEN CUNARD LINER "AQUITANIA."

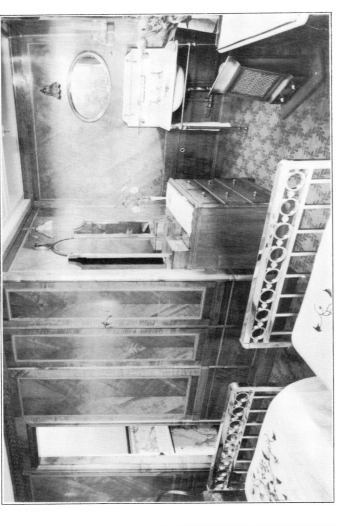

Fig. 227. Gainsborough Suite Bedroom — B52.

Fig. 228. Cabin-Class Suite Bedroom — B94.

Fig. 229. Cabin-Class Stateroom — B81.

Fig. 230. Cabin-Class Stateroom — B75.

PLATE XXV

THE QUADRUPLE-SCREW TURBINE-DRIVEN CUNARD LINER "AQUITANIA."

Fig. 231. Cabin-Class Stateroom — C12.

Fig. 232. Cabin-Class Stateroom — C47.

Fig. 233. Cabin-Class Stateroom — B76.

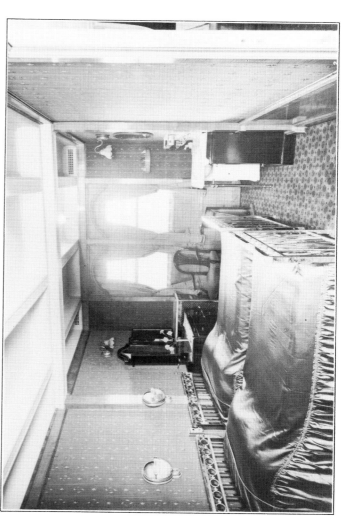

Fig. 234. Holbein Suite Bedroom — B104.

PLATE XXVI

THE QUADRUPLE-SCREW TURBINE-DRIVEN CUNARD LINER "AQUITANIA."

FIG. 236. RAEBURN SUITE BEDROOM — B101.

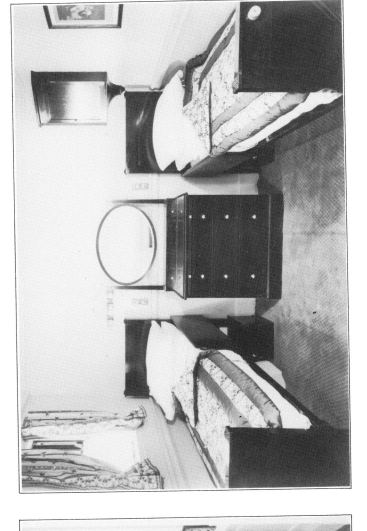

FIG. 238. FIRST-CLASS STATEROOM — C84.

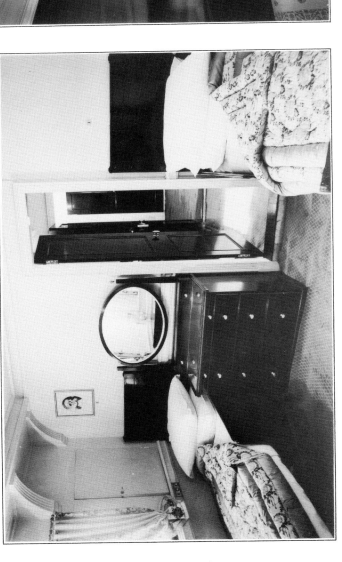

FIG. 235. FIRST-CLASS STATEROOM — C133.

FIG. 237. CABIN-CLASS STATEROOM — C88.

PLATE XXVII

THE QUADRUPLE-SCREW TURBINE-DRIVEN CUNARD LINER "AQUITANIA."

FIG. 239. SECOND-CLASS MAIN STAIRCASE.

FIG. 240. SECOND-CLASS VERANDAH CAFÉ.

FIG. 242. SECOND-CLASS SMOKING ROOM FIREPLACE.

FIG. 241. SECOND-CLASS SMOKING ROOM.

PLATE XXVIII

THE QUADRUPLE-SCREW TURBINE-DRIVEN CUNARD LINER "AQUITANIA."

FIG. 243. SECOND-CLASS LOUNGE.

FIG. 244. SECOND-CLASS DRAWING ROOM.

FIG. 245. SECOND-CLASS DINING SALOON, PORT SIDE, LOOKING FORWARD.

FIG. 246. SECOND-CLASS DINING SALOON, LOOKING AFT.

PLATE XXIX

THE QUADRUPLE-SCREW TURBINE-DRIVEN CUNARD LINER "AQUITANIA."

FIG. 247. FORWARD THIRD-CLASS DINING SALOON.

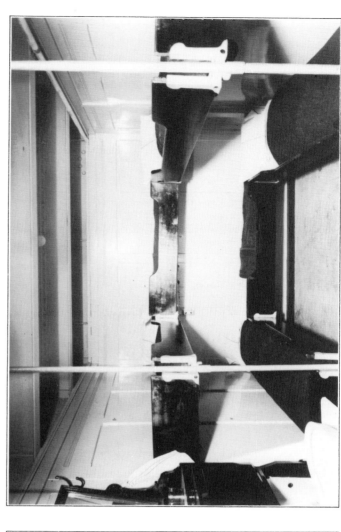

FIG. 248. THIRD-CLASS NON SMOKING COMPARTMENT.

FIG. 249. TOURIST-CLASS 4-BERTH STATEROOM — G4.

FIG. 250. THIRD-CLASS 6-BERTH STATEROOM — G24.

PLATE XXX

THE QUADRUPLE-SCREW TURBINE-DRIVEN CUNARD LINER "AQUITANIA."

FIG. 251. FIRST-CLASS SECONDARY STAIRCASE.

FIG. 252. GAINSBOROUGH SUITE VERANDAH.

FIG. 253. SECOND-CLASS 4-BERTH STATEROOM — C265.

FIG. 254. CORRIDOR TO GRILL ROOM.

PLATE XXXI

THE QUADRUPLE-SCREW TURBINE-DRIVEN CUNARD LINER "AQUITANIA."

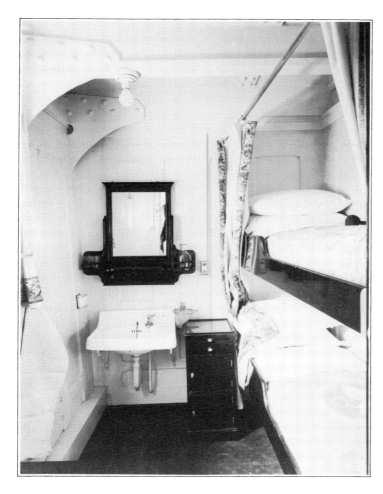

FIG. 255. SECOND-CLASS 2-BERTH STATEROOM — E27.

FIG. 256. TOURIST-CLASS 3-BERTH STATEROOM — F76.

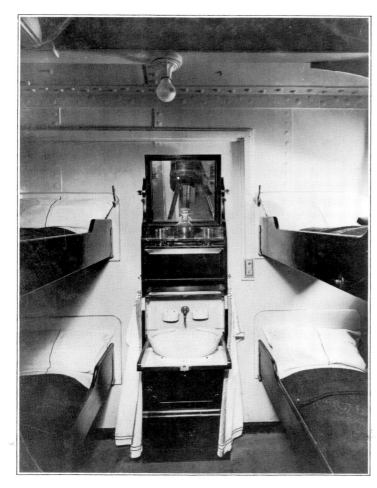

FIG. 257. SECOND-CLASS 4-BERTH STATEROOM — G38.

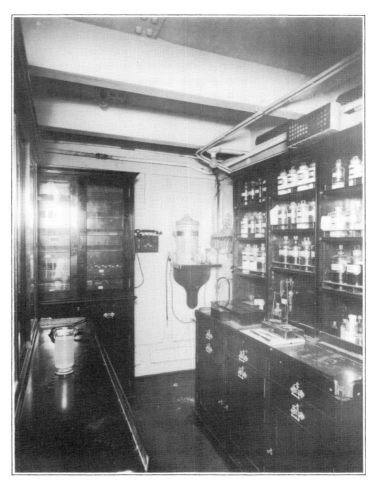

FIG. 258. DISPENSARY.

PLATE XXXII

THE QUADRUPLE-SCREW TURBINE-DRIVEN CUNARD LINER "AQUITANIA."

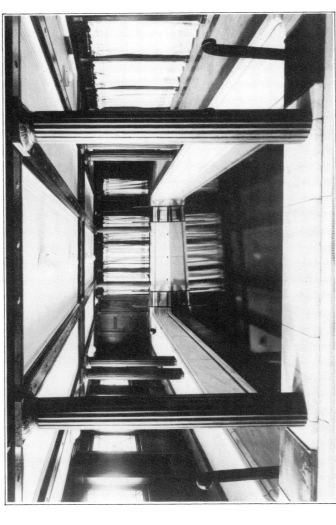

FIG. 260. MEN'S AFT HOSPITAL WARD.

FIG. 262. FIRST-CLASS SWIMMING BATH.

FIG. 259. MARCONI OFFICE.

FIG. 261. FIRST-CLASS GYMNASIUM.

PLATE XXXIII

THE QUADRUPLE-SCREW TURBINE-DRIVEN CUNARD LINER "AQUITANIA."

"AQUITANIA" AT THE SOUTHAMPTON OCEAN TERMINAL CIRCA 1930.

Inbound "Aquitania" Approaching New York. Mid-1930's.